Descartes

Philosophical Letters

# Descartes

## Philosophical Letters

*Translated and edited by*

Anthony Kenny

UNIVERSITY OF MINNESOTA PRESS

Minneapolis

Copyright © 1970 by Oxford University Press
First paperback edition, 1981
Published by the University of Minnesota Press,
2037 University Avenue Southeast, Minneapolis MN 55414
Printed in the United States of America

Library of Congress Cataloging in Publication Data

Descartes, René, 1596–1650.
    Descartes: philosophical letters.
    Reprint. Originally published : Oxford :
Clarendon Press, 1970.
    Includes indexes.
        1. Descartes, René, 1596–1650.    2. Philosophers
—France — Correspondence.    I. Kenny, Anthony
John Patrick.
[B1873.A4    1981]        194        81-3431
ISBN 0-8166-1060-6 (pbk.)            AACR2


The University of Minnesota
is an equal-opportunity
educator and employer.

# CONTENTS

# PREFATORY NOTE

Ten years ago the Clarendon Press at Oxford published this selection of Descartes' *Letters* in English translation. Many scholars have told me that they and their students have found it a valuable collection, and I have been proud to see the letter 'K' joining the familiar 'AT' and 'HR' in the footnotes to articles on Descartes. I was sorry when Clarendon Press felt obliged to let the edition go out of print and I am very pleased that the University of Minnesota Press and Basil Blackwell are now reissuing the collection in paperback. I have taken the opportunity to correct a number of misprints and minor mistranslations.

Anthony Kenny

# LIST OF ABBREVIATIONS

AM = ADAM, Charles, and MILHAUD, Gérard, *Descartes. Correspondance publiée avec une introduction et des notes.* (Vol. 1–2 Alcan; vol. 3–8 PUF Paris, 1936–63).

AT = ADAM, Charles, and TANNERY, Paul, *Oeuvres de Descartes.* (Cerf, Paris, 1897–1913. Reprinted: Vrin 1957–8.)

HR = HALDANE, Elizabeth S., and Ross, G. R. T., *The Philosophical works of Descartes, rendered into English.* (Second edition, Cambridge University Press, 1931, 2 vols. Reprinted: New York, Dover, 1955; Cambridge University Press, 1967.)

Olscamp = *DESCARTES, R.: Discourse on Method, Optics, Geometry and Meteorology. Translated with an introduction by Paul J. Olscamp.* (Bobbs-Merrill, Indianapolis, 1965.)

# INTRODUCTION

The correspondence of Descartes is of unique philosophical interest. No philosopher of comparable stature has left such a corpus of letters about epistemology, metaphysics, ethics, philosophy of mind, and many branches of science. Living in solitude and attached to no academic institution, Descartes depended for information and for stimulus to reflection upon his exchange of letters with philosophers and men of science in many parts of Europe. Almost half of the canonical edition of his works is devoted to correspondence. Surprisingly, less than two dozen of the seven hundred letters which survive have ever been translated into English. True, many of them deal with recondite mathematical and scientific matters likely to be of interest only to historians of science who will read them in the original French or Latin. But an equal number are philosophical treatises which retain a more than historical value and should interest any student of philosophy who seeks a real understanding of Descartes' published works.

Descartes himself took his correspondence very seriously. He set aside one day a week for letter writing and frequently had several thousand words written when the postman arrived. He preserved his drafts until his death at Stockholm in 1650, and as his biographer Baillet wrote 'the most important of his posthumous works was the inestimable treasure of the letters which were found in his coffer'. The correspondence was almost lost in 1653 when the vessel carrying it to France sank in the Seine; the manuscripts are said to have been recovered after three days in the water. They were first published by Descartes' disciple Clerselier between 1657 and 1667.

The standard modern edition of Descartes' works is that of Adam and Tannery, thirteen volumes published between 1897 and 1913. The first five volumes of this handsome

ix

edition were devoted to the correspondence, and included
very many letters unknown to Clerselier, with extremely
rich annotations and supplementary material. One hundred
and forty-one letters between Descartes and Constantijn
Huygens were discovered and edited by L. Roth at Oxford
in 1926. In 1936 Adam and Milhaud began a new edition
of the complete correspondence in eight volumes, of which
the last appeared in 1963. Though more complete than the
Adam and Tannery collection, this edition is in several ways
disappointing. The full annotations are missing, the spelling
has been modernized and is full of misprints, and no
justification is given for the changes in dates and identifica-
tion of recipients, definitive though these no doubt are.
However, a very useful index of names at the end of each
volume gives brief biographies of all persons referred to in
the letters, which are of great assistance to the reader.

There are a number of selections of Descartes' letters
available in French for those who do not possess the definitive editions. F. Alquié's valuable three-volume edition of
Descartes' *Oeuvres philosophiques*, of which the first two
volumes appeared in 1963 and 1967, prints all the letters
of philosophical interest in chronological sequence between
the published and unpublished works in the order in which
they were written. The Pléiade one-volume edition of
Descartes' works, edited by A. Bridoux, contains one hundred and forty-four letters occupying over four hundred
pages. A briefer selection was made by M. Alexandre in
1954 for the P.U.F. series *Les Grands Textes*, with
the title *Descartes: Lettres: Textes choisis*.

The English translation of Descartes' works by Haldane
and Ross (Cambridge University Press, 1911, 1967)
contains only two letters, to Clerselier and to Dinet, which
were written for publication in Descartes' lifetime. Extracts
from thirteen letters are given in a clear and vigorous
translation in the edition of Descartes' *Philosophical Writings*
by Elizabeth Anscombe and P. T. Geach (Nelson, 1954).

The present edition contains a hundred letters of
Descartes in whole or in part. I have selected the letters for
their philosophical rather than for their historical interest,
though I have taken care to include letters that describe the

preparation of Descartes' published works and throw light upon their meaning.

It was with some regret that I decided to translate, in many cases, extracts rather than complete letters. Archaic science and unfamiliar mathematics are so mingled with philosophy, especially in the letters to Mersenne, that the printing of all the letters in their entirety would have called for a wealth of scholarly annotation both beyond my capacity and irrelevant to my purpose. Throughout I have tried to keep in mind the needs of students of philosophy rather than of historians of science and mathematics.

I have not included any of the letters of Descartes' correspondents, even when these are extant, preferring to devote as much of the volume as possible to Descartes' own writing. I have, however, referred to correspondents' letters in footnotes when this seemed essential for the clarification of Descartes' replies.

A brief commentary links the letters and relates them to the publication of Descartes' works and other events of his life referred to in the correspondence. A footnote to the title of each letter gives references to the originals in the editions of Adam and Tannery and Adam and Milhaud, specifies the language of the original, and explains whether the letter is translated in its entirety or only in part.

Even in correspondence, Descartes was a clear and careful writer, and the letters selected presented no great problems of translation. The chief liberty which I have permitted myself in translation has been that of breaking up into smaller units Descartes' lengthy periods packed with relative clauses. On the rare occasions where it seemed impossible to give an untendentious translation, I have included the original expression in parenthesis or in a footnote. It has not been possible to preserve complete uniformity in the translation of philosophical terms, but wherever Descartes is consciously using jargon, an attempt has been made to reproduce it in English. Conventional flourishes at the ends of letters have been abbreviated.

There are three indexes. The first is a biographical index of persons addressed or mentioned in the letters. The second is an analytical index of philosophical topics treated. The third is an index of passages in Descartes' published works commented on or discussed.

I must acknowledge my debt to the French editions listed above, from which all the information in the footnotes and index is derived; and to the versions of Geach and Anscombe, which set a model to the translator of Descartes' letters. I wish to thank Professor Bernard Williams, Professor Harry Frankfurt, and Mr. L. J. Beck, for helpful suggestions about the selection of letters for translation. Finally I must express my gratitude to Miss P. Lloyd for typing a difficult manuscript very promptly and efficiently.

# LIST OF LETTERS

Descartes was born in Touraine in 1596. From his eleventh to his nineteenth year, as he tells us in the *Discourse on Method*, he followed a course of studies at the Jesuit College of La Flèche. After further studies in law at Poitiers he enrolled at the age of twenty-two in the army of Prince Maurice of Nassau. In Holland he met the savant Isaac Beeckman, for whom he wrote a treatise on music and to whom in 1619 he addressed his first surviving letters. In them he wrote of music, geometry, and navigation; he discussed the logical system of Raymond Lull and spoke of his own plan to publish 'a new science which will provide a general method of solving all questions, concerning quantity, whether continuous or discontinuous'. It was in November of the same year, meditating beside a stove in Bavaria, that Descartes acquired a conviction of his vocation to rebuild science and philosophy on fresh foundations.

The years 1620 to 1625 were spent in travels in Germany, Holland, and Italy; the surviving fragments of letters concern family business. From 1626 to 1629 Descartes lived in Paris and made some of the friends who were to be his lifelong correspondents, especially the erudite and indefatigable Franciscan Marin Mersenne. At the same time, most probably, he began work on the *Rules for the Direction of the Mind*, never completed and never published in his lifetime.

In 1629 Descartes migrated to Holland where he lived for all but one of his twenty-one remaining years of life. Frequently he changed his address, always in pursuit of greater seclusion. It is to his passion for solitude that we owe the volume and importance of his correspondence: most of his scientific and philosophical discussion with his contemporaries was conducted by letter. The letters which survive from 1629 concern lens-cutting, music, and a number of scientific curiosities. The first letter to Mersenne, of 8 October 1629, discusses the parhelia, or mock suns, which had recently been observed by the astronomer Scheiner, and which inspired Descartes to begin his treatise on meteors, and shortly afterwards to project a complete system of physics. The only letter of strictly philosophical interest in this year is the following, which discusses an otherwise unknown project for a universal language.

# Descartes to Mersenne, 20 November 1629[1]

Reverend Father,

This project for a new language seems more remarkable at first than I find it to be upon close examination. There are only two things to learn in any language: the meaning of the words and the grammar. As for the meaning of the words, your man does not promise anything extraordinary; because in his fourth proposition he says that *the language is to be translated with a dictionary*.[2] Any linguist can do as much in all common languages without his aid. I am sure that if you gave M. Hardy a good dictionary of Chinese or any other language, and a book in the same language, he would guarantee to work out its meaning.

The reason why not everyone could do the same is the difficulty of the grammar. That, I imagine, is your man's whole secret; but there is no difficulty in it. If you make a language with only one pattern of conjugation, declension, and construction, and with no defective or irregular verbs introduced by corrupt usage, and if the nouns and verbs are inflected and the sentences constructed by prefixes or suffixes attached to the primitive words, and all the prefixes and suffixes are listed in the dictionary, it is no wonder if ordinary people learn to write the language with a dictionary in less than six hours, which is the gist of his first proposition.

The second says that *once this language has been learnt, the others can be learnt as dialects of it*. This is just sales talk. He does not say how long it would take to learn them, but only that they could be regarded as dialects of his language, which he takes as primitive because it does not have the grammatical irregularities of the others. Notice that in his dictionary, for the primitive words, he could use the words of every language as synonyms of each other. For instance, to signify *love*, he could use *aimer, amare, philein*

[1] AT i. 76; AM i. 89; in French, complete.

[2] The italics, here and below, represent Latin words in a French context.

and so on; a Frenchman, adding to *aimer* the affix for a noun will form the noun corresponding to *amour*, a Greek will add the same affix to *philein*, and so on. Consequently his sixth proposition, about *inventing a script*, is very easy to understand. For if he put into his dictionary a single symbol corresponding to *aimer*, *amare*, *philein* and each of the synonyms, a book written in such symbols could be translated by all who possessed the dictionary.

The fifth proposition, too, it seems to me, is simply self-advertisement. As soon as I see the word *arcanum* (mystery) in any proposition I begin to suspect it. I think he merely means that he can teach the languages he names more easily than the average instructor, because he has reflected much about their grammars in order to simplify his own.

There remains the third proposition, which *is* altogether a mystery to me. He says that he will expound the thoughts of the writers of antiquity from the words they used, by taking each word as expressing the true definition of the thing spoken of. Strictly this means that he will expound the thoughts of those writers by giving their words a sense they never gave them themselves; which is absurd. But perhaps he means it differently.

However, this plan of reforming our grammar, or rather inventing a new one, to be learnt in five or six hours, and applicable to all languages, would be of general utility if everyone agreed to adopt it. But I see two difficulties which stand in the way.

The first is discordant combinations of letters which would often make the sounds unpleasant and intolerable to the ear. It is to remedy this defect that all the differences in inflexion of words have been introduced by usage; and it is impossible for your author to have avoided the difficulty while making his grammar universal among different nations; for what is easy and pleasant in our language is coarse and intolerable to Germans, and so on. The most that he can have done is to have avoided discordant combinations of syllables in one or two languages; and so his universal language would only do for a single country. But we do not need to learn a new language to talk only to Frenchmen.

The second difficulty is in learning the words of the language. It is true that if each man uses as primitive words the words of his own language, he will not have much difficulty; but in that case he will be understood only by the people of his own country unless he writes down what he wants to say and the person who wants to understand him takes the trouble to look up all the words in the dictionary; and this is too burdensome to become a regular practice. If your man wants people to learn primitive words common to every language he will not find anyone willing to take the trouble. It would be easier to get everyone to agree to learn Latin or some other existent language than one where there are as yet neither books for practice in reading nor speakers for practice in conversation. So the only possible benefit that I see from his invention would be in the case of the written word. Suppose he had a big dictionary printed of all the languages in which he wanted to make himself understood, and put for each primitive word a symbol corresponding to the meaning and not to the syllables, a single symbol, for instance, for *aimer*, *amare*, and *philein*: then those who had the dictionary and knew his grammar could translate what was written into their own language by looking up each symbol in turn. But this would be no good except for reading mysteries and revelations; in other cases no-one who had anything better to do would take the trouble to look up all these words in a dictionary. So I do not see that all this has much use. Perhaps I am wrong; I just wanted to write to you all I could conjecture on the basis of the six propositions which you sent me. When you have seen the system, you will be able to say if I worked it out correctly.

I believe, however, that it would be possible to devise a further system to enable one to make up the primitive words and their symbols in such a language so that it could be learnt very quickly. Order is what is needed: all the thoughts which can come into the human mind must be arranged in an order like the natural order of the numbers. In a single day one can learn to name every one of the infinite series of numbers, and thus to write infinitely many different words in an unknown language. The same could be done for all the other words necessary to express all the other things which fall within the purview of the human mind. If this secret were discovered I am sure that the language would soon spread throughout the world. Many people would willingly spend five or six days in learning how to make themselves understood by the whole human race.

But I do not think that your author has thought of this. There is nothing in all his propositions to suggest it, and in any case the discovery of such a language depends upon the true philosophy. For without that philosophy it is impossible to number and order all the thoughts of men or even to separate them out into clear and simple thoughts, which in my opinion is the great secret for acquiring true scientific knowledge. If someone were to explain correctly what are the simple ideas in the human imagination out of which all human thoughts are compounded, and if his explanation were generally received, I would dare to hope for a universal language very easy to learn, to speak, and to write. The greatest advantage of such a language would be the assistance it would give to men's judgement, representing matters so clearly that it would be almost impossible to go wrong. As it is, almost all our words have confused meanings, and men's minds are so accustomed to them that there is hardly anything which they can perfectly understand.

I think it is possible to invent such a language and to discover the science on which it depends: it would make peasants better judges of the truth about the world than philosophers are now. But do not hope ever to see such a language in use. For that, the order of nature would have to change so that the world turned into a terrestrial paradise; and that is too much to suggest outside of fairyland.

Descartes' next letter to Mersenne, of 18 December 1629, concerns scientific matters: it contains a statement of a principle of inertia, and an inquiry whether the Church has decided the created universe to be finite or infinite. Further letters during the winter of 1629–30 treat of optics, music, acoustics, linguistics, astronomy, and aesthetics. The following extract from the letter of 18 March 1630 contains a sketch of an aesthetic theory and a startling anticipation of the theory of conditioned reflexes.

## From the letter to Mersenne, 18 March 1630[1]

... You ask whether one can discover the essence of beauty. This is the same as your earlier question, why one sound is more pleasant than another, except that the word 'beauty' seems to have a special relation to the sense of sight. But in general 'beautiful' and 'pleasant' signify simply a relation between our judgement and an object; and because the judgements of men differ so much from each other neither beauty nor pleasantness can be said to have any definite measure. I cannot give any better explanation than the one I gave long ago in my treatise on music; I will quote it word for word, since I have the book before me.

'*The most pleasing sense-objects are neither those which are most easy to perceive nor those which are most difficult; but those which are not so easy as to fail to satisfy the natural desire of the senses to operate on their objects nor yet so difficult as to tire the senses.*'[2]

To explain what I meant by difficult or easy perception I instanced the divisions of a flower bed. If there are only one or two types of shape arranged in the same pattern, they will be taken in more easily than if there are ten or twelve arranged in different ways. But this does not mean that one design can be called absolutely more beautiful than another; to some men's fancy one with three shapes will be the most beautiful, to others it will be one with four or five and so on. But whatever will please most men could be called the most beautiful without qualification; but what this is cannot be determined.

Secondly, what makes one man want to dance may make another want to cry. This is because it evokes ideas in our

[1] AT i. 128; AM i. 124; in French; extract.
[2] Cf. *Compendium of Music*, trans. Roberts, American Institute of Musicology 13 (1961).

memory: for instance those who have in the past enjoyed dancing to a certain tune feel a fresh wish to dance when they hear a similar one; on the other hand, if a man had never heard a galliard without some affliction befalling him, he would certainly grow sad when he heard it again. This is so certain that I reckon that if you whipped a dog five or six times to the sound of a violin, he would begin to howl and run away as soon as he heard that music again.

## Descartes to Mersenne, 15 April 1630[1]

Reverend Father,

Your letter of the 14th of March, which I think is the one you are worried about, reached me ten or twelve days later; but because you indicated that others were on the way, and because it was only eight days since I had written to you, I put off replying to you until today when I received your last dated the 4th of April. I beg you to believe that I am greatly obliged to you for all the kind services you do me, which are too numerous for me to be able to thank you for each individually. I assure you that I will repay you in any way you ask if it is in my power; and I will always tell you my address provided that you tell no-one else. If anybody has the idea that I plan to write, please try to remove this impression, not to confirm it; I swear that if I had not already told people I planned to do so, so that they would say I have not been able to carry out my plan, I would never undertake the task at all. If people are going to think about me, I am civilized enough to be glad that they should think well of me; but I would much prefer them to have no thought of me at all. I fear fame more than I desire it; I think that those who acquire it always lose some degree of liberty and leisure, which are two things I possess so perfectly and value so highly that there is no monarch in the world rich enough to buy them away from me. This will not prevent me from completing the little treatise I have begun, but I do not want

---

[1] AT i. 135; AM i. 129; parts omitted.

this to be known so that I shall always be free to disavow it. My work on it is going very slowly, because I take much more pleasure in acquiring knowledge than in putting into writing the little that I know. I am now studying chemistry and anatomy simultaneously; every day I learn something that I cannot find in any book. I wish I had already started to research into diseases and their remedies, so that I could find some cure for your erysipelas, which I am sorry has troubled you for such a long time. Moreover, I pass the time so contentedly in the acquisition of knowledge that I never settle down to write any of my treatise except under duress, in order to carry out my resolution, which is, if I am still living, to have it ready for posting to you by the beginning of the year 1633. I am telling you a definite time so as to put myself under a greater obligation, so that you can reproach me if I fail to keep to the date. Moreover, you will be amazed that I am taking such a long time to write a discourse which will be so short that I reckon it will take only an afternoon to read. This is because I take more trouble, and think it more important, to learn what I need for the conduct of my life than to spend my time in publishing the little I have learnt. Perhaps you find it strange that I have not persevered with some other treatises I began while I was at Paris. I will tell you the reason: while I was working on them I acquired a little more knowledge than I had when I began them, and when I tried to take account of this I was forced to start a new project rather larger than the first. It is as if a man began building a house and then acquired unexpected riches and so changed his status that the building he had begun was now too small for him. No-one could blame such a man if he saw him starting to build another house more suitable to his condition. But I am sure that I will not change my mind again; because what I now possess will stand me in good stead no matter what else I may learn; and even if I learn nothing more I shall still carry out my plan.

\*     \*     \*

As for your questions: 1. The corpuscles, which enter a thing during rarefaction and exit during condensation, and

which can penetrate the hardest solids, are of the same substance as visible and tangible bodies; but you must not
imagine that they are atoms, or that they are at all hard.
Think of them as an extremely fluid and subtle substance
filling the orifices in other bodies. You must admit that even
in gold and diamonds there are certain orifices, however
tiny they may be; and if you agree also that there is no such
thing as a vacuum, as I think I can prove, you are forced to
admit that these orifices are full of some matter which can
penetrate everywhere with ease. Now heat and rarefaction
are simply an admixture of the matter I speak of.

To convince you of this would take a longer discussion
than is possible within the bounds of a letter. I have said the
same about many other questions which you have put to me;
please believe that it has never been an excuse to conceal from
you what I propose to write in my treatise on Physics. I
assure you that there is nothing of what I know that I am
keeping a secret from anyone; much less from you whom I
honour and esteem and to whom I am obliged in countless
ways. But the difficulties of physics which I told you I had
taken on are all so linked and interdependent that it would
be impossible for me to give the solution to one without
giving the solution to all; and I do not know how to do that
more quickly or more simply than I shall do in the treatise
which I am writing.

\*       \*       \*

Your question of theology is beyond my mental capacity,
but it does not seem to me outside my province, since it has
no concern with anything dependent on revelation, which is
what I call theology in the strict sense; it is a metaphysical
question which is to be examined by human reason. I think
that all those to whom God has given the use of this reason
have an obligation to employ it principally in the endeavour to
know Him and to know themselves. That is the task with
which I began my studies; and I can say that I would not
have been able to discover the foundations of Physics if I
had not looked for them along that road. It is the topic which
I have studied more than anything and in which, thank God,

I have not altogether wasted my time. At least I think that
I have found how to prove metaphysical truths in a manner
which is more evident than the proofs of geometry—in my
own opinion, that is: I do not know if I shall be able to
convince others of it. During my first nine months in this
country I worked on nothing else. I think that you heard
me speak once before of my plan to write something on the
topic; but I do not think it opportune to do so before I have
seen how my treatise of Physics is received. But if the book
which you mention was very well written and fell into my
hands I might perhaps feel obliged to reply to it immediately
because if the report you heard is accurate it says things
which are very dangerous and, I believe, very false. However in my treatise on Physics I shall discuss a number of
metaphysical topics and especially the following. The
mathematical truths which you call eternal have been laid
down by God and depend on Him entirely no less than the
rest of his creatures. Indeed to say that these truths are
independent of God is to talk of Him as if He were Jupiter
or Saturn and to subject Him to the Styx and the Fates.
Please do not hesitate to assert and proclaim everywhere
that it is God who has laid down these laws in nature just
as a king lays down laws in his kingdom. There is no single
one that we cannot understand if our mind turns to consider
it. They are all *inborn in our minds*[1] just as a king would
imprint his laws on the hearts of all his subjects if he had
enough power to do so. The greatness of God, on the other
hand, is something which we cannot comprehend even
though we know it. But the very fact that we judge it
incomprehensible makes us esteem it the more greatly; just
as a king has more majesty when he is less familiarly known
by his subjects, provided of course that they do not get the
idea that they have no king—they must know him enough to
be in no doubt about that.

It will be said that if God had established these truths He
could change them as a king changes his laws. To this the
answer is: 'Yes he can, if his will can change.' 'But I
understand them to be eternal and unchangeable.'—'I make
the same judgement about God.' 'But His will is free.'—

[1] Italics represent Latin words in a French context (as also below).

'Yes, but his power is incomprehensible.' In general we can assert that God can do everything that we can comprehend but not that he cannot do what we cannot comprehend. It would be rash to think that our imagination reaches as far as His power.

I hope to put this in writing, within the next fortnight, in my treatise on Physics; but I do not want you to keep it secret. On the contrary I beg you to tell people as often as the occasion demands, provided that you do not mention my name. I should be glad to know the objections which can be made against this view; and I want people to get used to speaking of God in a manner worthier, I think, than the common and almost universal way of imagining him as a finite being.

A propos of infinity, you asked me a question in your letter of 14 March, which is the only thing I find in it which is not in the last letter. You said that if there were an infinite line it would have an infinite number of feet and of fathoms, and consequently that the infinite number of feet would be six times as great as the number of fathoms. *I agree entirely.* 'Then this latter number is not infinite.' *I deny the consequence.* 'But one infinity cannot be greater than another.' Why not? *Where is the absurdity?* Especially if it is only greater *by a finite ratio, as in this case multiplication by 6, a finite ratio, in no way affects the infinity.* In any case, what right have we to judge whether one infinity can be greater than another or not? It would no longer be infinite if we could comprehend it. Continue to honour me by thinking kindly of me.

I am, etc.

Descartes to Mersenne, 6 May 1630[1]

Reverend Father, •

Thank you for M. Gassendi's account of the corona.[2] As for the bad book[3] I no longer want you to send it to me;

[1] AT i. 147; AM i. 129; in French, complete
[2] Cf. *Meteors*, Disc ix and x, Olscamp 346ff.
[3] See the preceding letter.

because I have now decided on other projects, and I think
that it would be too late to carry out the plan which made me
say to you in the last post that if it was a well-written book
and fell into my hands I would try to reply immediately. I
thought that even if there were only thirty-five copies of the
book, still, if it was well written it would go to a second
impression, and circulate widely among curious people however much it might be prohibited. I had thought of a remedy
which seemed more effective than any legal prohibition. My
idea was that before the book was reprinted secretly it
should be printed with permission with the addition, after
each paragraph or each chapter, of arguments in refutation
of its conclusions to expose their fallaciousness. I thought
that if it was sold thus publicly in its entirety with a reply,
nobody would care to sell it in secret without a reply and
thus nobody would learn its false doctrine without at the
same time being disabused of it. The Answers to such books
which appear separately are customarily of little use because
nobody reads books which do not suit his humour; and so the
people who take the time to examine the replies are never
the same as those who have read the bad books. I expect
that you will say that we do not know whether I would have
been able to reply to the author's arguments. To that I can
only say that at least I would have done all I could; and
since I have many arguments that persuade and convince me
of the contrary of what you told me was in the book I dared to
hope that they might also persuade others. I trusted that truth
expounded by an undistinguished mind would be stronger than
falsehood maintained by the cleverest people in the world.

As for the eternal truths, I say once more that *they are true
or possible only because God knows them as true or possible.*[1] *They
are not known as true by God in any way which would imply that
they are true independently of Him.* If men really understood
the sense of their words they could never say without
blasphemy that the truth of anything is prior to the knowledge which God has of it. In God willing and knowing
are a single thing in such a way that *by the very fact of willing
something he knows it and it is only for this reason that such a*

---

[1] Here and below the italics represent Latin words in a French context.

*thing is true.* So we must not say that if *God did not exist nonetheless these truths would be true*; for the existence of God is the first and the most eternal of all possible truths and the one from which alone all others derive. It is easy to be mistaken about this because most men do not regard God as an infinite and incomprehensible being, the sole author on whom all things depend; they stick at the syllables of His name and think it sufficient knowledge of Him to know that 'God' means what is meant by 'Deus' in Latin and what is adored by men. Those who have no higher thoughts than these can easily become atheists; and because they perfectly comprehend mathematical truths and do not perfectly comprehend the truth of God's existence, it is no wonder they do not think the former depend on the latter. But they should rather judge on the contrary, that since God is a cause whose power surpasses the bounds of human understanding, and since the necessity of these truths does not exceed our knowledge, they must be something less than, and subject to, the incomprehensible power of God. What you say about the production of the Word[1] does not conflict, I think, with what I say; but I do not want to involve myself in theology, and I am already afraid that you will think my philosophy too presumptuous for daring to express an opinion on such lofty matters.


## Descartes to Mersenne, 27 May 1630[2]

Reverend Father,

You ask me *by what kind of causality God established the eternal truths.*[3] I reply: *by the same kind of causality* as he created all things, that is to say, as their *efficient and total cause.* For it is certain that he is no less the author of creatures' essence than he is of their existence; and this essence is nothing other than the eternal truths. I do not conceive them as emanating from God like rays from the sun; but I know

[1] The generation of the Second Person of the Trinity by the First.
[2] AT i. 151; AM i. 141; in French; complete.
[3] Italics represent Latin words in a French context.

that God is the author of everything and that these truths are something and consequently that he is their author. I say that I know this, not that I can conceive it or comprehend it; because it is possible to know that God is infinite and all-powerful although our soul, being finite, cannot comprehend or conceive Him. In the same way we can touch a mountain with our hands but we cannot put our arms around it as we could put them around a tree or something else not too large for them. To comprehend something is to embrace it in one's thought; to know something it is sufficient to touch it with one's thought.

You ask also what necessitated God to create these truths; and I reply that just as He was free not to create the world, so He was no less free to make it untrue that all the lines drawn from the centre of a circle to its circumference are equal. And it is certain that these truths are no more necessarily attached to his essence than other creatures are. You ask what God did in order to produce them. I reply that *from all eternity he willed and understood them to be, and by that very fact he created them*. Or, if you reserve the word *created* for the existence of things, then he *established them and made them*. In God, willing, understanding, and creating are all the same thing without one being prior to the other even *conceptually*.

2. As for the question whether *it is in accord with the goodness of God to damn men for eternity*, that is a theological question: so if you please you will allow me to say nothing about it. It is not that the arguments of free thinkers on this topic have any force, indeed they seem frivolous and ridiculous to me; but I think that when truths depend on faith and cannot be proved by natural argument, it degrades them if one tries to support them by human reasoning and mere probabilities.

3. As for the liberty of God I completely share the view which you tell me was expounded by Father Gibieuf. I did not know that he had published anything, but I will try to have his treatise sent from Paris as soon as possible so that I can see it. I am very pleased that my opinions coincide with his because that assures me at least that they are not too extravagant to be defended by very able men.

The fourth, fifth, sixth, eighth, and last points of your letter are all theological matters, so if you please I will say nothing about them. As for the seventh point concerning such things as the birthmarks caused on children by their mothers' imagination, I agree it is worth examination but I am not yet convinced.

In your tenth point you start from the supposition that God leads everything to perfection and that nothing is annihilated, and then you ask what is the perfection of dumb animals and what becomes of their souls after death. That question is within my competence, and I reply that God leads everything to perfection, in one sense, i.e. collectively, but not in another, i.e. in particular. The very fact that particular things perish and that others appear to take their place is one of the principal perfections of the universe. As for animals' souls and other forms and qualities, do not worry about what happens to them. I am about to explain all this in my treatise, and I hope that I will make it all so clear that no one will be left in any doubt.

In autumn 1630 Descartes quarrelled with Beeckman, whom he accused of trying to steal the credit for the treatise on music written twelve years earlier. The correspondence between the two contains little of philosophical interest—though Descartes spoke of publishing it as part of a treatise on ethics—except for the following passages from a long letter of reproach.

## From the letter to Beeckman, 17 October 1630[1]

... Consider first what are the things which one person can learn from another: you will find they are languages, history, empirical facts, and clear and certain proofs, like those of geometers, which bring conviction to the mind. Merely to repeat the views and maxims of philosophers is not to teach them. Plato says one thing, Aristotle another, Epicurus another, Telesio, Campanella, Bruno, Basson,

[1] AT i. 156; AM i. 147; in Latin; extracts.

Vanini, and the innovators all say something different. Of all these people, I ask you, who is it who really teaches me, or indeed anyone who loves wisdom? Doubtless it is the man who can first convince someone by his arguments, or at least his authority. But if someone merely comes to believe something, without being swayed by any authority or argument which he has learnt from others, this does not mean that he has been taught it by anyone even though he may have heard many people say it. It may even happen that he really knows it, being impelled to believe it by true reasons, and that no-one before him has ever known it, although they may have been of the same opinion because they deduced it from false principles. . . . Many people can know the same thing without any of them having learnt it from the others. It is ridiculous and offensive to take trouble as you do to distinguish, in the possession of science, what is your own from what is not, as if it was the possession of a piece of land or sum of money. If you know something, it is completely yours, even if you have learnt it from someone else.

. . . You reproach me, without any reason or basis, for having sometimes put myself on a level with angels. I still cannot convince myself that you are so out of your mind as to believe this. But I realise that your sickness may be very far gone, and so I will explain what may have given you the occasion to make this complaint. Philosophers and theologians are accustomed, when they want to show that something's being the case is repugnant to reason, to say that not even God could make it the case. This way of speaking has always seemed too bold to me; so in order to use a more modest expression, whenever—as happens more often in mathematics than in philosophy—an occasion arose on which others would say that God cannot do something, I would merely say that an angel could not do it. If this is the reason that you say I put myself on a level with the angels, you could as well say that the wisest people in the world put themselves on a level with God. I am very unfortunate to have been suspected of vanity on a point in which I can say I was behaving with extraordinary modesty.

Descartes' two letters to Mersenne in November 1630 concern his quarrel with Beeckman and his disappointment in Jean Ferrier, a craftsman with whom he had hoped to co-operate in the construction of optical instruments. In the course of the second letter he explains his plans for publication.

## From the letter to Mersenne, 25 November 1630[1]

...I am sorry for the troubles of M. (Ferrier) even though he has brought them on himself. Since you thought it proper, I do not object to your showing my letter about him to M. (Mydorge); but I would have preferred you not to put it actually in his hands. My letters are normally written with too little care to be fit to be seen by anyone except their addressee. Moreover, I am afraid that he may have inferred from it that I want to have my *treatise on Dioptrics* printed, because I think I mentioned in other places beside the last paragraph which you say you cut off. I would like this project to remain unknown; because it cannot be ready for a long time owing to the way I am working on it. I want to include a discourse explaining the nature of colours and light. This has held me up for six months and is still not half finished; but it will be longer than I thought and contain almost a whole treatise of Physics. I am hoping that it will serve to keep my promise to you, to have my *Treatise on the World* finished in three years, because it will be more or less an abstract of it. After that I do not think I will ever bring myself to have anything else printed, at least in my lifetime. I am too much in love with the fable of my *World* to give it up if God lets me live long enough to finish it; but I cannot answer for the future. I think I will send you this treatise on light as soon as it is complete, and before sending you the rest of the treatise on *Dioptrics*, because in it I want to give my own account of colours and consequently I am obliged to explain how the whiteness of the bread remains in the Blessed Sacrament.[2] I would be glad to have this examined first by my friends before it is seen by the world at

[1] AT i. 177; AM i. 169; in French; extracts.
[2] See the *Fourth Replies*, HR ii. 116.

large. However, although I am not hurrying to finish my *treatise on Dioptrics*, I am not afraid of anyone *stealing a march on me*[1] because I am sure that whatever others may write will not coincide with my account unless they learn it from the letters I have written to M. F(errier).

*       *       *

I am most obliged to you for sending me an extract from the manuscript you mentioned. The shortest way I know to reply to the arguments which he brings against the Godhead, and to all the arguments of other atheists, is to find an evident proof which will make everyone believe that there is a God. I can boast of having found one myself which satisfies me entirely, and which makes me know that there is a God with more certainty than I know the truth of any proposition of geometry; but I do not know whether I would be able to make everyone understand it the way I can. I think that it is better not to treat of this matter at all than to treat of it imperfectly. The universal agreement of all races is sufficient to maintain the Godhead against the insults of atheists, and no individual should enter into dispute with them unless he is very certain of refuting them.

I will test in my *treatise on Dioptrics* whether I am capable of explaining my conceptions and convincing others of truths of which I have convinced myself. I doubt it very much; but if I find by experience that it is so, perhaps I may some day complete a little treatise of Metaphysics, which I began when in Frisia, in which I set out principally to prove the existence of God and of our souls when they are separate from the body, from which their immortality follows. I am enraged when I see that there are people in the world so bold and so impudent as to fight against God.

In 1631 the only extant correspondence of philosophical interest consists in some fragments, preserved in Baillet's *Life* of Descartes, of a letter to Etienne de Villebressieu, an engineer in the service of Louis XIII.

[1] Italics denote Latin words in a French context.

## From the letter to Villebressieu, summer 1631[1]

You saw these two results of my fine Rule or Natural Method in the discussion which was forced on me in the presence of the Papal Nuncio, Cardinal de Berulle, Father Mersenne and all that great and learned company assembled at the Nuncio's palace to hear M. de Chandoux lecture about his new philosophy. I made the whole company avow what great power the art of right reasoning has over the minds of those who have no learning beyond the ordinary. I showed them that my principles are more certain, more true and more natural than any of those which are currently received in the learned world. You were as convinced as everybody else, and you were all good enough to beg me to put them in writing and to publish them.

\*     \*     \*

I advise you to put your ideas for the most part in the form of propositions, problems, and theorems and to publish them so as to force somebody else to supply them with research and observation. That is what I would like everybody to do, so that many people's experience may help to discover the finest things in nature, and to build a science of physics which would be clear, and certain, and based on proof and more useful than that commonly taught. You for your part could greatly help to disabuse poor sick minds concerning the *sophistication*[2] of metals on which you have worked so hard and so uselessly without having found any truth in the idea in twelve years of assiduous work and numerous experiments. Your experience would be generally useful as a warning to certain people of their errors.

It seems to me too that you have already discovered some general principles of nature, such as, that there is only one material substance which receives from an exter-

---

[1] AT i. 212; AM i. 198; in French; extracts.     [2] Adulteration.

nal agent its action or its ability to move from one place to another, and that from this it acquires the different shapes or modes which make it into the kind of thing we see in the primary compounds which are called Elements. Moreover you have observed that the nature of these Elements or primary compounds which are called Earth, Water, Air, and Fire consists only in the difference between the fragments, the smaller or large particles of this matter; and that matter changes daily from one element into another. Heat and movement make the large particles change into small ones, and when the action of heat and movement ceases matter turns into ignoble substances, that is to say, from subtle particles into large ones. You have seen too that the primary mingling of these four compounds results in a mixture which can be called the fifth element. This is what you call the principle, or most noble preparation of the elements; since it is, you say, a productive seed or a material life which takes specific form in all the noble particular individuals to which we cannot refuse our admiration. I am quite in agreement with your view that the four elements which constitute matter and the fifth which results from them are so changed in such a case that none of them continues to be what it was but that all together constitute the animal or the plant or the mineral. All this suits my style of philosophizing very well, and it accords admirably with all the mechanical experiments which I have performed upon nature in this field.

The letters which survive from the first three months of 1632 concern geometry and dioptrics. The following letter records the progress of Descartes' *Treatise on the World*.

## Descartes to Mersenne, 5 April 1632[1]

Reverend Father,

It is a long time since I heard from you, and I shall begin to worry about your health if you do not write to me soon. I expect that you have been waiting for me to send you the Treatise which I promised you for this Easter. It is almost finished, and I could keep my promise if I thought that you would want to hold me to the letter; but I would prefer to keep it for a few months, to revise it and rewrite it, and draw some diagrams which are necessary. They are quite a trouble to me, for as you know I am a very poor draughtsman and careless about matters which are unconnected with learning. If you blame me for having so often failed to keep my promise, I will say in excuse that my only reason for so long putting off writing the little I know has been the hope of learning more and adding to my knowledge. For instance, in the treatise which I now have in hand, after the general description of the stars, the heavens and the earth, I did not originally intend to give an account of particular bodies on the earth but only to treat of their various qualities. In fact, I am now discussing in addition some of their substantial forms, and trying to show the way to discover them all in time by a combination of experiment and reasoning. This is what has occupied me these last days; for I have been making various experiments to discover the essential differences between oils, ardent spirits, common and strong waters, salts etc. Altogether, if I postpone the payment of my debt it is with the intention of paying you interest on it. I tell you all this only for lack of better matter; when you receive what I plan to send you it will be for you to judge whether it is worth anything. I am very much afraid that it may be so much less than your expectation that you will not be willing to accept it in payment.

---

[1] AT i. 242; AM I. 220; in French; complete.

Last time you wrote to me about a man who boasted of being able to solve mathematical problems of all kinds. I would be glad to know if you have set him the problem of Pappus, which I sent to you. I must admit that I took five or six weeks to find the solution; and if anyone else discovers it, I will not believe that he is ignorant of algebra.

I am, etc.

## Descartes to Mersenne, 10 May 1632[1]

Reverend Father,

Eight days ago I put you to the trouble of sending on a letter for me to Poitou; but I was in a hurry when writing it, having negligently put off writing, as usual, until the postman was almost ready to leave, and so I forgot to include the address for a reply. This forces me to burden you once more with a letter to send on.

You tell me that you have Scheiner's description of the phenomenon at Rome. If it is more detailed than the one which you sent me before, I will be most obliged if you will take the trouble to send me a copy.

If you know any author who has made a special collection of the various accounts of comets I will be very obliged if you will inform me of it. For the last two or three months I have been rapt in the heavens. I have discovered their nature and the nature of the stars we see there and many other things which a few years ago I would not even have dared to hope; and now become so rash as to seek the cause of the position of each fixed star. For although they seem very irregularly distributed in various places in the heavens, I do not doubt that there is a natural order among them which is regular and determinate. The discovery of this order is the key and foundation of the highest and most perfect science of material things which men can ever attain. For if we possessed it we could discover *a priori* all the different forms and essences of terrestrial bodies, whereas without it

---

[1] AT i. 249; AM i. 225; in French; complete.

we have to content ourselves with guessing them *a posteriori* from their effects. I cannot think of anything which could be of greater help towards the discovery of this order than the description of many comets; and, as you know, I have no books and even if I had I would begrudge the time spent in reading them, so I would be very glad to find somebody who had collected together the things which could cost me a lot of trouble to glean from several authors each writing about only one or two comets.

You once told me that you knew some people who were so dedicated to the advancement of science that they were willing to make every kind of experiment at their own expense. It would be very useful if some such person were to write the history of celestial phenomena in accordance with the Baconian method and to describe the present appearance of the heavens without any arguments or hypotheses, reporting the position of each fixed star in relation to its neighbours, listing their differences in size and colour and visibility and brilliance and so on. He should tell us how far this accords with what ancient astronomers have written and what differences are to be found; for I have no doubt that the stars are constantly changing their relative position, in spite of being called fixed. He should add the observations which have been made of comets, with a table of the track of each like the ones Tycho made of the three or four that he observed, and he should include the variations in the ecliptic and apogee of planets. Such a work would be more generally useful than might seem possible at first sight, and it would relieve me of a great deal of trouble. But I have no hope that anyone will do it, just as I do not hope to discover the answers to my present questions about the stars. I think that the science I describe is beyond the reach of the human mind; and yet I am so foolish that I cannot help dreaming of it though I know that this will only make me waste my time as it has already done for the last two months. In that time I have made no progress with my treatise; but I will not fail to finish it before the date I told you. I have written all this needlessly so as to fill up my letter and not send you empty paper. Tell me if M. de Beaune is publishing anything. I would be glad to see MM. Mydorge and Hardy's method of doubling a cube as well as the books you sent me. I think that you told me that it would be there but I have not been able to find it.

I am, etc.

In letters to Mersenne later in 1632 Descartes reported the progress of his *Treatise on the World*, enunciated the law of sines in Dioptrics, and compared the anatomical theories of Harvey's *De Motu Cordis* with his own independent results. In 1633 he was apparently working so hard on his treatise as to have no time for correspondence. Only two letters survive from the first ten months of the year; that of 22 July informs Mersenne that the treatise is complete except for final corrections. But while Descartes was revising his work, he learnt that the Roman Inquisition had condemned Galileo's book *Massimi Sistemi* for maintaining that the earth is in motion around the sun. As his own *World* was explicitly heliocentric, he resolved to suppress the treatise rather than, in the words of Baillet's translator, 'to expose himself to the scurvy humour of the Inquisition of Rome, by publishing that hypothesis they had condemned without understanding it'. He wrote to Mersenne to inform him of his decision in November 1633 and again in February 1634; but these letters seem to have gone astray, and in the following letter their content is summarized.

## From the letter to Mersenne, April 1634[1]

Reverend Father,

From your last I learn that my latest letters to you have been lost, though I thought I had addressed them very safely. In them I told you at length the reason why I did not send you my treatise. I am sure you will find it so just that far from blaming me for resolving never to show it to anyone, you would be the first to exhort me to do so, if I were not already fully so resolved.

Doubtless you know that Galileo was recently censured by the Inquisitors of the Faith, and that his views about the movement of the earth were condemned as heretical. I must tell you that all the things I explained in my treatise, which

[1] AT i. 284; AM i. 252; in French; extracts.

25

included the doctrine of the movement of the earth, were so interdependent that it is enough to discover that one of them is false to know that all the arguments I was using are unsound. Though I thought they were based on very certain and evident proofs, I would not wish, for anything in the world, to maintain them against the authority of the Church. I know that it might be said that not everything which the Roman Inquisitors decide is automatically an article of faith, before it is decided upon by a General Council. But I am not so fond of my own opinions as to want to use such quibbles to be able to maintain them. I desire to live in peace and to continue the life I have begun under the motto *to live well you must live unseen.*[1] And so I am more happy to be delivered from the fear of my work's making unwanted acquaintances than I am unhappy at having lost the time and trouble which I spent on its composition.

\*      \*      \*

As for the results you tell me of Galileo's experiments I deny them all; but I do not conclude the motion of the earth to be any less probable. I do indeed agree that the movement of a chariot, a boat, or a horse remains in some manner in a stone thrown from them, but there are other reasons which prevent it from remaining undiminished. As for a cannon ball shot off a high tower, it must take much longer descending than one allowed to fall vertically; for it meets a lot of air on its way, which resists its vertical motion as well as its horizontal motion.

I am astonished that an ecclesiastic should dare to write about the motion of the earth, whatever excuses he may give. For I have seen letters patent about Galileo's condemnation, printed at Liège on 20 September 1633, which contained the words '*though he pretended he put forward his view only hypothetically*'[2]; so that they seem to forbid even the use of this hypothesis in astronomy. For this reason I do not dare to tell him any of my thoughts on the topic. Moreover, I do not see that this censure has been endorsed by the Pope or

---

[1] Bene vixit, bene qui latuit (Ovid, *Tristia* III. iv. 25).
[2] Quamvis hypothetice a se illam proponi simularet.

by any Council, but only by a single congregation of the
Cardinals of the Inquisition; so I do not altogether lose hope
that the case may turn out like that of the Antipodes, which
were similarly condemned long ago. So in time my World
may yet see the day; and in that case I shall need my own
arguments to use myself.

Further criticisms of Galileo are to be found in a letter to Mersenne of
14 August 1634. In a letter to Beeckman later in the same month Descartes
defends the instantaneous propagation of light, a theory with which, he says,
his whole philosophy stands or falls.

No letters of strictly philosophical interest have survived from the year
1635. Descartes showed the manuscript of his *Dioptrics* to Constantijn
Huygens, and his letters to him at this period concern the topics treated in it,
and especially the cutting of lenses. A letter to an unknown correspondent in
the summer of the year concludes as follows:

'I do not think that heavy bodies fall because of a real quality called
heaviness, as philosophers imagine, or because of some attraction of the earth;
but I could not explain my views on all these topics without publishing my
*World* with the forbidden movement, which I now think inopportune; and
I am surprised that you intend to refute the book *Against the Movement of the
Earth*; but I leave it to your prudence.'

# Descartes to Mersenne, March 1636[1]

Reverend Father,

About five weeks ago I received your last of 18 January
and I had not received the previous letter until four or five
days before. I postponed replying to you in the hope of
being able to tell you soon that I had sent my work to the
printer. That was why I came to this town,[2] because the
Elzevirs earlier said they would like to be my publishers.
But having seen me here they imagine, I think, that I will
not escape from them, and so they have been making
difficulties, so that I have resolved to go to someone else.
Although I could find here several other publishers I will not

---

[1] AT i. 338; AM i. 300; in French; complete.          [2] Leyden.

settle with any of them until I have news from you, provided that I do not have to wait too long. If you think that my manuscripts could be printed in Paris more conveniently than here and if you would be willing to take charge of them as you once kindly offered to do, I could send them to you immediately after receiving word from you. However, there is this difficulty: my manuscript is no better written than this letter; the spelling and punctuation is equally careless and the diagrams are drawn by myself, that is to say, very badly. So if you cannot make out from the text how to explain them to the engraver it would be impossible for him to understand them. Moreover I would like to have the whole thing printed in a handsome fount on handsome paper, and I would like the publisher to give me at least two hundred copies because I want to distribute them to a number of people.

So that you may know what it is that I want to have printed, there will be four treatises, all in French, and the general title will be as follows. 'The Plan of a Universal Science to raise our Nature to its Highest Degree of Perfection, with the Dioptrics, the Meteors and the Geometry; in which the most Curious Topics which the Author has been able to choose in order to give Proof of his Universal Science are Explained in such a Manner that even those who have Never Studied them can Understand them.' In this *Plan* I explain a part of my method, I try to prove the existence of God and of the soul apart from the body, and I add many other things which I imagine will not displease the reader. In the Dioptrics besides treating of refraction and the manufacture of lenses I give detailed descriptions of the eye, of light, of vision, and of everything belonging to Catoptrics and Optics.[1] In the *Meteors* I dwell principally on the nature of salt, the causes of winds and thunder, the shapes of snowflakes, the colours of the rainbow—here I try also to demonstrate what is the nature of each colour—and the crowns or haloes and the mock suns or parhelia like those which appeared at Rome six or seven years ago. Finally, in the *Geometry* I try to give a general method of solving all the

---

[1] Dioptrics is the part of optics which treats of refraction, catoptrics that which treats of reflection.

problems that have never yet been solved. All this I think will make a volume no bigger than fifty or sixty sheets. I do not want to put my name to it, as I resolved long ago; please do not say anything about it to anybody unless you judge proper to mention it to some publisher to find out whether he is willing to co-operate with me. Do not make any contract for me, please, until you hear my reply; I will make my decision on the basis of what you tell me. I would prefer to employ somebody who has no connection with Elzevir, who will probably have warned his correspondents because he knows that I am writing to you.

I have used up all my paper in telling you this. There remains only enough to tell you that in order to examine the things which Galileo says about motion I would need more time than I can spare at present.

I think that the experiment showing that sounds travel no more quickly with the wind than against the wind is correct, at least so far as the senses can perceive; because the movement of sound is something of a quite different nature from the movement of wind.

Thank you for the account of the ball shot vertically which does not return; it is very remarkable.

As for the rarefied matter of which I have often spoken, I think it to be of the same matter as terrestrial bodies; but as air is more fluid than water so I imagine this matter much more fluid, liquid and penetrating than air.

A bow bends back because when the shape of its orifices is distorted, the rarefied matter which passes through tends to restore whichever side it enters from.

I am, etc.

In the end the *Discourse* and its accompanying essays were published by Maire of Leyden. Descartes' letters to Huygens in 1636 record how it was seen through the press; a slow business because of the diagrams. He decided to abbreviate the title to 'Discourse on the Method etc., with the Dioptrics, the Meteors, and the Geometry, which are Essays in that Method'. Mersenne urged him to publish in addition his suppressed treatise on physics.

## Descartes to Mersenne, 27 February 1637[1]

I find that you have a very poor opinion of me and consider me very inconstant and irresolute, since you think that because of what you tell me I ought to change my plan, and attach my Physics to my first *Discourse*. You seem to think I should give it to the publisher this very day on seeing your letter. I could not help laughing when I read the passage where you say that I am forcing the public to kill me so that it can see my writings the sooner. To this I can only reply that they are now in such a place and condition that those who would kill me would never be able to lay hands on them; and if I do not die in my own good time and in a good humour with the men who remain living, they will certainly not see them for more than a hundred years after my death.

I am very grateful to you for the objections which you have sent me and I beg you to continue to tell me all those you hear. Make them as unfavourable to me as you can; that will be the greatest pleasure you can give me. I am not in the habit of crying when people are treating my wounds, and those who are kind enough to instruct and inform me will always find me very docile.

However, I have not been able to understand your objection to the title; because I have not put *Treatise on Method* but *Discourse on Method*, which means *Preface* or *Notice* on method, to show that I do not intend to teach the method but only to describe it. As can be seen from what I say, it is a practice rather than a theory. I call the following treatises *Essays in this Method*, because I claim that what they contain could never have been discovered without it so that they show how much it is worth. I have also inserted a certain amount of Metaphysics, Physics, and Medicine in the first *Discourse* in order to show that my method extends to topics of all kinds.

Your second objection is that I have not explained at

[1] AT i. 347; AM i. 328; in French; complete.

sufficient length how I know that the soul is a substance distinct from the body and that its nature is nothing but thought. This, you say, is the only thing that makes obscure the proof of the existence of God. I admit that what you say is very true and that this makes my proof of the existence of God difficult to understand. But I could not deal any better with this topic without explaining in detail the falsehood or uncertainty to be found in all the judgements that depend on the senses and the imagination, so as to show in the sequel which judgements depend only on the pure understanding, and what evidence and certainty they possess. I left this out on purpose and after deliberation, mainly because I wrote in the vernacular. I was afraid that weak minds might avidly embrace the doubts and scruples which I would have had to propound, and afterwards been unable to follow as fully the arguments by which I would have endeavoured to remove them. Thus I would have set them on a false path and been unable to bring them back. Eight years ago, however, I wrote in Latin the beginnings of a treatise of metaphysics in which this argument is conducted at some length; if a Latin version of my present book is made, as is planned, I could have it included. However I am convinced that those who study my arguments for the existence of God will find them the more probative the more they try to fault them. I claim that they are clearer in themselves than any of the demonstrations of geometers; in my view they are obscure only to those who cannot *withdraw their mind from the senses* as I wrote on page 38.[1]

I am extremely grateful to you for the trouble which you offer to take concerning the printing of my manuscripts. However, I could not allow anyone but myself to be put to any expense; I would not fail to send you whatever was necessary. Indeed I do not think that there will be any great expense necessary; some publishers have promised me gifts to induce me to offer them my work, even before I had left Paris or begun writing. So I think that there may still be enough foolish publishers to print them at their own expense, and enough gullible readers to buy copies and save them from their folly. Whatever I do I shall not hide myself

[1] Cf. AT vi. 37; HR i. 104.

as if I had committed a crime, but only to avoid disturbance and to keep the liberty I have always enjoyed. I will not be very alarmed if some people know my name; but for the present I prefer people not to speak of it at all, so that no expectations may be raised and my work may not fall short of expectation.

Like you I am amused by the fantasies of the chemist of whom you wrote. I think that such chimaeras are unworthy to occupy the thoughts of a decent man for a single moment.

I am, etc.

Apart from a letter of condolence to Huygens on the death of his wife, Descartes' correspondence in the spring of 1637 concerns the final preparation for the publication of the *Discourse* and the obtaining of a Privilege or Copyright from the King of France. This was granted, thanks to Mersenne's efforts, on 4 May 1637, but the news took some time to reach Descartes.

## Descartes to Mersenne, end of May 1637[1]

You argue that if the nature of man is simply to think, then he has no will. I do not see that this follows; because willing, understanding, imagining, sensing and so on are just different ways of thinking, and all belong to the soul.

You reject my statement that in order to do well it is sufficient to judge well; yet it seems to me that the common scholastic doctrine is that *the will does not tend towards evil except in so far as it is presented to it by the intellect under some aspect of goodness*[2]—that is why they say that *whoever sins does so in ignorance*—so that if the intellect never presented anything to the will as good without its actually being so, the will could never go wrong in its choice. But the intellect often presents different things to the will at the same time; and that is why they say, 'I see and praise the better, but I follow the worse,' which applies only to weak minds, as I

[1] AT i. 365; AM I. 351; in French; complete.
[2] Latin words in a French context.

said on page 26.[1] The welldoing of which I speak cannot be understood in a theological sense—for there Grace comes into the question—but simply in the sense of moral and natural philosophy where no account is taken of Grace. So I cannot be accused, on these grounds, of the error of the Pelagians. It is as if I said that good sense was the only thing necessary to make a man of honour; it would be altogether beside the point to object that it was necessary also to have the right sex and not to be a woman.

Similarly, when I say that it is probable (I mean according to human reason) that the world was created just as it should be, I am not denying that it may be certain by faith that it is perfect.

As to those who asked you what my religion was, they should have looked at what I wrote on p. 29,[2] namely, that I would not have thought that I should be content with the opinions of others for a single moment if I had not proposed to examine them by my own judgement when the time came. Then they would see that it cannot be inferred from my Discourse that infidels should remain in the religion of their parents.

I do not find anything else in your two letters which needs a reply, except that it seems that you are afraid that the publication of my first *Discourse* may commit me never afterwards to publish my *Physics*. You need not be afraid of that, because I do not anywhere promise never to publish it during my life time. I merely say that in the past I planned to publish it, but that more recently, for the reasons which I give, I have decided not to do so during my lifetime; and that now I have made up my mind to publish the treatises contained in this volume. It can indeed be inferred from that that if the reasons which prevent me from publishing should be altered, I could make a fresh resolve, without thereby being inconstant; because *when a cause is removed its effect is removed*. You say also that what I say about my *Physics* may be attributed to vainglory since I do not include it. It may be, by people who do not know me and have only read my first *Discourse*. But those who look at the

---

[1] AT vi. 25; HR i. 96. The quotation is from Ovid, *Metamorphoses* vii. 20.
[2] AT vi. 28; HR i. 98.

whole book, or who know me in person, will not, I think, accuse me of that vice. Nor will they reproach me for despising my fellow men, as you do, because I do not press upon them a gift that I am not yet sure they want. I spoke of my *Physics* as I did solely in order to urge those who want to see it to put an end to the causes which prevent me from publishing it.

Once more, I ask you to send us either the Privilege or the refusal of it, as promptly as possible. I would prefer it one day earlier in the simplest form than one day later in the most ample form.

I am, etc.

## Descartes to [Silhon], May 1637[1]

Sir,

I agree, as you observe, that there is a great defect in the work you have seen, and that I have not expounded, in a manner that everyone can easily grasp, the arguments by which I think I can prove that there is nothing at all so evident and certain in itself as the existence of God and of the human soul. But I did not dare to try to do so, since I would have had to explain at length the strongest arguments of the sceptics to show that there is no material thing of whose existence one can be certain. Thus I would have accustomed the reader to detach his thought from sensible things; and then I would have shown that a man who thus doubts everything material cannot for all that doubt his own existence. From this it follows that he, that is his soul, is a being or substance which is not at all corporeal, whose nature is solely to think, and that this is the first thing one can know with certainty. If you spend a sufficient time on this meditation, you acquire by degrees a very clear, dare I say intuitive, notion of intellectual nature in general. This is the idea which, if considered without limitation, represents God, and if limited, is the

[1] AT i. 352; AM i. 354; in French; complete.

idea of an angel or a human soul. Now it is not possible fully to understand what I later say about the existence of God unless you begin in this way, as I hinted on p. 38.[1] But I was afraid that this introduction would look at first as if it was designed to bring in scepticism, and would disturb weaker minds, especially as I was writing in the vernacular. So I did not dare to put in even the little on p. 32 without some words of warning.[2] But as for intelligent people like yourself, Sir, if they take the trouble not only to read but also to meditate in order the things I say I meditated, spending a long time on each point, to see whether I have gone wrong, I trust that they will come to the same conclusions as I did. I shall be glad, as soon as I have time, to try to explain this further. I am pleased to have had this opportunity to show you that I am, etc.

The *Discourse* and *Essays* were published on 8 June 1637. Descartes sent copies of the book to the King of France, to Cardinal Richelieu, to the Prince of Orange, and to his Jesuit teachers at La Flèche. Some of his covering letters have been preserved. In one letter he explains that the whole purpose of publishing the *Discourse* is to prepare the way for a complete publication of his *Physics*. 'To this end I propose a general method, which I do not really expound, but merely give samples of in the three *Essays* which I attach to the *Discourse*. The subject of the first is partly philosophical and partly mathematical; of the second, wholly philosophical; of the third, wholly mathematical . . . And to show that this method is of universal application I inserted briefly something of metaphysics, physics, and medicine in the first *Discourse*' (AT i. 368; AM i. 356). In the following letters Descartes replies to some of the first critics of his work.

# Descartes to Plempius for Fromondus, 3 October 1637[3]

At the beginning of his objections the learned and distinguished M. Fromondus reminds me of the fable of Ixion.[4]

[1] AT vi. 37; HR i. 104.    [2] AT vi. 31; HR i. 101.
[3] AT i. 412; AM ii. 5; in Latin; with omissions.
[4] In classical mythology Ixion made love to a cloud, mistaking it for Juno.

This seems very apt. He does well to warn me to keep to the truth and shun cloudy speculations: I protest that as far as in me lies I have always done so and will always do so. But the story fits him too: he thinks that he is attacking my philosophy, but he refutes only empty theories which have nothing to do with me, such as the system of atoms and void attributed to Democritus and Epicurus.

1. *A propos* of pp. 46 and 47[1] he comments that noble actions like sight cannot result from so ignoble and brutish a cause as heat. He supposes that I think that animals see just as we do, i.e. feeling or thinking they see, which is said to have been Epicurus' view and is still almost universal. But in the whole of that part up to p. 60[2] I explain quite explicitly that my view is that animals do not see as we do when we are aware that we see, but only as we do when our mind is elsewhere. In such a case the images of external objects are depicted on our retinas, and perhaps the impressions they leave in the optic nerves cause our limbs to make various movements, although we are quite unaware of this. In such a case we too move just like automata, and nobody thinks that the force of heat is insufficient to cause their movements.

2. *A propos* of p. 56[3] he asks what is the point of attributing substantial souls to animals, and goes on to say that my views will perhaps open the way for atheists to deny the presence of a rational soul even in the human body. I am the last person to deserve this criticism, since, like the Bible, I believe, and I thought I had clearly explained, that the souls of animals are nothing but their blood, the blood which is turned into spirits[4] by the warmth of the heart and travels through the arteries to the brain and from it to the nerves and muscles. This theory involves such an enormous difference between the souls of animals and our own that it provides a better argument than any yet thought of to refute the atheists and establish that human minds cannot be drawn out of the potentiality of matter. And on the other side, I do not see how those who credit animals with some

[1] AT vi. 46; HR i. 109.        [2] AT vi. 60; HR i. 118.
[3] AT vi. 56; HR i. 116.        [4] i.e. animal spirits, or volatile fluids.

sort of substantial soul distinct from blood, heat, and spirits, can answer such Scripture texts as Leviticus 17, 14 (The soul of all flesh is in its blood, and you shall not eat the blood of any flesh, because the soul of flesh is in its blood) and Deuteronomy 12, 23 (Only take care not to eat their blood, for their blood is their soul, and you must not eat their soul with their flesh). Such texts seem much clearer than others which are quoted against certain other opinions which have been condemned solely because they contradict the Bible or appear to. Moreover, since these people posit so little difference between the operations of a man and of an animal, I do not see how they can convince themselves there is such a great difference between the natures of the rational and sensitive souls. On their view, when the sensitive soul is alone, its nature is corporeal and mortal; when it is joined to the rational soul it is spiritual and immortal. For how do they think sensation is distinguished from reason? Sense-cognition, they say, is a matter of simple apprehension and therefore cannot be false; but the cognition of reason is a little more complex, and can make its way through tortuous syllogisms. This in no way seems to show its greater perfection; especially when the same people say that God's knowledge and that of the angels is utterly simple and intuitive, a sheer apprehension free from any discursive wrapping. With respect, then, it seems that on their view the senses of animals are closer to the knowledge of God and the angels than human reasoning is. I could have said many such things to support my theses, not only about the soul, but about almost everything else I have discussed. I did not do so, partly for fear of writing something false while refuting falsehood, partly for fear of seeming to want to ridicule received Scholastic opinions.

*        *        *

9. He expresses surprise that on p. 30[1] I recognize no sensation save that which takes place in the brain. On this point I hope that all doctors and surgeons will help me to

---

[1] Of the *Dioptrics* (AT vi. 110; Olscamp 87).

persuade him; for they know that those whose limbs have recently been amputated often think they still feel pain in the parts they no longer possess. I once knew a girl who had a serious wound in her hands and had her whole arm amputated because of creeping gangrene. Whenever the surgeon approached her they blindfolded her eyes so that she would be more tractable, and the place where her arm had been was so covered with bandages that for some weeks she did not know that she had lost it. Meanwhile she complained of feeling various pains in her fingers, wrist, and forearm; and this was obviously due to the condition of the nerves in her arm which formerly led from her brain to those parts of her body. This would certainly not have happened, if the feeling or, as he says, sensation of pain had occurred outside the brain.

10. I do not understand his objections to pp. 159 and 163.[1] If my philosophy seems too crass to him, because, like Mechanics, it considers shapes and sizes and motions, he is condemning what seems to me its most praiseworthy feature, of which I am particularly proud. I mean that in my kind of philosophy I use no reasoning which is not mathematical and evident, and all my conclusions are confirmed by true experiments. Whatever I concluded to be possible from the principles of my philosophy actually happens whenever the appropriate agents are applied to the appropriate matter. I am surprised that he does not realize that the Mechanics now current is nothing but a part of the true Physics, which not being welcomed by the common sort of philosophers, took refuge with the mathematicians. This part of philosophy has in fact remained truer and less corrupt than the others, because since it has useful and practical consequences, any mistakes in it result in financial loss. So if he despises my style of philosophy because it is like Mechanics, it is the same to me as if he despised it for being true.

He does not agree that water and other bodies are made up of any parts which are actually distinct. He should observe that in many cases we can perceive such parts with the naked eye: specks of dust in stones, strands in wood, and the

---

[1] Of the *Meteors* (AT vi. 233; Olscamp 264).

warp and woof of flesh, to quote his own example. It is perfectly reasonable to judge of things which are too small for the senses to perceive on the model of those we see. He should remember that he said himself in his objection to p. 164[1] that the air and spirits enclosed in water raise its topmost parts as they leave it: and this is unintelligible unless he admits that the air and spirits consist of various parts scattered throughout the water. Perhaps he is worried about his integral union, and the other shadowy entities with which a subtle philosophy stuffs its continuum, and that is why he will not agree that terrestrial bodies are composed of actually divided parts. If so, he should re-read p. 164 and he will find that I conceive each of these particles as a continuous body, divisible to infinity, about which could be said everything that he has proved in his most subtle tract *On the Composition of the Continuum*.[2] I do not explicitly deny in bodies any of the things which others admit in addition to the elements of my theory; but my crass unsubtle philosophy is content with this simple apparatus.

11. He is convinced that my supposition that the parts of water are oblong like eels is rash and baseless. He should remember what is said on p. 76 of the *Discourse on Method*.[3] If he would be good enough to read with sufficient attention everything I wrote in the *Meteors* and the *Dioptrics*, he would find six hundred reasons from which six hundred syllogisms could be constructed to prove what I say. They would go like this.

If water is more fluid and harder to freeze than oil, this is a sign that oil is made of parts which stick together easily, like the branches of trees, while water is made of more slippery parts, like those which have the shape of eels. But experience shows that water is more fluid and harder to freeze than oil. Ergo . . .

Again, if cloths soaked in water are easier to dry than cloths soaked in oil, that is a sign that the parts of water have the shapes of eels, and can thus easily come out through the holes in the cloth, and that the parts of oil have the shapes

---

[1] AT vi. 238; Olscamp 265.
[2] *Labyrinthus, sive de Compositione Continui* . . . (Antwerp, 1631).
[3] AT vi. 76; HR i. 128.

of branches, and thus get entangled in the same holes; but experience shows etc.

Again, if water is heavier than oil, this is a sign that the parts of oil are branch-shaped, and so leave many spaces around them, and that the parts of water are like eels, and therefore are satisfied with less space; but etc.

Again, if water is more easy to turn into vapour, or is, as the chemists say, more volatile than oil, that is a sign that it is made up of parts which can easily be separated from each other like eels; and that oil is made up of branch-like parts which are more closely intertwined. But etc.

Although each of these points taken by itself gives only probability to the conclusion, taken together they amount to a proof of it. But if I had tried to derive all these conclusions like a dialectician, I would have worn out the printers' hands and the readers' eyes with an enormous volume.

12. What I say on p. 162[1] seems paradoxical to him: that a slow motion produces the sensation of cold, and a fast motion the sensation of heat. On the same showing it should seem paradoxical to him that a gentle rubbing on the hand should produce a sensation of titillation and pleasure, and a harder rubbing produce a sensation of pain; for pleasure and pain are no less different from each other than heat and cold. Moreover, if we put a warm hand on a tepid body, it will seem cold to us, though we shall think it to be warm if we touch it with another hand which is colder.


## Descartes to Plempius, 3 October 1637[2]

Sir,

I received your letter with M. Fromondus' comments, and they were very welcome, though I must admit they arrived sooner than I expected. A few weeks ago I had heard that the book had not yet been sent to you, and many of those to whom I gave it to read here told me that they were not in a position

---

[1] AT vi. 237; Olscamp 266.     [2] AT i. 410; AM ii. 1; in Latin; complete.

to judge it until they had re-read it several times. I am the more grateful to you both: to yourself for your generous praise, which I fear is beyond my deserts and is doubtless mostly due to your friendship for me; and to M. Fromondus for the care with which he has read my book and the trouble he has taken to send me his opinion of it. The judgement of a man so gifted, and so learned in the topics I treated, will enable me to assess the opinion of many others. In many points, however, I see that he has not understood my meaning, so that I cannot yet tell what he and others will say after a closer examination. I cannot altogether agree with your judgement that my explanations can be rejected and ignored, but cannot be refuted or disproved. I used only very evident principles, and like a mathematician I took account of nothing but sizes, shapes, and motions, and so I cut myself off from all the subterfuges of philosophers. Consequently, the slightest error which occurs will be easily detectable and refutable by a mathematical proof. On the other hand, if something is so true and solid that it cannot be overthrown by any such proof, then nobody, at least no teacher, can afford to ignore it. It is true that in appearance I expounded my opinions without proving them; but it is not difficult to extract from my explanations syllogisms which so evidently destroy the rival accounts of the same topics, that those who want to defend them will find it difficult, without making themselves a laughing stock, to reply to people who have understood what I say. I am aware that my geometry will have very few readers; for I left out things which I thought others knew, and tried in a few words to include, or touch on, many things—indeed everything which can ever be discovered in that science. So it demands readers who are not only skilled in the whole of geometry and algebra so far discovered, but also industrious, intelligent, and attentive. I have heard that in your university[1] there are two such men, Wendel and van der Waegen. I will be very pleased to hear from you what they, or any others, judge of it. I am very anxious to see what you are writing about the motion of the heart. Send me it as soon as possible, please, and let me know how M.

---

[1] Louvain.

Fromondus took my replies. Greet him warmly in my name. I have nothing to say about the philosophers of Leyden; I left there before the book was published; and so far as I know, they have all held their peace, as you predicted of others also.

I am, etc.

## From the letter to Mersenne, 5 October 1637[1]

Reverend Father,

You tell me that one of your friends[2] who saw the *Dioptrics* had certain objections to make. The first was that he doubts whether the tendency to move should follow the same laws as movement itself, since the two differ from each other as much as potentiality and actuality. I am convinced that he conceived this doubt because he imagined that I was doubtful on the point myself, and because I put these words on line 24 of page 8: 'It is very easy to believe that the tendency to move must follow in this the same laws as does movement.'[3] He thought that when I said that something was easy to believe, I meant that it was no more than probable; but in this he has altogether mistaken my meaning. I consider almost as false whatever is only a matter of verisimilitude; and when I say that something is easy to believe I do not mean that it is only probable, but that it is so clear and so evident that there is no need for me to stop to prove it. As in fact it cannot reasonably be doubted that the laws which govern movement, which is the actuality, as he says himself, must govern also the tendency to move, which is the potentiality of the same actuality; for although it is not always true that what has once been in potentiality is later in actuality, it is altogether impossible for something to be in actuality without having been in potentiality.

---

[1] AT i. 450; AM i. ii. 44; in French; extract.
[2] Fermat.    [3] AT vi. 89, Olscamp 70.

## Descartes to Plempius, 20 December 1637[1]

Sir,

I am glad that my answers to M. Fromondus' objections have at last reached you. But I am very surprised that he should conclude from them that I was annoyed or irritated by his paper. I was not at all; and I do not think that I uttered the slightest word against him without his having said similar or harder things to me first. I concluded that he liked that style of writing, and so I went rather against my own nature, which is disinclined to any contention, because I was afraid that he might enjoy the game less if I received his attack too gently and softly. People who play draughts or chess against each other do not cease thereby to be friends; indeed their very skill in the game is often a cause and bond of friendship between them. I only wanted by my reply to earn his goodwill.

I do not know why my book is not yet obtainable in your shops: if your booksellers want a copy from mine, I know he will be very glad to send one. I do not expect to have a sufficiently ripe judgement on my book from anyone who only reads hurriedly through a borrowed copy. The points near the end of each treatise cannot be understood unless everything which goes before is memorized; and the proofs of the propositions at the beginning depend on everything which follows. The things which I say in the first chapters about the nature of light, and about the shape of the particles of salt and fresh water, are not my principles, as you seem to object, but rather conclusions which are proved by everything that comes after. Sizes, shapes, positions, and motions are my formal object (in Philosophers' jargon) and the physical objects which I explain are my material object. The principles or premisses from which I derive these conclusions are only the axioms on which geometers base their demonstrations: for instance, 'the whole is greater than

[1] AT i. 475; AM ii. 61; in Latin; complete.

the part', 'if equals are taken from equals the remainders are equal'; but they are not abstracted from all sensible matter, as in geometry, but applied to various experimental data known indubitably by the senses. For instance, from the oblong and inflexible shape of the particles of salt, I deduced the square shape of its grains, and many other things which are obvious to the senses; I wanted to explain the latter by the former as effects by their cause. I did not want to prove things which are already well enough known, but rather to demonstrate the cause by the effects *a posteriori*, as I remember I wrote at length in my reply to the eleventh objection of M. Fromondus.

I will be glad if the Jesuit to whom you recommended my book writes to me about it; whatever comes from the men of that Society is likely to be well thought out, and the stronger the objections he puts forward, the more pleased I shall be with them. For the same reason I eagerly await your objections about the motion of the heart.

I am, etc.

In the year 1638 Descartes was involved in a number of controversies arising out of his scientific work. The mathematician Fermat sent him five pages of objections to the *Dioptrics* and a treatise to rival his *Geometry*. Thus began a debate which drew in a number of other famous mathematicians, Roberval and Etienne Pascal supporting Fermat, and Mydorge and Hardy supporting Descartes. The correspondence between Descartes and Fermat grew heated, but the two were finally reconciled through Mersenne. The arrival of Plempius' paper on the motion of the heart engaged Descartes in another controversy about the circulation of the blood. Morin, the professor of mathematics at Paris, attacked Descartes' theories of the nature and transmission of light. Most of Descartes' correspondence in 1638 is taken up with these controversies. In the course of them he was drawn to develop a number of crucial points in philosophy of science, as the following letters show.

## From the letter to Mersenne, January 1638 (?)

... You ask whether I think that water is in its natural state when it is liquid or when it is frozen. I reply that I do not regard anything in nature as violent, except in relation to the human intellect, which calls 'violent' anything which is not in accordance with its will, or not in accordance with what it judges ought to be the case. It is no less natural for water to be frozen when it is very cold, than to be liquid when it is less cold, because the causes of each are equally natural.

## Descartes to Vatier, 22 February 1638[1]

Reverend Father,

I am overwhelmed by your kindness in studying my book of essays with such great care, and sending me your opinion of it with so many marks of goodwill. When I sent it to you I should have enclosed a letter assuring you of my very humble service, were it not that I was hoping—vainly as it turned out—to circulate the book anonymously. I must believe that it is your affection for the father rather than any deserts of the child which has made you welcome it so favourably. I am extremely grateful to you. Perhaps I am too flattered by the very favourable things you say in your two letters, but I must say frankly that no one, among all those who have been good enough to express an opinion of my work, has done me such good justice as you. No one else's criticism has been so favourable, so unbiassed, and so well-informed. By the way, I am surprised that your second letter followed so closely on your first. I received them more or less at the same time, though when I saw your first I was sure that I must not expect another before your vacation.

I will answer you point by point. I must say first that my purpose was not to teach the whole of my Method in the Discourse in which I propound it, but only to say enough to show that the new views in the *Dioptrics* and the *Meteors* were not random notions, and were perhaps worth the trouble of examining. I could not demonstrate the use of this Method in the three treatises which I gave, because it prescribes an order of research which is quite different from

---

[1] AT i. 558; AM ii. 133; in French; complete.

the one I thought proper for exposition. I have however given a brief sample of it in my account of the rainbow, and if you take the trouble to re-read it, I hope that it will satisfy you more than it did the first time; the matter is, after all, quite difficult in itself. I attached these three treatises to the discourse which precedes them because I am convinced that if people examine them carefully and compare them with what has previously been written on the same topics, they will have grounds for judging that the Method I adopt is no ordinary one and is perhaps better than some others.

It is true that I have been too obscure in what I wrote about the existence of God in this treatise on Method, and I admit that although it is the most important, it is the least worked out section in the whole book. This is partly because I did not decide to include it until I had nearly completed it and the publisher was becoming impatient. But the principal reason for its obscurity is that I did not dare to go into detail about the arguments of the sceptics, nor to say everything which is necessary *to withdraw the mind from the senses.*[1] The certainty and evidence of my kind of argument for the existence of God cannot really be known without a distinct memory of the arguments which display the uncertainty of all our knowledge of material things; and these thoughts did not seem to me suitable for inclusion in a book which I wished to be intelligible even to women while providing matter for thought for the finest minds. I confess also that this obscurity arises partly—as you rightly observed—because I supposed that certain notions, which the habit of thought had made familiar and evident to me, ought to be equally so to everyone. Such, for instance, is the notion that since our ideas cannot receive their forms or their being except from external objects or from ourselves, they cannot represent any reality or perfection which is not either in those objects or in ourselves. On this point I propose to give some further explanation in a second impression.

I realized that what I said I had put in my *Treatise on Light* about the creation of the Universe would be incredible;

---

[1] Latin words in a French context.

because only ten years ago if someone else had written it I would not have been willing to believe myself that the human mind could attain to such knowledge. But my conscience, and the force of truth, gave me the courage to say it; I thought I could not omit it without betraying my own case, and there are already many people who can bear witness to it. Moreover, a part of my *Physics* was completed and prepared for publication some time ago; if it is ever published, I hope that future generations will be unable to doubt what I say.

I am grateful to you for the care with which you have examined my views on the movement of the heart. If your doctor has any objections to make to it, I will be very pleased to have them, and will not fail to reply. Only eight days ago I received seven or eight objections on the same topic from a Professor of Medicine at Louvain, a friend of mine, to whom I sent two sheets in reply. I would like to receive more of the same kind about all the difficulties which people find in what I have tried to explain. I shall not fail to reply carefully to them, and I trust that I can do so without disobliging any of their propounders. This is the kind of thing which a number of people together can do more easily than one man on his own, and there are no people who can do it better than the members of your Society. I should count it a great honour and favour if they would be willing to take the trouble; it would doubtless be the shortest method of finding out all the errors, or all the truths in my works.

As for light, if you look at the third page of the *Dioptrics*, you will see that I said there expressly that I was going to speak about it only hypothetically. Indeed, since the treatise which contains the whole body of my physical theory is named *On Light*, and since in it I explain light with greater detail and at greater length than anything else, I did not wish to write again what I had written there, but only to convey some idea of it by comparisons and hints, so far as seemed necessary for the subject matter of the *Dioptrics*.

I am obliged to you for expressing your pleasure that I did not allow others to anticipate me in publishing my thoughts; but that is something of which I have never been afraid. It matters little to me whether I am the first or the last to write what I write, provided that what I write is true. Moreover, all my thoughts are so closely connected and so interdependent, that no one could steal any of them without knowing them all.

Please tell me without delay the difficulties which you find in what I have written on refraction, or any other topic; because if you wait until my more detailed views on light are published you may have to wait a long time. I cannot prove *a priori* the hypotheses I proposed at the beginning of the *Meteors* without expounding my whole physical theory; but the phenomena which I have deduced necessarily from them, and which cannot be deduced in the same way from other principles, seem to me to prove them sufficiently *a posteriori*.[1] I foresaw that this manner of writing would shock my readers at first, and I think I could easily have prevented this by refraining from calling these propositions 'hypotheses' and by enunciating them only after I had given some reasons to prove them. However, I will tell you candidly that I chose this manner of expounding my thoughts for two reasons. First, believing that I could deduce them in order from the first principles of my Metaphysics, I wanted to pay no attention to other kinds of proofs; secondly, I wanted to try whether the simple exposition of truth would be sufficient to carry conviction without any disputations or refutations of contrary opinions. Those of my friends who have read most carefully my treatises on *Dioptrics* and *Meteors* assure me that in this I have succeeded; because although at first they found them as difficult as everyone else, after reading and re-reading them three or four times they say that they no longer find anything there which they think can be called into question. And indeed it is not always necessary to have *a priori* reasons to convince people of a truth. Thales, or whoever it was who first said that the moon received its light from the sun, probably gave no other proof of it except that the different phases of its light could be easily explained on that hypothesis. That was enough to ensure that from that time to this his view has been generally accepted as incontrovertible.

[1] AT vi. 233.

My thoughts are so interconnected that I dare to hope that people will find my principles, once they have become familiar by frequent study and are considered all together, are as well proved by the consequences I derive from them as the borrowed nature of the moon's light is proved by its waxing and waning.

The only other point to which I must reply concerns the publication of my Physics and Metaphysics. I can tell you briefly that I desire it as much or more than anyone, but only under certain conditions, without which I would be foolish to desire it. I will say also that I do not fear at all, basically, that they contain anything against the faith. On the contrary, I am vain enough to think that the faith has never been so strongly supported by human arguments as it may be if my principles are adopted. Transubstantiation, in particular, which the Calvinists regard as impossible to explain by the ordinary philosophy, is very easily explained by mine. But I see no signs that the conditions which could oblige me to do so will be fulfilled, at least for a long time; and so I resign myself to do for my part whatever I regard as my duty and submit myself for the rest to the Providence which rules the world. I know that it is that Providence which gave me the small beginnings of which you have seen the samples, and I hope that the same Providence will give me the grace to complete it, if it is useful for its glory, and if not, I wish to give up all desire to do so. I assure you that nothing which I have gained from my publications has been more delightful to me than the approval which you were good enough to give me in your letter. It is particularly precious and welcome to me because it comes from a person of your worth and cloth, and from the very place where I had the good fortune to receive my entire education in youth, and the home of my masters, towards whom I will never fail in gratitude.

I am, etc.

## Descartes to Reneri for Pollot, April 1638[1]

Your friend need not have been so ceremonious. People of such worth and intelligence need no formal introduction, and I will always count it a favour when they do me the honour of consulting me about my writings. Please tell your friend not to hesitate to do so. This time, however, since he wanted it so, I will ask you to pass on my replies to him.

First, if I had said without qualification that one should hold to opinions that one has once decided to follow, even though they are doubtful, I should indeed have been no less to blame than if I had said that one should be opinionated and stubborn; because holding to an opinion is the same as persisting in a judgement that one has made. But I said something quite different. I said that one must be decided in one's actions even when one was undecided in one's judgements, and that one should follow the most doubtful opinions with no less constancy than if they were thoroughly certain.[2] By this I meant that once one has settled on opinions which one judges doubtful—that is, once one has decided that there are no others that one judges better or more certain—one should act on them with no less constancy than if one knew that they were the best: which indeed they are when so considered. There is no danger that this constancy in action will lead us further and further into error or vice, since there can be error only in the intellect which, I am supposing, remains free throughout and regards what is doubtful as doubtful. Moreover, I apply this rule mainly to actions in life which admit of no delay, and I use it only provisionally, intending to change my opinions as soon as I can find better, and to lose no opportunity of looking for such. Finally, I was forced to speak of firmness and resolution in action for the sake of relief of conscience and to prevent people blaming me for saying

[1] AT ii. 34; AM ii. 236; in French; with omissions.
[2] Cf. AT vi. 24; HR i. 96.

that in order to avoid rashness we must once in our lifetime put aside all the opinions we have hitherto believed. Otherwise it seemed that people would have objected that such a universal doubt could give rise to great indecision and moral chaos. Altogether it seems to me that I could not have been more careful to set the virtue of resoluteness between its two contrary vices, indecision and obstinacy.

2. It does not seem to me a fiction, but a truth which nobody should deny, that there is nothing entirely in our power except our thoughts[1]; at least if you take the word 'thought' as I do, to cover all the operations of the soul, so that not only meditations and acts of the will, but the activities of seeing and hearing and deciding on one movement rather than another, so far as depends on the soul, are all thoughts. In philosophical language there is nothing strictly attributable to a man apart from what is covered by the word 'thought'; for the activities which belong to the body alone are said to take place in a man rather than to be performed by him. Notice too the word *completely* and what follows: 'when we have done our best about external things, everything which we fail to achieve is an absolute impossibility so far as we are concerned'. This shows that I did not mean that external things were not at all in our power, but that they are in our power only in so far as they can be affected by our thoughts, and not *absolutely* or *completely* in our power because there are other powers outside us which can frustrate our designs. To make myself clearer I even put side by side the two expressions *absolutely* and *so far as we are concerned*, which a critic, if he did not understand the sense of the passage, might complain contradicted each other. Nothing exterior, then, is in our power except in so far as it is at the command of the soul, and nothing is absolutely in our power except our thoughts. But though this is very true, and no one when he thinks of it explicitly could find it hard to accept, yet I did say that it was a belief which one had to grow accustomed to, and that long practice and repeated meditation were necessary to do so. This is because our desires and our passions are constantly telling us the opposite. We have so frequently

[1] AT vi. 25; HR i. 97.

experienced since childhood that by crying or commanding we could make our nurses obey us and get what we want, that we have gradually convinced ourselves that the world was made only for us, and that everything was our due. Those who are born to greatness and fortune are the more likely to deceive themselves in this way; they too are commonly seen to be the most impatient when they have to bear misfortune. It seems to me that there is no more fitting occupation for a philosopher than to accustom himself to believe what true reason tells him, and to beware of the false opinions which his natural appetites urge upon him.

3. When someone says 'I am breathing, therefore I am' if he wants to prove he exists from the fact that there cannot be breathing without existence, he proves nothing, because he would have to prove first that it is true that he is breathing, which is impossible unless he has also proved that he exists. But if he wants to prove his existence from the feeling or opinion that he has that he is breathing, so that he judges that even if the opinion was untrue he could not have it if he did not exist, then his proof is sound. For in such a case the thought of breathing is present to our mind before the thought of our existing, and we cannot doubt that we have it while we have it.[1] To say 'I am breathing, therefore I am', in this sense, is simply to say 'I am thinking, therefore I am'. You will find on examination that all the other propositions from which we can thus prove our existence reduce to the same one; so that one cannot prove from them the existence of the body, i.e. of a nature which occupies space, etc., but only that of the soul, i.e. of a nature which thinks. Of course one may wonder whether the nature which thinks may perhaps be the same as the nature which occupies space, so that there is one nature which is both intellectual and corporeal; but by the method which I suggested it is known only as intellectual.

4. From the very fact that we conceive clearly and distinctly the two natures of the body and the soul as different, we know that in reality they are different, and consequently that the soul can think without the body, even

---

[1] Cf. AT vi. 35; HR i. 103.

though, when it is joined to it, it can have its operation disturbed by the bad disposition of the bodily organs.

5. Although the Pyrrhonians reached no certain conclusion from their doubts, it does not follow that no one can. I would try now to show how they can be used to prove God's existence and to clear up the difficulties which remain in what I wrote, were it not that someone has promised to send me soon a summary of all that can be doubted on this topic, which will perhaps enable me to do it better. So I must ask the person who wrote these queries to allow me to put off my reply until I have received the summary.

6. Most of the actions of animals resemble ours, and throughout our lives this has given us many occasions to judge that they act by an interior principle like the one within ourselves, that is to say, by means of a soul which has feelings and passions like ours. All of us are deeply imbued with this opinion by nature. Whatever reasons there may be for denying it, it is hard to say publicly how the case stands without exposing oneself to the ridicule of children and feeble minds. But those who want to discover truth must distrust opinions rashly acquired in childhood. To make the right judgement about this, it seems to me, we must consider the following. Suppose that a man had been brought up all his life in some place where he had never seen any animals except men; and suppose that he was very devoted to the study of mechanics, and had made, or helped to make, various automata shaped like a man, a horse, a dog, a bird and so on, which walked, and ate, and breathed, and so far as possible imitated all the other actions of the animals they resembled, including the signs we use to express our passions, like crying when struck and running away when subjected to a loud noise. Suppose that sometimes he found it impossible to tell the difference between the real men and those which had only the shape of men, and had learned by experience that there were only the two ways of telling them apart which I explained on p. 57 of my Discourse on Method[1]: first, that these automata never answered in word or sign, except by chance, to questions

---

[1] AT vi. 56; HR i. 116.

put to them; and secondly, that though their movements were often more regular and certain than those of the wisest men, yet in many things which they would have to do to imitate us, they failed more disastrously than the greatest fools. Now, I say, you must consider what would be the judgement of such a man when he saw the animals we have; especially if he was gifted with the knowledge of God, or at least had noticed how inferior is the best skill shown by men in their artefacts when compared with that shown by nature in the composition of plants. Nature has packed plants with an infinity of tiny invisible ducts to convey certain liquids in such a way as to form leaves and flowers and fruits. Let us suppose that our man had noticed this, and so believed firmly that if there were automata made by God or nature to imitate our actions, they would imitate them more perfectly, and be incomparably more skilfully constructed than any which could be invented by men. Now suppose that this man were to see the animals we have, and noticed in their actions the same two things which make them differ from ours, and which he had already been accustomed to notice in his automata. There is no doubt that he would not come to the conclusion that there was any real feeling or emotion in them as in us, but would think they were automata, which, being made by nature, were incomparably more accomplished than any of those he had previously made himself. It only remains to consider whether the verdict he would give, with knowledge of the facts and unprejudiced by any false opinion, would be less credible than the one we made when we were children and have kept only through habit. We base our judgement solely on the resemblance between some exterior actions of animals and our own; but this is not at all a sufficient basis to prove that there is any resemblance between the corresponding interior actions.

7. I tried to show that the soul was a substance really distinct from the body. This was sufficient, I believe, in discussion with people who believe God to be creator of all, to force the admission that our souls must necessarily be created by Him. And those who acquire certainty of God's existence in the way I have shown cannot fail to recognize Him as universal creator.

From the letter to Mersenne, 17 May 1638[1]

...2. You ask whether there would be real space, as there is now, if God had created nothing. At first this question seems to be beyond the capacity of the human mind, like infinity, so that it would be unreasonable to discuss it; but in fact I think that it is merely beyond the capacity of our imagination, like the questions of the existence of God and the human soul. I believe that the intellect can reach the truth of the matter, which is, in my opinion, that not only would there not be any space, but even those truths which are called eternal—as that the whole is greater than its part— would not be truths if God had not so established, as I think I wrote you once before.

*       *       *

You ask if I regard what I have written about refraction as a demonstration. I think it is, in so far as one can be given in this field without a previous demonstration of the principles of physics by metaphysics—that is something I hope to do some day but it has not yet been done—and so far as it is possible to demonstrate the solution to any problem of mechanics, or optics, or astronomy, or anything else which is not pure geometry or arithmetic. But to ask for geometrical demonstrations in a field within the range of physics is to ask the impossible. And if you will not call demonstrations anything except geometers' proofs, then you must say that Archimedes never demonstrated anything in mechanics, nor Vitellio in optics, nor Ptolemy in astronomy. But of course nobody says this. In such matters people are satisfied if the authors' hypotheses are not obviously contrary to experience and if their discussion is coherent and free from logical error, even though their hypotheses may not be strictly true. I could demonstrate,

[1] AT ii. 134; AM ii. 261; in French; extracts.

for instance, that even the definition of a centre of gravity given by Archimedes is false, and that there is no such centre; and the other hypotheses he frames elsewhere are not strictly true either. The hypotheses of Ptolemy and Vitellio are much less certain again; but that is not a sufficient reason for rejecting the demonstrations which they have based on them. Now what I claim to have demonstrated about refraction does not depend on the truth of the nature of light, nor on whether its propagation is instantaneous or not, but only on my hypothesis that it is an action, or a power, which in its propagation from place to place follows the same laws as local motion, and is transmitted by means of an extremely rarefied liquid in the orifices of transparent bodies. Your difficulty about instantaneous propagation arises from an ambiguity in the word 'instantaneous': you seem to take it as denying every kind of priority, as if the light of the sun could be propagated here without first passing through all the intermediate space. But 'instantaneous' excludes only temporal priority; it is compatible with each of the lower parts of a ray of light being dependent on all of the upper ones, in the same way as the end of a successive movement depends on all its preceding parts. I say that there are only two ways to refute what I have written. One is to prove by experience or reason that the hypotheses I have made are false; the other is to show that what I have deduced from them cannot be deduced from them. M. de Fermat understood this very well; for he tried to refute what I wrote about refraction by attempting to prove that it contained a logical error. But if people simply say that they do not believe what I have written, because I deduce it from certain hypotheses which I have not proved, then they do not know what they are asking or what they ought to ask.

## Descartes to Morin, 13 July 1638[1]

Sir,

The objections which you kindly sent me are such that I would have received them gladly from anybody; but your rank among the learned, and the reputation which your writings have earned you, make them more gratifying from you than from anyone else. I think there is no better way of showing this than by the care I shall take to answer you in every point.

You begin with my hypotheses. You say that the phenomena of the heavenly movements can be deduced with no less certainty from the hypothesis that the earth is stationary than from the hypothesis that it moves. I agree readily. I hope that people will take in the same way what I have written in the *Dioptrics* about the nature of light, so that the force of the mathematical demonstrations which I have tried to set out there will not be dependent on any opinion in Physics, as I said sufficiently clearly on p. 3.[2] If there is some other way of imagining light which will explain all the properties of it that we know from experience, it will be seen that all that I have demonstrated about refraction, vision, and so on, can be derived from it just as well as from the hypothesis I proposed.

You say also that there is a vicious circle in proving effects from a cause, and then proving the cause by the same effects. I agree: but I do not agree that it is circular to explain effects by a cause, and then prove the cause by the effects; because there is a big difference between proving and explaining. I should add that the word 'demonstrate' can be used to signify either, if it is used according to common usage and not in the technical philosophical sense. I should add also that there is nothing circular in proving a cause by several effects which are independently known, and then

1 AT ii. 196; AM ii. 310; in French; with omissions.
2 AT vi. 83.

proving certain other effects from this cause. I have combined these two senses together on p. 76[1]: 'As my last conclusions are demonstrated by the first, which are their causes, so the first may in turn be demonstrated from the last which are their effects.' But that does not leave me open to the accusation of speaking ambiguously, because I explained what I meant immediately afterwards when I said that 'the effects are for the most part certain from experience and so the causes from which I derive them serve not so much to prove them as to explain them'. And I put 'serve not so much to prove them' rather than 'do not serve at all', so that people could tell that each of these effects could also be proved from this cause, in case there was any doubt about it, provided that the cause had already been proved from other effects. I do not see what other term I could have used to explain myself better.

You say also that astronomers often make hypotheses which cause them to fall into grave errors; as when they wrongly hypothesise parallax, or the obliquity of the ecliptic, and so on. To this I reply that these items do not belong to the class of suppositions or hypotheses I was speaking of; I marked out this class clearly when I said that one could draw very true and certain consequences from them even though they were false and uncertain. For the parallax, the obliquity of the ecliptic and so on cannot be hypothesised as false or uncertain, but only as true; whereas the Equator, the Zodiac, the epicycles and other such circles are commonly hypothesised as false, and the movement of the earth as uncertain, and yet for all that true conclusions are drawn from them.

Finally, you say that nothing is easier than to fit a cause to an effect. It is true that there are many effects to which it is easy to fit many separate causes; but it is not at all so easy to fit a single cause to many effects, unless it is the cause which truly produces them. There are often cases in which in order to prove what is the true cause of a number of effects, it is sufficient to give a single one from which they can all clearly be deduced. I claim that all the effects of

[1] AT vi. 76.

which I spoke belong to this class. You must remember that in the whole history of Physics people have only tried to imagine some causes to explain the phenomena of nature, without hardly ever having succeeded. Compare my hypotheses with the hypotheses of others. Compare all their real qualities, their substantial forms, their elements and their other countless hypotheses with my single hypothesis that all bodies are composed of parts. This is something which is visible to the naked eye in many cases and can be proved by countless reasons in others. All that I add to this is that the parts of certain kinds of bodies are of one shape rather than another. This in turn is easy to prove to those who agree that bodies are composed of parts. Compare the deductions I have made from my hypothesis—about vision, salt, winds, clouds, snow, thunder, the rainbow and so on—with what the others have derived from their hypotheses on the same topics! I hope this will be enough to convince anyone unbiassed that the effects which I explain have no other causes than the ones from which I have derived them. None the less, I intend to give a demonstration of it in another place.

## Descartes to [Hogelande], August 1638 (?)[1]

Sir,

I have read carefully the book you kindly sent me, and I thank you for it.[2] The author is clearly an intelligent and learned man, of great integrity and public spirit. All his criticisms of the accepted sciences and teaching methods are only too true, and his complaints are only too justified.

His plan of collecting into a single book all that is useful in every other book would be a very good one if it were practicable; but I think that it is not. It is often very difficult to judge accurately what others have written, and to draw the good out of them without taking the bad too. Moreover, the

---

[1] AT ii. 345; AM iii. 21; in French; complete.
[2] Comenius' *Conatuum comeniorum Praeludia* (London, 1637).

particular truths which are scattered in books are so detached
and so independent of each other, that I think one would
need more talent and energy to assemble them into a well-
proportioned and ordered collection, as your author plans
to do, than to make up such a collection out of one's own
discoveries. I do not mean that one should neglect other
people's discoveries when one encounters useful ones; but I
do not think one should spend the greater part of one's
time in collecting them. If a man were capable of finding the
foundations of the sciences, he would be wrong to waste his
life in finding scraps of knowledge hidden in the corners of
libraries; and if he was no good for anything else but that,
he would not be capable of choosing and ordering what he
found. It is true that the author says that he has already
composed or started such a book, and I am prepared to
believe that he would succeed in the task better than anybody; but the specimens which he exhibits here do not give
one great hope. The aphorisms he prints on p. 31ff contain
only such generalities that he seems to have a long way to
go to reach the particular truths which alone are required for
conduct.

Besides this, I find two things in his programme which I
cannot altogether approve. The first is that he seems to
want to combine religion and revealed truths too closely
with the sciences which are acquired by natural reasoning.
The other is that he imagines a universal science which
could be learnt by young scholars before they reach the
age of twenty-four. He does not seem to notice that there
is a great difference in this respect between acquired and
revealed truths. The knowledge of revealed truths depends
only on grace, which God denies to no one, even though it
is not efficacious for all; so the most stupid and the most
simple can acquire it as well as the most sophisticated. But
unless you have a mind out of the ordinary, you cannot hope
to do anything extraordinary in the human sciences. It is
true that we are obliged to take care that our reasonings do
not lead us to any conclusions which contradict what God
has commanded us to believe; but I think that to try to
derive from the Bible knowledge of truths which belong only
to human sciences, and which are useless for our salvation, is

to apply the holy Scripture to a purpose for which God did not give it, and so to abuse it. But perhaps the author did not intend to use the Bible in that way, nor to mix sacred and profane things. In everything else his intentions seem so good that even though he has some defects he still deserves great respect.

I thank you for the warning which you give me of the slanders of N. They are so weak and ill founded that I think they do more harm to himself, in revealing the sickness of his mind, than they can do to anyone else.

I am, etc.

## From the letter to Morin, 12 September 1638[1]

... You say that if light is nothing but the action of the Sun, then there is no light in the sun's nature; and that light is a more actual and more absolute being than movement is; and that only God acts by his essence, and so on. You are making difficulties in words where there are none in reality. There is no more problem than if I said that a clock only shows the time by the movement of its finger, and that its quality of showing the time is not a more actual or absolute being than its movement, and that this movement belongs to it by its nature and essence, because it would cease to be a clock if it did not have it. I know that you will say that the form of the clock is only an artificial form, while the form of the sun is natural and substantial; but I reply that this distinction concerns only the origin of these forms, and not at all their nature; or that the substantial form of the sun, in so far as it differs from the qualities to be found in the matter of which it consists, is an altogether philosophical entity which is unknown to me.

Throughout 1639 Descartes continued, in his letters to Mersenne, to answer innumerable questions concerning mechanics, chemistry, anatomy,

[1] AT ii. 362; AM iii. 64; in French; extract.

optics. He defended his *Essays* pertinaciously against critics, and told Mersenne, a propos of an attack on his (false) account of the movement of the heart, 'If what I have written on that topic, or about refractions, or about anything else on which I spent more than three lines, turns out to be false, then I agree that all the rest of my philosophy is worthless.' The extracts which follow have been chosen to illustrate Descartes' method and philosophy of science and nature.

## From the letter to Mersenne, 9 January 1639[1]

4. If you make the supposition that God removes all the air in a room without putting any other body in its place, you will have to suppose *eo ipso* that the walls of the room will touch each other; otherwise you will be thinking a self-contradictory thought. Just as you cannot imagine Him to flatten all the mountains in the world while leaving all the valleys, so you cannot think that He removes every kind of body and yet leaves space behind. For the idea that we have of body, or matter in general, is contained in the idea that we have of space, i.e. of something which has length and breadth and depth, just as the idea of a mountain is contained in the idea of a valley.

5. To suppose a body moving in a non-resistant medium is to suppose that all the parts of the surrounding liquid body are disposed to move at the same speed as the original body in such a way as to leave room for it and take up its room. That is why every kind of liquid resists some movement or other. To imagine matter which resisted none of the different movements of different bodies, you would have to pretend that God or an angel was moving its parts at various speeds to correspond with the speed of the movements of the body they surround.

Hitherto I have not told you what, on my view, prevents there being a void between the parts of rarefied matter. This was because I could not explain it except by discussing another extremely rarefied matter, which I wished not to mention in my *Essays*, but to keep for my *treatise on the*

---

[1] AT ii. 479; AM iii. 161; in French; extracts.

*World.* However, I am too much in your debt to keep secrets from you. So I will tell you that I imagine, or rather I have proof, that besides the matter which makes up earthly bodies, there are two other kinds. One is very rarefied and has parts which are round, or almost round, like grains of sand; this fills up the orifices of earthly bodies and is the material of which all the heavens are made. The other is incomparably more rarefied still, and its parts are so small and so fast-moving that they have no fixed shape but at each moment assume with ease the shape required to fill up all the little interstices which are not occupied by other bodies. To understand this, you must first consider that the smaller a body is, the less force is required, *ceteris paribus,*[1] to change its shape: for instance, if you have two balls of lead of unequal size, you need less force to flatten the smaller than to flatten the larger; and if they collide with each other, the shape of the smaller one will undergo a greater change. Secondly, you must observe that when several different bodies are set in motion together the smaller ones receive more of this motion, that is to say move more quickly, than the larger ones (once again, *ceteris paribus*). From this it follows *by logical necessity*[2] that since there are moving bodies in the universe, and since there is no vacuum, there must be a type of matter whose parts are so small and so fast-moving that the force of their collision with other bodies is sufficient to change their shape and mould them to fit the places they occupy. But I have said too much on a topic on which I intended to say nothing.

From the letter to Mersenne, 20 February 1639[3]

... The number and the orderly arrangement of the nerves, veins, bones, and other parts of an animal do not show that nature is insufficient to form them, provided you suppose that in everything nature acts in exact accord with

---

[1] Other things being equal.          [2] Latin expression in a French context.
[3] AT ii. 523; AM iii. 195; in French; extract.

the laws of mechanics, and that these laws have been imposed on it by God. In fact, I have taken into consideration not only what Vesalius and the others write about anatomy, but also many details unmentioned by them that I have observed myself while dissecting various animals. I have spent much time on dissection during the last eleven years, and I doubt whether there is any doctor who has made such detailed observations as I. But I have found nothing whose formation seems inexplicable by natural causes. I can explain it all in detail, just as in my *Meteors* I explained the origin of a grain of salt or a crystal of snow. In my *Treatise on the World* I supposed the body of an animal already formed, and merely exhibited its functions; if I were to start it again I should undertake to include also the causes of its formation and birth. But for all that I do not yet know enough to be able to heal even a fever. Because I claim to know only animal in general, which is not subject to fevers, and not yet man in particular, who is.

## From the letter to [Debeaune], 30 April 1639[1]

... I think that in the whole of created matter there is a certain quantity of motion which never increases or diminishes. So, when one body moves another, it loses as much of its own motion as it gives away; thus, when a stone falls to earth from a high place, if it stops and does not bounce, I think that this is because it moves the earth, and so transfers its motion to it; but if the earth it moves contains a thousand times as much matter as itself, when it transfers the whole of its motion to it it gives it only one thousandth of its velocity. So if two unequal bodies receive the same amount of movement as each other, this equal quantity of movement does not give the same velocity to the larger one as to the smaller. In this sense, then, one can say that the more matter a body contains the more 'natural inertia' it has.[2] One can say too that a body which is large is better able than a small one

---

[1] AT ii. 530; AM iii. 213; in French; extracts.
[2] 'Natural inertia' was an expression of Debeaune's.

to transfer its motion to other bodies; and a larger body is harder to move than a smaller one. So there is one sort of inertia which depends on the quantity of the matter, and another which depends on the extent of its surfaces.

My theory of weight is as follows. All the rarefied matter which is between here and the moon, rotates rapidly round the earth, and pushes towards it all the bodies which cannot move so fast. It pushes them with greater force when they have not yet begun to fall than when they are already falling; for, after all, if they fell as fast as it moved, it would not push them at all, and if they fell faster, it would actually resist them.

## From the letter to Mersenne, 16 October 1639[1]

... Since my last I have taken the time to read the book which you kindly sent me.[2] Since you ask my opinion of it, and since it deals with a subject on which I have worked all my life, I think I should write something about it in this letter. I find in it many good things, *but not to everyone's taste*, since there are few who are capable of understanding metaphysics. In the general plan of the book the author takes a route very different from the one I have followed. He examines what truth is; I have never thought of doing so, because it seems a notion so transcendentally clear that nobody can be ignorant of it. There are many ways of examining a balance before using it, but there is no way to learn what truth is, if one does not know it by nature. What reason would we have for accepting anything which could teach us the nature of truth if we did not know that it was true, that is to say, if we did not know truth? Of course it is possible to tell the *meaning of the word*[3] to someone who does not know the language, and tell him that the word *truth*, in the strict sense, denotes the conformity of thought

[1] AT ii. 587; AM iii. 247; in French; extracts.
[2] Lord Herbert of Cherbury's *De Veritate*. In an earlier letter of 27 August, Descartes had complained that the book mingled religion with philosophy.
[3] Latin words in a French context.

with its object and that when it is attributed to things outside thought, it means only that they can be the objects of
true thoughts, whether in our minds or in God's. But no
definition of logic can be given which will help anyone to
discover its nature. I think the same of many other things
which are very simply and naturally known, such as shape,
size, movement, place, time and so on: if you try to define
these things you only obscure them and cause confusion.
For instance, a man who walks across a room shows much
better what movement is, than a man who says 'it is the act
of a being in potency, in so far as it is in potency' and so on.[1]

The author takes universal consent as the criterion of his
truths; whereas I have no criterion for mine except the light
of nature. The two criteria agree in part: for since all men
have the same natural light, it seems that they should have
the same notions; but there is also a great difference between
them, because hardly anyone makes good use of that light
of nature, so that many people—perhaps all those we know
—may consent to the same error. Also there are many things
which can be known by the light of nature, but which no
one has yet reflected on.

He claims that we have as many faculties as there are
different objects of knowledge. This seems to me like saying
that because wax can take an infinite number of shapes, it
has an infinite number of faculties for taking them. In that
sense it is true, but such a mode of speech seems to me
quite useless, and indeed rather dangerous, since it may give
occasion to ignorant people to imagine so many little
entities in our soul. So I prefer to think that wax, simply by
its flexibility, takes on all sorts of shapes, and that the soul
acquires all its information by the reflexion which it makes
either on itself (in the case of intellectual matters) or (in
the case of corporeal matters) on the various dispositions of
the brain to which it is joined which may result from the
action of the senses or from other causes. But it is a useful
practice not to accept any belief without considering on
what title or for what cause one accepts it; and this comes to
the same thing as his advice always to consider what faculty
one is using etc.

[1] Aristotle, *Physics* iii. 201 a 10.

66

There is no doubt also that in order not to be deceived by the senses one should, as he says, take care that nothing is lacking on the part of the object, or the medium, or the organ.

He recommends especially that one should follow natural instinct, from which he derives all his common notions. For my part, I distinguish two kinds of instinct. One is in us *qua* men, and is purely intellectual: it is the light of nature or *eye of the mind*,[1] to which alone I think one should trust. The other belongs to us *qua* animals, and is a certain impulse of nature towards the preservation of our body, towards the enjoyment of bodily pleasures and so on. This should not always be followed.

His Zetetics are useful to help in making the enumerations of which I speak on p. 20[2]; for once one has duly examined everything they contain, one can be sure of having omitted nothing.

What he says about religion, I leave to be examined by the gentlemen of the Sorbonne. I can only say that I found much less difficulty in reading it in French than I did before in going through it in Latin. He has many maxims which seem to me so pious, and so much in conformity with common sense, that I hope they may be approved by orthodox theology. Finally, though I cannot agree in everything with the opinions of this author, I regard him as a person of quite extraordinary talent.

I am, etc.

Descartes' next letters to Mersenne contain the first indication that he has begun work on what was later to become the *Meditations*.

---

[1] Latin words in French context.          [2] AT vi. 19; HR i. 92.

## From the letter to Mersenne, 13 November 1639[1]

... The opinions of your Analysts[2] about the existence of God and the honour he should be given are, as you write, very difficult to cure. It is not that it is impossible to give reasons strong enough to convince them; but such people, convinced of their own intelligence, are often less capable of listening to reason than others. The imagination, which is the part of the mind that most helps mathematics, is more of a hindrance than a help in metaphysical speculation. I am now working on a discourse in which I try to clarify what I have hitherto written on this topic. It will be only five or six printed sheets but I hope it will contain a great part of Metaphysics. To make it as good as possible, I plan to have only twenty or thirty copies printed, and send them to the twenty or thirty most learned theologians I can find, so as to have their criticisms and learn what should be changed, corrected or added before publication.

## From the letter to Mersenne, 25 December 1639

... 10. I have noticed that Lord Herbert takes many things as common notions which are nothing of the kind. It is certain that nothing should be taken as such unless it cannot be denied by anybody.

I turn to your letter of 4 December and thank you for the advice you give me about my essay on Metaphysics. The arguments of Raymond Lull are sophistries which I do not take seriously. As for the objections of your Analysts, I shall try to solve them without setting them out; that is, I shall lay the foundations, from which those who know the objections to them may derive their solution, without teaching

[1] AT ii. 617; AM iii. 259; in French; extracts.     [2] The geometers of Paris.

them to those who have never heard of them. I think this is how one should treat the matter. In any case, I am not so short of books as you think; I have here a *Summa* of St. Thomas and a Bible which I brought from France.

Throughout the winter of 1639–40, Descartes was working on his *Medita-tions*. His correspondence, however, gives little evidence of this. Most of the surviving letters are taken up with the Stampioen-Waessenaer affair, a dispute between two mathematicians at Leyden into which Descartes was drawn in defence of his *Geometry*. But the following letters inform us about the develop-ment of one of the best-known Cartesian doctrines, the location of the soul in the pineal gland. (Cf. *Dioptrics* v, AT vi. 129; Olscamp 100.)

## Descartes to Meyssonnier, 29 January 1640[1]

Sir,

I would have been the first to write to you, if I had known you to be such as you describe yourself in the letter which you so kindly sent me; for the search after truth is so urgent and so unending as to need the united effort of many thousands; and there are so few people in the world who join it wholeheartedly that those who do should cherish each other and seek to help each other by sharing their observations and their thoughts. This I am most willing to do with every kind of affection.

As a beginning, I will answer the question you asked me about the function of the little gland called *conarion*.[2] My view is that this gland is the principal seat of the soul, and the place in which all our thoughts are formed. The reason I believe this is that I cannot find any part of the brain, except this, which is not double. Since we see only one thing with two eyes, and hear only one voice with two ears, and alto-gether have only one thought at a time, it must necessarily be the case that the impressions which enter by the two eyes or by the two ears, and so on, unite with each other in

---

[1] AT iii. 18; AM iv. 19; complete, in French.      [2] The pineal gland.

some part of the body before being considered by the soul. Now it is impossible to find any such place, in the whole head, except this gland; moreover it is situated in the most suitable possible place for this purpose, in the middle of all the concavities; and it is supported and surrounded by the little branches of the carotid arteries which bring the spirits into the brain. As for the impressions preserved in the memory, I imagine they are not unlike the folds which remain in this paper after it has once been folded; and so I think that they are mainly located in the whole substance of the brain. But I do not deny that they can also be partly located in this gland, especially in people whose minds are sluggish. As for very good and subtle minds, I think their glands must be free from outside influence and easy to move, just as we observe that the gland is smaller in man than it is in animals, unlike the other parts of the brain. I think also that some of the impressions which serve the memory can be in various other parts of the body: for instance the skill of a lute player is not only in his head, but also partly in the muscles of his hands and so on. As for the likenesses of little dogs, which are said to appear in the urine of those who have been bitten by mad dogs, I must admit that I have always thought it was a fable, and unless you tell me that you have seen very distinct and well formed specimens I shall still find it difficult to believe in them. However, if it is true that they can be seen, they could be explained in some way similar to the birthmarks which children receive from the cravings of their mothers.[1]

I am, etc.

## From the letter to Mersenne, 11 March 1640[2]

...I would think I knew nothing in Physics if I could only say how things could be, without proving that they could not be otherwise. This is perfectly possible once one

[1] See *Dioptrics* v; AT vi. 129; Olscamp 100.
[2] AT iii. 33; AM iv. 35; in French; extract.

has reduced everything to laws of mathematics; I think I can do it for the small area to which my knowledge extends. But I did not do it in my essays, because I did not want to present my Principles there, and I do not yet see anything to persuade me to present them in future.


## From the letter to Mersenne, 1 April 1640[1]

... Your second letter, of March 10th, contained another of M. Meyssonnier, which I would answer if I thought this was going to find you still at Paris; but if it has to be sent on to you, it is not a good idea to weigh it down so much, and I can put here, in a few words, all that I have to tell him, which you will pass on to him, please, when next you write to him. After thanking him for his kindness, say this to him. I do not altogether deny that the impressions which serve memory may be partly in the gland called *conarium*, especially in dumb animals and in people who have a coarse mind. But it seems to me that others would not have the great facility which they have in imagining an infinity of things which they have never seen, if their souls were not joined to some part of the brain capable of receiving all kinds of new impressions, and consequently not at all suitable for preserving old ones. Now there is only this gland to which the soul can be so joined; for there is nothing else in the whole head which is not double. But I think that it is the other parts of the brain, especially the interior parts, which most serve memory. I think that all the nerves and muscles can serve it, too, so that a lute player, for instance, has a part of his memory in his hands: for the ease of bending and disposing his fingers in various ways, which he has acquired by practice, helps him to remember the passages which need these dispositions when they are played. You will find this easy to believe if you bear in mind that what people call Local Memory is outside us: for instance, when we have read a book, not all the impressions which can remind us of its

[1] AT iii. 45; AM iv. 45; in French; extracts.

71

contents are in our brain. Many of them are on the paper of the copy which we have read. It does not matter that these impressions have no resemblance to the things of which they remind us; often the impressions in the brain have no resemblance either, as I said in the fourth discourse of my *Dioptrics*.[1] But besides this memory, which depends on the body, I believe there is also another one, entirely intellectual, which depends on the soul alone.

I would not find it strange that the gland *conarium* should be found decayed when the bodies of lethargic persons are dissected, because it decays very rapidly in all other cases too. Three years ago at Leyden, when I wanted to see it in a woman who was being autopsied, I found it impossible to recognize it, even though I looked very thoroughly, and knew well where it should be, being accustomed to find it without any difficulty in freshly killed animals. An old professor who was performing the autopsy, named Valcher, admitted to me that he had never been able to see it in any human body. I think this is because they usually spend some days looking at the intestines and other parts before opening the head.

I need no proof of the mobility of this gland apart from its situation; because since it is supported only by the little arteries which surround it, it is certain that very little will suffice to move it. But for all that I do not think that it can go far one way or the other.

In April 1640 Descartes completed the *Meditations*. He began to circulate the manuscript among his friends and invited criticisms and suggestions for its revision. The first to receive it and to reply were two professors of the University of Utrecht, Regius and Emilius.

[1] AT vi. 112; Olscamp 90.

## From the letter to Regius, 24 May 1640[1]

Sir,

I am much obliged to you and M. Emilius for examining and correcting the manuscript which I sent you. I see that you were even kind enough to correct the punctuation and spelling. You would have put me under an even greater obligation if you had been willing to make some changes in the words and the thoughts. For however small the changes were, they would have given me hope that what you had left was less at fault; but now I fear that you may have refrained from criticism only because too much needed correction, or the whole needed to be cancelled.

Now for your objections. In your first you say that it is because we have in ourselves some degree of wisdom and power and goodness that we form the idea of an infinite, or at least indefinite, degree of wisdom and power and goodness and the other attributes of God; just as it is because we have some degree of quantity that we form the idea of infinite quantity. I entirely agree, and am quite convinced that we have no idea of God except the one formed in this manner. But the whole point of my argument is this. These perfections are so slight in me that unless we derived our origin from a being in which they are actually infinite my nature could not enable me to extend them in thought to an infinite degree. Similarly, I could not form the idea of an indefinite quantity by looking at a very small quantity unless the size of the world was actually or at least possibly indefinite.

In your second objection you say that the truth of axioms which are clearly and distinctly conceived is self-evident. This too, I agree, is true, during the time they are clearly and distinctly conceived; because our mind is of such a nature that it cannot help assenting to what it clearly conceives. But because we often remember conclusions

[1] AT iii. 63; AM iv. 57; in Latin; extracts.

that we have derived from such premises without actually attending to the premises, I say that in such a case, if we lack knowledge of God, we can pretend that they are uncertain even though we remember that they were deduced from clear principles; because perhaps our nature is such that we go wrong even in the most evident matters. Consequently, even at the moment when we deduced them from those principles, we did not have scientific knowledge (*scientia*) of them, but only a conviction (*persuasio*) of them. I distinguish the two as follows: there is conviction when there remains some reason which might lead us to doubt, but scientific knowledge is conviction based on an argument so strong that it can never be shaken by any stronger argument. Nobody can have the latter unless he also has knowledge of God. But a man who has once understood the arguments which prove that God exists and is not a deceiver, provided that he remembers the conclusion 'God is no deceiver' whether or not he continues to attend to the arguments for it, will continue to possess not only the conviction, but real scientific knowledge of this and all other conclusions whose premises he remembers he once clearly perceived.

In your latest objections—which I received yesterday, and which reminded me to reply to your earlier ones—you say that rashness of judgement depends on innate or acquired temperament of body. I do not agree. That would take away the liberty and power of our will, which can remedy such rashness. If it does not remedy it, the error which results is a privation in relation to us, but a mere negation in relation to God.

\*　　\*　　\*

[The rest of the letter, except for the following remark, concerns some theses on medical topics which Regius had sent to Descartes.]

I do not see why you think that the perception of Universals belongs to the imagination rather than to the intellect. I attribute it to the intellect alone, which relates to many things an idea which is in itself singular.

The following letter contains an answer to some objections to Descartes'
theory of the pineal gland forwarded by Mersenne from a physician of Sens
named Villiers. It alludes also to criticisms of his optical theory circulated by
the Jesuit Father Bourdin, later to write the *Seventh Objections.*

## From the letter to Mersenne, 30 July 1640[1]

. . . The letter of the learned doctor contains no argument
to refute what I have said about the gland called *conarium*[2]
except that it can suffer alteration[3] like the rest of the brain.
This is no reason why it should not be the principal seat of
the soul; for it is certain that the soul must be joined to some
part of the body, and there is no other part which is not at least
as subject to alteration as this gland. Although it is very
small and very soft, it is situated in such a well-protected
place that it is almost immune from illness, like the vitreous
or crystalline humour of the eye. It happens much more often
that people become troubled in their minds without any
known cause—which could be attributed to some malady
of this gland—than it happens that sight is lost through a
malady of the crystalline humour. Moreover, all the alterations which take place in the mind, when a man sleeps after
drinking, for instance, can be attributed to some alterations
taking place in this gland.

He says that the soul can utilize double parts, or use the
spirits, which do not all reside in this gland. I agree, because
I do not think that the soul is so imprisoned in the gland
that it cannot act elsewhere. But utilizing a thing is not the
same as being immediately joined or united to it; and since
our soul is not double, but single and indivisible, it seems to
me that the part of the body to which it is most immediately
joined should also be single and not divided into a pair of
similar parts. I cannot find such a part in the whole brain
except this gland.

\*        \*        \*

[1] AT iii. 119; AM iv. 112; in French; extracts.        [2] The pineal gland.
[3] A Scholastic technical term, meaning qualitative change.

I have not yet had my five or six sheets of Metaphysics printed, though they have been ready for some time. I delayed because I do not want them to fall into the hands of pseudo-theologians—nor, now, into the hands of the Jesuits whom I see I shall have to fight—before I have had them seen and approved by various doctors, and if I can, by the Sorbonne as a whole. I intended to visit France this summer, and so planned to bring them myself; and I did not want to have them printed until I was about to depart for fear that the publisher would steal some copies to sell without my knowledge, as often happens. But the summer is already so far gone that I fear I will not be able to make the journey. If not, I will send you ten or twelve copies, or more if you think they will be needed. I will have printed no more than will be necessary for this purpose, and I will ask you to distribute and look after them. Please give them only to those theologians that you consider to be the most able, and the least prejudiced by, and committed to, scholastic errors—really good people who are more moved by truth and the glory of God than by envy and jealousy.

## From the letter to Mersenne, 6 August 1640[1]

Reverend Father,

I left myself so short a period to write to you eight days ago that I did not have time to answer all the points of your last, and I stopped at the ninth which concerned the folds of memory. I do not think that there has to be a very large number of these folds to supply all the things we remember, because a single fold will do for all the things which resemble each other. Moreover, in addition to the bodily memory, whose impressions can be explained by these folds in the brain, I believe that there is also in our intellect another sort of memory, which is altogether spiritual, and is not found in animals. It is this that we mainly use.

Moreover, it is a mistake to believe that we remember

---

[1] AT iii. 142; AM iv. 130; in French; extract.

best what we did when we were young; for we did then a
multitude of things which we no longer remember at all.
Those we do remember are remembered not only because of
the impressions we received when we were young, but mainly
because we have done the same things again and renewed
the impressions by remembering the events from time to
time.

Descartes' quarrel with the Jesuits forced him to renew his acquaintance
with traditional philosophy, and led ultimately to the writing of the *Principles
of Philosophy*, which was designed to replace the Scholastic textbooks.

## From the letter to Mersenne, 30 September 1640[1]

Reverend Father,

I did not intend to write to you by this post, but I have
thought of something on which I would be glad to have your
advice and information. As I told you, I intended to have
printed only twenty or thirty copies of my little *treatise on
Metaphysics*, so as to send them to the same number of
theologians for their opinion of it. But I do not see that I can
carry out that plan without the book's being seen by almost
everyone who has any curiosity to see it; either they will
borrow it from one of those to whom I send it, or they will
get it from the publisher who will certainly print more
copies than I want. So it seems that perhaps I will do
better to have a public printing of it from the start. I have no
fear that it contains anything which could displease the
theologians; but I would have liked to have the approbation
of a number of people so as to prevent the cavils of ignorant
contradiction-mongers. The less such people understand it,
and the less they expect it to be understood by the general
public, the more eloquent they will be unless they are re-
strained by the authority of a number of learned people. So I

[1] AT iii. 183; AM iv. 164; in French; extracts.

thought that I might send you my treatise in manuscript for
you to show to Father Gibieuf, and that I might write to
him myself to ask him to examine it. He will, unless I am
much mistaken, be kind enough to approve it. You could
also show it to a few others, as you judge fit. Once approved
by three or four such people, it could be printed; and if you
agree I would dedicate it to all the masters of the Sorbonne,
asking them to be my protectors in God's cause. For I
must confess that the quibbles of Father Bourdin have made
me determine to fortify myself henceforth with the authority
of others, as far as I can, since truth by itself is so little
esteemed.

I will not travel during this winter, because in the next
four or five months I am due to receive the objections of the
Jesuits, and I think I should hold myself in readiness for
them. Meanwhile I should like to re-read some of their
Philosophy, which I have not looked at for twenty years.
I want to see if I like it better now than I did before. For
this purpose, I beg you to send me the names of the authors
who have written textbooks of philosophy, and to tell me
which are the most commonly used, and whether they have
any new ones since twenty years ago. I remember only
Conimbricenses, Toletus, and Rubius. I would also like to
know if there is in current use any abstract of the whole of
scholastic philosophy; this would save me the time it would
take to read their huge tomes. There was, I think, a Carthus-
ian or Feuillant who made such an abstract but I do not
remember his name.

* * *

I entirely agree with the argument which you were sent
from Blaye, to the effect that whatever we conceive distinctly
to be possible is possible, and that we conceive distinctly
that it is possible that the world has been made, and therefore
it has been made. It is certain that it is impossible to conceive distinctly that the sun or any other finite thing is
independent, because independence, conceived distinctly,
involves infinity. It is a serious mistake to believe that one
can conceive distinctly that an atom, or even a part of matter,

can occupy indifferently a larger or smaller space. First of all, an atom can never be conceived distinctly, since the very meaning of the word involves a contradiction, that of being a body and being indivisible. And as for a genuine part of matter, the determinate quantity of the space which it occupies is necessarily involved in any distinct thought which one can have of it. The principal aim of my metaphysics is to show which are the things that can be distinctly conceived.

## From the letter to Mersenne, 28 October 1640[1]

... I come to the second letter sent by one of your friars from Blaye.[2] Because I do not know which are the two points on which you want my opinion, I will go through them all.

1. I agree that a single effect can be explained in several possible ways; but I do not think that the possibility of things in general can be explained except in one way, which is the true one.

2. He is right in saying that it is a mistake to accept the principle that no body moves of itself. For it is certain that a body, once it has begun to move, has in itself for that reason alone the power to continue to move, just as, once it is stationary in a certain place, it has for that reason alone the power to continue to remain there. But the individual principle of movement which he postulates in each several body is altogether imaginary.

3. I cannot accept his indivisible bodies, nor the natural inclinations which he attributes to them. I cannot conceive such inclinations in things which lack understanding, and I do not even attribute them to irrational animals. Everything in them which we call natural appetites or inclinations is explained on my theory solely in terms of the rules of mechanics. I cannot accept his elements either; they are at least as difficult to understand as the things he tries to explain by them.

---

[1] AT iii. 205; AM iv. 164; in French; extracts.  [2] Father Lacombe.

4. Two indivisible things could only make a single thing divisible into two parts at most; but before saying that they could make up a body, you must know what is meant by the term 'body'. In fact it means a thing which has length and breadth and extension, and so cannot be composed of indivisible things, since an indivisible thing cannot have any length or breadth or depth. If it had, we could divide it at least in our imagination, which would suffice to guarantee that it was not indivisible: for if we could divide it in imagination an angel could divide it in reality. He thinks movement and shape by themselves are inadequate as principles of explanation, because he does not see how all the various properties of such things as wine could be explained in terms of them. You can remove this difficulty by telling him that they have all been explained already, and so have all other properties perceptible by the senses. But not a word about miracles.

\*        \*        \*

8. I do not see why he associates atheism with the explanation of nature in terms of shape and movement as if the two doctrines were somehow akin. He says that the idea of a simple Being, which we conceive to contain all Being, could not be conceived if there was not a real exemplar of this Being, because we can only conceive—you should add 'distinctly'—things which are possible and true. This makes it look as if he has read my works, which contain this very argument; but he adds many things which I cannot agree with, as that this Being has dimensions, and that dimensions can be conceived without composition of parts, i.e. without the thing which has the dimensions being divisible etc. He is also right in saying that not everything which we do not conceive distinctly is thereby false. He does well to apply this to the mystery of the Trinity which is an article of faith and cannot be known by natural reason alone. I do not find anything to mention in the other articles, and I have no paper left.

Since you are willing to take my *Metaphysics* under your protection, I hope to send it to you in a week or two at most.

I would send it now, but I want to have it copied first.
Perhaps I will send it by M. de Zuylichem.[1]

I am, etc.

For some years Cartesian doctrines had been taught at the newly-founded
University of Utrecht by the professor of philosophy, Reneri. After Reneri's
death in 1639 the propagation of Descartes' views at Utrecht was continued
by Regius, professor of medicine. Regius' tactless manner of exposition
alienated many of his colleagues and an anti-Cartesian reaction was led by
Gisbert Voetius, the professor of theology, who wrote to Mersenne for
support. The following letter was written on Descartes' receipt of this news,
and contains also details of the progress of the *Meditations* and the project
of the *Principles*.

# From the letter to Mersenne, 11 November 1640[2]

Reverend Father,

Thank you for your news of M. Voetius. I find nothing
strange in it except his not knowing our friendship for each
other; everyone here who knows me at all knows about that.
He is the most pendantic fellow in the world, and he is
bursting with rage because there is a professor in their
university of Utrecht[3] who openly teaches my philosophy,
and even gives private lectures in physics, which in a few
months enable his pupils to make fun of the ancient philosophy. Voetius and the other professors have done all they
can to get the magistrates to forbid him to teach; but despite
their efforts the magistrates allow him to continue. This
Voetius has also spoilt Mlle de Schurmans: she had excellent
gifts for poetry, painting and other gentle arts, but these last
five or six years he has taken her over completely so that she
cares for nothing but theological controversies, and all
decent people shun her. Her brother has always been known
as a man of poor intelligence. Your letter to Voetius I have

[1] Constantijn Huygens.    [2] AT iii. 230; AM iv. 198; in French; extracts.
[3] Regius.

given back to the postman, so that he will pay the postage of it, as if it had not been enclosed in your letter to me. This will take revenge for the six livres he made you pay for his theses.

I do not think that the diversity of the opinions of scholastics makes their philosophy difficult to refute. It is easy to overturn the foundations on which they all agree, and once that has been done all their disagreements over detail will seem foolish. I have bought the Philosophy of Fr. Eustache of S Paul,[1] which seems to me the best book of its kind ever made. I would be glad to know if the author is still alive.

\*     \*     \*

I would willingly answer your question about the flame of a candle and similar things; but I see that I can never really satisfy you on this until you have seen all the principles of my philosophy. So I must tell you that I have resolved to write them before leaving this country, and to publish them perhaps within a year. My plan is to write a series of theses which will constitute a complete textbook of my philosophy. I will not waste any words, but simply put down all my conclusions, with the true premises from which I derive them. I think I could do this without many words. In the same volume I plan to have printed an ordinary textbook of philosophy, perhaps Fr. Eustache's, with notes by me at the end of each question. In the notes I will add the different opinions of others, and what one should think of them all, and perhaps at the end I will make a comparison between the two philosophies. But please do not tell anyone yet of this plan, especially before my *Metaphysics* is published; because perhaps if the Regents knew of it they would do their best to make trouble for me—though once the thing is done I hope they will all be pleased. It might also hold up the approbation of the Sorbonne, which I want, and which seems very useful for my purposes. Because I must confess that the small *treatise on Metaphysics* which I sent you contains all the principles of my Physics.

[1] *Summa philosophica quadripartita* (Paris, 1609).

The argument for Godhead in the book you write about—that if the sun has shone eternally, it cannot have illuminated one hemisphere before the other—proves nothing except that our finite mind cannot comprehend the infinite.

\*   \*   \*

Yesterday I sent my *Metaphysics* to M. de Zuylichem[1] to post on to you; but he will not do so for a week since I have allowed him that length of time to look at it. I have not put any title on it, but it seems to me that the most suitable would be *René Descartes' Meditations on First Philosophy*[2] because I do not confine my discussion to God and the soul, but treat in general of all the first things to be discovered by philosophizing. You will see its scope from the letters which I have attached to it. I will not say any more now, except that I think it would be a good idea, before printing, to settle with the publisher to give us as many copies as we need, and to let us have them ready bound. There is no pleasure in buying one's own writings, and I am sure the publisher can do what I suggest without loss. Here I will need no more than thirty copies; as for Paris, it is for you to judge how many are necessary.

I am, etc.

The manuscript of the *Meditations* sent to Huygens included the *First Objections* and the *Reply* to them: for Descartes wrote on 12 November urging Huygens to read the first five meditations at a single sitting, and with them the answer to the letter at the end.

## Descartes to Colvius, 14 November 1640[3]

I am obliged to you for drawing my attention to the passage of St. Augustine relevant to my *I am thinking*,

---

[1] Constantijn Huygens.     [2] *Renati Descartes Meditationes de prima Philosophia.*
[3] AT iii. 247; AM iv. 209; in French; complete.

*therefore I exist*.¹ I went today to the library of this town² to read it, and I find that he does really use it to prove the certainty of our existence. He goes on to show that there is a certain likeness of the Trinity in us, in that we exist, we know that we exist, and we love the existence and the knowledge we have. I, on the other hand, use the argument to show that this I which is thinking is an immaterial substance with no bodily element. These are two very different things. In itself it is such a simple and natural thing to infer that one exists from the fact that one is doubting that it could have occurred to any writer. But I am very glad to find myself in agreement with St. Augustine, if only to hush the little minds who have tried to find fault with the principle. My little *treatise on Metaphysics* is already on the way to Paris, where I think it will be printed; all that I have left is a draft so full of crossings out that I could scarcely read it myself, which is why I cannot let you have it. But as soon as it is printed, I will see that you receive a copy as soon as anyone, since you are kind enough to want to read it, and I will be very glad to have your opinion of it.


## From the letter to Mersenne, 3 December 1640³

Reverend Father,

You tell me that St. Augustine and St. Ambrose say that our heart and our thoughts are not in our power, and that they confuse the mind and distract it and so on. This applies only to the sensitive part of the soul, which receives the impressions of exterior and interior objects, perhaps in the form of temptations. So far I entirely agree with them, and I have never said that all our thoughts were in our power, but only that, if there is anything absolutely in our power, it is our thoughts, that is to say, those which come from our will and free choice. I said this only in order to show that

¹ This refers to the *Discourse*, not to the *Meditations* in which the famous catchphrase does not occur; see below.
² Leyden.         ³ AT iii. 248; AM iv. 213; in French; extract.

our free will has no absolute jurisdiction over any corporeal thing. This is true and undeniable.

The following letter is a reply to one written by Mersenne immediately after receiving the manuscript of the *Meditations* and *First Objections* and *Replies*.

## Descartes to Mersenne, 24 December 1640[1]

Reverend Father,

I have just received your letters only an hour or two before the postman has to return; so I shall not be able this time to answer you point by point. The difficulty you raise about the *conarium*[2] seems to be the most urgent, and the man who wants to defend publicly what I said about it in my *Dioptrics*[3] does me so much honour that I must try to answer his queries. So without waiting for the next post I will say that the pituitary gland is akin to the pineal gland in that both are situated between the carotid arteries and on the path which the spirits take in rising from the heart to the brain. But this gives no ground to suppose that the two have the same function; for the pituitary gland is not, like the pineal gland, in the brain, but beneath it and entirely separate, in a concavity of the sphenoid bone specially made to take it, and even beneath the *dura mater* if I remember correctly. Moreover, it is entirely immobile, whereas we experience, when we imagine, that the seat of the common sense, that is to say the part of the brain in which the soul performs all its principal operations, must be mobile. It is not surprising that the pituitary gland should be situated as it is between the heart and the *conarium*, because there are many little arteries there, forming the carotid plexus[4] also, which come together there without reaching the brain. For

---

[1] AT iii. 262; AM iv. 237; in French; complete.
[2] The pineal gland.    [3] AT vi. 129; Olscamp 100.    [4] *Plexus mirabilis.*

it is a general rule throughout the body that there are glands at the meeting points of large numbers of branches of veins or arteries. It is not surprising either that the carotids send many branches to that point: that is necessary to feed the bones and other parts, and also to separate the coarser parts of the blood from the more rarefied parts which alone travel through the straightest branches of the carotids to reach the interior of the brain, where the *conarium* is located. There is no need to suppose that this separation takes place in any but a purely mechanical manner. When reeds and foam are floating on a stream which splits into two branches, the reeds and foam will be seen to go into the branch in which the water flows in a less straight line. The present case is similar. There is good reason for the *conarium* to be like a gland, because the main function of every gland is to take in the most rarefied parts of the blood which are exhaled by the surrounding vessels, and the function of the *conarium* is to take in the animal spirits in the same manner. Since it is the only solid part in the whole brain which is single, it must necessarily be the seat of the common sense, i.e. of thought, and consequently of the soul; for one cannot be separate from the other. The only alternative is to say that the soul is not joined immediately to any solid part of the body, but only to the animal spirits which are in its concavities, and which enter it and leave it continually like the water of a river. That would certainly be thought too absurd. Moreover, the *conarium* is so placed that it is easy to understand how the images which come from the two eyes, or the sounds which enter by the two ears, must come together at the place where it is situated. They could not do this in the concavities, except in the middle one, or in the channel just below the *conarium*; and this would not do, because these cavities are not distinct from the others in which the images are necessarily double. If I can offer any further help to the man who put these questions to you, please assure him that I will gladly do my best to give him satisfaction.

I am very much indebted to you for the care you are taking of my book of metaphysics, and I trust to you to correct or change whatever you think fit. But I am surprised that you promise me objections from various theologians within eight days, because I am convinced that it would take longer to absorb all that is in it. This was the opinion also of the man who made the objections at the end[1]; he is a priest of Alkmaar, who wishes to remain anonymous, so please remove his name if it occurs in any place. You should also please warn the printer to alter the numbers in the objections by which the pages of the *Meditations* are cited, to make them fit the printed pages.

You say that I have not said a word about the immortality of the soul. You should not be surprised. I could not prove that God could not annihilate the soul but only that it is by nature entirely distinct from the body, and so that it is not bound by nature to die with it. This is all that is required as a foundation for religion, and is all that I had any intention of proving.

You should not find it strange, either, that I do not prove in my second *Meditation* that the soul is really distinct from the body, but merely show how to conceive it without the body. This is because I do not yet have, at that point, the premisses needed for the conclusion. You find it later on, in the sixth *Meditation*.

It should be noted that in all my writing I do not follow the order of topics, but the order of arguments. I mean that I do not attempt to say in a single place everything about a topic, for in that way I could not give proper proofs since some of my arguments involve more distant researches than others. But in orderly reasoning *from easier matters to more difficult matters*[2] I make what deductions I can, first on one topic, then on another. This is the right way, in my opinion, to find and explain the truth. The order of topics is only good for people whose arguments are disjointed, and who can say as much about one difficulty as about another. So I do not think that it would be useful, or even possible, to insert into my meditations the answers to the objections which may be made to them. That would interrupt the flow and even destroy the force of my arguments. The majority of the objections would be drawn from perceptible

---

[1] Caterus, author of the *First Objections*.     [2] Latin words in a French context.

things, whereas my arguments get their force from the withdrawal of thought from objects of sense. So I have put Caterus' objections at the end, to show where any others which come might be placed.

But I hope that people will take their time in composing them; it does not matter if the treatise remains unpublished two or three more years. The manuscript is very ill written and can only be seen by one person at a time: so it seems to me that it would be useful to have twenty or thirty copies printed in advance. I would be glad to pay whatever it costs; I would have had it done here, if there was any publisher that I could trust; but I did not want the ministers of this country to see it before our theologians.

As for the style, I would be very glad if it were better than it is; but apart from grammatical faults, if there are any, or gallicisms such as '*in dubium ponere*' for '*revocare*', I am afraid that nothing could be changed without detriment to the sense. For instance, where the text has '*nempe quicquid hactenus ut maxime verum admisi, vel a sensibus vel per sensus accepi*',[1] to add '*falsum esse*'[2] as you suggest would entirely change the meaning, which is that I have got from the senses, or by the senses, all that up to now I have thought most true. It would not do so much harm to substitute '*erutis fundamentis*' for '*suffosis*' since both expressions are good Latin and mean more or less the same.[3] But it seems to me that the latter, which has only the single meaning which I want it to have, is at least as good as the former, which has several.

I will send you perhaps within a week an abstract of the principal points which concern God and the Soul, which can be printed in front of the Meditations, so that people can see where such matters are to be found. Otherwise I realize that many people will be annoyed at not finding in a single place all the things they are looking for. I shall be very glad to have M. Desargues for one of my judges, if he is willing to take the trouble, and I have more trust in him alone than in three theologians. I will not be at all unhappy to have

---

[1] Whatever I have hitherto admitted as most true, I learnt either from, or by, my senses.
[2] To be false.  [3] i.e. overturning the foundations.

many objections, because I feel sure they will serve to make truth better known. Thank God, I have no fear of being unable to reply adequately. It is time to finish.

I am, etc.

## From the letter to Mersenne, 31 December 1640[1]

Reverend Father,

I received no letter from you by this post; but since I did not have time a week ago to answer all your points, I will add now what I then left out. First, I send you an abstract of my *Metaphysics*, which, if you approve, can be prefaced to my six Meditations. After the preceding words '*will draw the same conclusions from them as I do*', should be added '*But because in the six following Meditations etc.*'[2] In the Abstract the reader will be able to see all that I have proved of the immortality of the soul, and all that I can add to it when I publish my *Physics*. Without wrecking the order I could not prove that the soul is distinct from the body before proving the existence of God.

You say that we do not know that the idea of a most perfect Being may not be the same as that of the corporeal world. This difficulty is easy to solve in the same way as the soul is proved to be distinct from the body, that is, because we conceive something altogether different in each case. But for this purpose we have to form distinct ideas of the things we want to judge about, and this is what most men fail to do and what I have mainly tried to teach by my *Meditations*. But I will spend no longer on these objections, because you promise to send me shortly all those which may be made. I only ask you to be in no hurry about it: people who do not study everything carefully, and who merely read the second *Meditation* to find out what I say of the soul, or the third, to find out what I say of God, will very likely make objections out of difficulties which I have already explained.

---

[1] AT iii. 271; AM iv. 242; in French; extracts.
[2] These expressions do not appear in the published text.

89

In the place where I put '*in accordance with the laws of my Logic*' please put '*in accordance with the laws of the true Logic*'; it is about the middle of my replies to Caterus, where he objects that I have borrowed my argument from St. Thomas.[1] The reason why I add '*my*' or '*the true*' to '*logic*' is that I have read theologians who follow the ordinary logic and *inquire what God is before inquiring whether there is a God.*[2]

Where I wrote '*the power to possess the idea of God could not belong to our intellect, if that etc.* you are right that it would be better to write '*this*' instead of '*that*'; it is about the fourth or fifth page of my reply to the Objections.[3] It is better also to put '*cause of itself*' instead of '*cause*' in the following line, as you suggest.

What I say later, that *nothing can be in me, that is to say, in my mind, of which I am not conscious,*[4] this is something which I proved in my *Meditations*, and it follows from the fact that the soul is distinct from the body and that its essence is to think.

You find obscure the sentence where I say that whatever has the power to create or keep in being something separate from itself has *a fortiori* the power to keep itself in being.[5] But I do not see how to make it clearer without adding many words, which would be inelegant since I only mention the matter briefly by the way.

At the place where I speak of infinity, it is a good idea to insert, as you say, that *the infinite qua infinite is in no way comprehended by us.*[6]

The world *perhaps lacks limits as regards extension, but not as regards power, intelligence etc. And so it does not altogether lack limits.*[7]

A little further on, we could, as you suggest, put '*about which there can be no doubt*', after the expression 'anything real' and between parentheses.[8] But as it stands it does not seem obscure to me; you could find a thousand places in Cicero which are more so.

It seems very clear to me that *possible existence is contained*

---

[1] AT vii. 107; HR ii. 13.    [2] Latin words in a French context.
[3] AT vii. 105; HR ii. 12.    [4] AT vii. 107; HR ii. 13.
[5] AT vii. 111; HR ii. 16.    [6] AT vii. 112; HR ii. 17.
[7] These Latin phrases do not appear in the published *Replies*.
[8] AT vii. 114; HR ii. 18.

*in everything which we clearly conceive; because from the fact
that we clearly conceive something it follows that it can be
created by God.*[1]

As for the mystery of the Trinity, I share St. Thomas'
opinion that it is a sheer article of faith and cannot be known
by the light of nature. But I do not deny that there are
things in God which we do not understand, just as even in a
triangle there are many properties which no mathematician
will ever know; which does not prevent everyone knowing
what a triangle is.

It is certain that there is nothing in an effect *which is not
contained formally or eminently in its EFFICIENT and
TOTAL cause.*[2] I added these two words on purpose. The
sun and the rain are not the total cause of the animals they
generate.

I was finishing this when I received your last letter which
reminds me to ask you to tell me if you know why you did
not receive my *Metaphysics* by the post by which I sent them,
nor even with the letters which I wrote you a week later,
and whether the packet was opened; for I gave it to the
same postman.

Thank you for correcting '*maiorem*' to '*maius*'. I am not
surprised that there are such mistakes in my writing, I have
often come across them myself; they happen when I am
writing with my mind on something else. But I am surprised
that three or four of my friends who read it did not notice the
solecism.

I have no objection to seeing what M. Morin has written
about God, because you say that he uses a mathematical
method; but I do not hope for much from it, because I
never heard before that he went in for that sort of writing.
Nor have I great hopes of the other books printed at la
Rochelle. M. de Zuylichem[3] has returned and if you send
it to him with the paper written by the Englishman[4] I can
get them from him. But do ask him to send them on
promptly, because he has so much other business that he
might forget.

---

[1] Latin words in a French context.
[2] Latin words in a French context; cf. AT vii. 40; HR i. 162.
[3] Constantijn Huygens.          [4] Thomas Hobbes.

I will not fail to answer immediately anything you send me about my *Metaphysics*. But otherwise I should be very glad to have as few distractions as possible, for the coming year at least, since I have resolved to spend it in writing my philosophy in an order which will make it easy to teach.[1] The first part, which I am working on at present, contains almost the same things as the *Meditations* which you have, except that it is in an entirely different style, and what is written at length in one is abbreviated in the other, and *vice versa*.

Descartes' correspondence with Mersenne in the first part of 1641 mainly concerns the compilation of the *Objections* and *Replies* to the *Meditations*.

## From the letter to Mersenne, 28 January 1641[2]

This note is to tell you that I am not able to send you my reply to the objections by today's post. This is partly because I have had other business which has not left me a day free, and partly because the objectors seem to have understood nothing of what I wrote, and merely to have read it through post-haste.[3] They merely oblige me to repeat what I have already said, and this is more troublesome than if they had put forward difficulties which gave more exercise to my mind. This is between ourselves, because I should be very sorry to offend them, and you will see by the trouble I take in replying that I consider myself indebted to them and also to the author of the latest objections which I received only last Tuesday.[4] (That was why I did not mention them in my last, because our postman leaves on a Monday.)

I have read M. Morin's book.[5] Its main fault is that he

---

[1] i.e. in writing the *Principles of Philosophy*.
[2] AT iii. 292; AM iv. 265; in French; with omissions.
[3] The *Second Objections* were, in fact, largely the work of Mersenne.
[4] The *Third Objections*, by Thomas Hobbes.
[5] J. B. Morin, *Quod Deus sit Mundusque ab ipso creatus fuerit in tempore* (1635).

always discusses the infinite as if he had completely mastered it and could comprehend all its properties. This is an almost universal fault, which I have tried carefully to avoid. I have never written about the infinite except to submit myself to it, and not to determine what it is or what it is not. Then, before giving any explanation of matters in controversy, in his sixteenth theorem, where he sets about proving that God exists, he rests his argument on his alleged refutation of the earth's movement, and on the revolution of the whole sky around it, which he has in no way proved. He supposes also that there cannot be an infinite number, which he could never prove. Right up to the end everything that he says is very far from the geometrical self-evidence and certainty which he seemed to promise at the beginning. This also is between ourselves, please, since I have no desire to hurt his feelings.

*          *          *

I claim that we have ideas not only of all that is in our intellect, but also of all that is in the will. For we cannot will anything without knowing that we will it, nor could we know this without an idea; but I do not claim that the idea is different from the action itself.

There will be no difficulty, so far as I can see, in adapting theology to my style of philosophy. I do not see that any-anything in it needs changing except in the case of tran-substantiation, which is very clear and easy to explain on my principles. I shall have to explain it in my *Physics*, along with the first chapter of Genesis; I propose to send my explanation to the Sorbonne to be examined before it is printed. If you think that there are other things which call for the writing of a whole new course of theology, and are willing to undertake this yourself, I shall count it a favour and do my best to help you.

*          *          *

I will be very glad if people make me many objections, the strongest they can find; I hope that truth will stand out all the better from them. But when people want to do so, please show them my replies and the objections which you have already sent to me, so that they will not put forward points which I have already answered.

I proved quite explicitly that God was the creator of all things, and I prove all his other attributes at the same time, because I proved his existence from the idea which we have of Him; and also from the fact that since we have this idea in ourselves, we must have been created by Him. But I see that people take more notice of the headings in books than of anything else. This makes me think that the title of the second meditation, '*Of the human mind*' could have added to it '*that it is better known than body*', so that people will not think that I was trying to prove its immortality in that place. So in the third: '*Of God—that he exists.*' And the fifth: '*Of the essence of material things, and again of God, that he exists.*' In the sixth: '*Of the existence of material things, and of the real distinction between mind and body.*' These are the things that I want people mainly to notice. But I think I included many other things besides; and I may tell you, between ourselves, that these six *Meditations* contain all the foundations of my *Physics*. But please do not tell people, for that might make it harder for supporters of Aristotle to approve them. I hope that readers will gradually get used to my principles, and recognize their truth, before they notice that they destroy the principles of Aristotle.

## From the letter to Mersenne, 4 March 1641[1]

...I must also ask you to correct these words, which come in my reply to the penultimate objection made by the theologian.[2] '*Because we cannot think of His existence as being possible without at the same time thinking that there must be possible some power by means of which He exists, and because that power cannot be conceived to be in anything other than that same*

---

[1] AT iii. 318; AM iv. 299; in French; extracts.
[2] The *First Replies*, AT vii. 119; HR ii. 21.

*supremely powerful Being, we conclude that He can exist by his own might.'* In place of that, put simply: '*Because we cannot think of His existence as being possible, without at the same time, bearing in mind His immense power, recognizing that He can exist by His own might etc.*'. But please correct it in all the copies in such a way that no one will be able to read or decipher the words '*thinking that there must be possible some power by means of which He exists, and because that power cannot be conceived to be in anything other than that same supremely powerful Being, we conclude'*. For many people are more curious to read and examine words that have been erased than any other words, so as to see where the author thinks he has gone wrong, and to discover there some ground for objections, attacking him in the place which he himself judged to be the weakest.

## From the letter to Mersenne, 18 March 1641[1]

Reverend Father,

I send you at last my reply to the objections of M. Arnauld[2]; and I ask you to change the following things in my *Metaphysics*, to let it be known that I have deferred to his judgement, so that others seeing how ready I am to take advice, may tell me more frankly what reasons they have for disagreeing with me, and may be less stubborn in opposing me if they have none.

The first correction is in the synopsis of the *Fourth Meditation*. After the words '*for the understanding of the rest*' please add '*But note meanwhile that this meditation is not about sin, the error which is committed in the pursuit of good and evil, but only about the error which occurs in judging between truth and falsehood. It does not concern matters of faith and conduct, but only speculative truths which can be known by the light of nature.*' Put the words between square brackets so that it can be seen that they have been added.[3]

[1] AT iii. 334; AM iv. 311; in French; with omissions.
[2] The *Fourth Objections*.      [3] See AT vii. 15; HR i. 142.

2. In the *Sixth Meditation*, p. 96, after the words 'since I did not yet know the author of my being' please add, again in square brackets, the words 'or at least I pretended not to know'.[1]

3. Then, in my reply to the first objections, where I discuss *whether God can be said to be caused by himself*, at the words '*So if I thought nothing could stand in somewhat the same relation to itself . . . etc.*'[2] please put in the margin '*Note that these words mean only that there may be a thing whose essence is such that it needs no efficient cause in order to exist.*'

4. A little further on, at the words '*Thus, even though there was never a time when there was no God, yet because no one but Himself keeps Him in being . . .*' put in the margin '*The keeping in being is not meant to be any positive influence of an efficient cause; it is simply that God's essence is such that He cannot help existing for ever.*'[3]

5. Three lines later there occur the words '*Though even those who think that it is impossible for anything to be its own efficient cause do not normally . . . etc.*'. Please correct the text as follows: '*Though those who recognize only the proper and strict sense of the word 'efficient', who think it impossible for anything to be its own efficient cause and who do not recognize the presence here of any other type of cause analogous to the efficient, do not normally . . .*'[4] For I did not mean to say that anything could be its own efficient cause if 'efficient' is taken in the strict sense; I meant that when we ask *whether anything can be self-dependent*[5] the question must not be taken to concern *efficient causality strictly so called, or it would be vacuous,*[6] as I said. It is because of the common scholastic axiom, '*nothing can be its own efficient cause*', that 'self-dependent' has not been taken in the appropriate sense. None the less, I did not want to blame the scholastics for this openly.

6. Please do not forget the correction which I mentioned in my last letter, at the end of the same replies: '*Because we cannot think*' etc. Because until my book is published, I think I have the right to change it as I think fit.

---

[1] AT vii. 77; HR i. 189.          [2] AT vii. 108; HR ii. 14.
[3] AT vii. 109; HR ii. 14.          [4] AT vii. 109; HR ii. 15.
[5] *an aliquid possit esse a se.*
[6] Latin words in a French context, here and below.

I think also that I have the right to ask that in M. Arnauld's objections, where he is inquiring whether *God is the cause of himself*, and he quotes my words '*So if I thought nothing could stand in the same relation to itself*', the quotation should read '*stand in somewhat the same relation*'. For the word 'somewhat', which he has forgotten, changes the sense. I think it is better to ask you to insert it in his text than for me to accuse him in my reply of quoting me inaccurately; especially as he seems to have left it out inadvertently, since he concludes '*Since it is evident that nothing can stand in at all the same relation*' where his '*at all*' corresponds to my '*somewhat*'.[1]

In the same way I might ask you, at the beginning of the same objection, where he quotes me as saying '*so that God performs somewhat the same function for himself* etc.' to put '*so that we may think that God performs somewhat the same*, etc.' as my text has it.[2] A little further on, where he quotes me as saying *that the meaning of 'efficient' should not in my view be so restricted*, he quotes only the less important of the reasons I gave, and omits the main one, which is *that the question would be vacuous* etc. But I have gently put this right in my reply; so it is less important to change it, and the change should not be made without his permission.

\*       \*       \*

I leave you to take care of the titles of my *Metaphysics*; you will be, if you please, its godfather. For the objections, it is a good idea to call them *First Objections, Second Objections* and so on, and then to put '*Replies to the Objections*' rather than '*Solutions of the difficulties*' so as to leave the reader to judge whether the replies contain solutions or not. Let those who give false answers call them solutions; it is not those who boast loudest of nobility who are most nobly born.

I am not yet sending you the last sheet of my reply to M. Arnauld, where I give an explanation of transubstantiation according to my principles; because I want first to read the

[1] AT vii. 213; HR ii. 92.    [2] AT vii. 208; HR ii. 88.

Councils on this topic, and I have not yet been able to obtain them.

I am, etc.

Descartes to Mersenne, 31 March 1641[1]

Reverend Father,

I have not much to tell you by this post, because I have not had a letter from you; but I did not want to put off sending you the remainder of my reply to M. Arnauld's objections.[2] You will see that in it I show that the teaching of the Councils about the Blessed Sacrament fits my philosophy so well that I claim that it cannot be explained in accordance with the common philosophy. I think that philosophy would have been rejected as clashing with faith if mine had been known first. I swear to you in all seriousness that I believe it is as I say. So I have decided to say so publicly, and to fight with their own weapons the people who confound Aristotle with the Bible and abuse the authority of the church in order to vent their passions—I mean the people who had Galileo condemned. They would have my views condemned likewise if they had the power; but if there is ever any question of that, I am confident I can show that none of the tenets of their philosophy accords with the Faith so well as my doctrines.

As soon as M. Arnauld has seen my replies, I think it will be time to give the complete work to the doctors of the Sorbonne, so that it can be printed when they have expressed their opinion. I leave entirely to you such matters as the size of the volume, the type face, the titles I have left out, and any notes for the reader which need adding to what I have written. You have already taken so much trouble over the book that the greater part of it belongs to you.

I am, etc.

---

[1] AT iii. 349; AM iv. 330; in French; complete.        [2] The *Fourth Objections*.

98

Easter Day 1641

I send you a note for the publisher, which you will find is not dated from Leyden, because I no longer live there, but at a house half a league away.[1] I have retired here to work more easily at philosophy and experimentation. You do not need to change the address on your letters—or rather you do not need to put any address except my name, because the Leyden postman knows where he should deliver them.

## From the letter to Mersenne, 21 April 1641 [2]

Reverend Father,

... I am surprised at the objections of your doctors, namely that we have no certainty, according to my philosophy, that the priest is holding the Host at the altar, or that he has water to baptise, etc. Even among scholastic philosophers who ever said that there was any more than moral certainty of such things? Theologians say that it is a matter of faith to believe that the body of Jesus Christ is in the Eucharist, but they do not say that it is a matter of faith to believe that it is in this particular Host. *For that you have to suppose, as a matter of ordinary human credence, that the priest had the intention to consecrate, and that he pronounced the words, and is duly ordained, and other such things which are by no means matters of faith.*[3]

Those who say that God continually deceives the damned, and that he might similarly be continually deceiving us, contradict the foundation of faith and all our belief, which is that *God cannot lie*.[3] This is stated over and over again in so many places in St. Augustine, St. Thomas and others that I am surprised that any theologian denies it. They will have to abandon all certainty if they do not admit as an axiom that *God cannot deceive us*.[3]

I wrote that indifference in our case is rather a defect than

<hr>

[1] At Endegeest.       [2] AT iii. 358; AM iv. 335; in French; with omissions.
[3] Latin words in a French context.

a perfection of freedom; but it does not follow that the same is the case with God. Nevertheless, I do not know that it is *an article of faith*[1] to believe that He is indifferent, and I feel confident that Fr Gibieuf will defend my position well on this matter; because I wrote nothing which is not in accord with what he said in his book *De Libertate*.[2]

I nowhere said that God does not co-operate immediately in everything, and I asserted the opposite explicitly in my reply to the theologian.[3]

I did not think I should have made my replies to the Englishman[4] any longer, since his objections seemed so implausible to me that to answer them at greater length would have been giving them too much importance.

The doctor who says that we can doubt whether or not we are thinking as well as we can doubt anything is so much in conflict with the natural light that I am sure that no one who thinks about what he says will share his opinion.

You told me earlier that in my reply to the Englishman I used the word '*idea*' two or three times very close to each other. It did not seem superfluous to me, because it refers to different ideas. Repetitions may be offensive in some places, but they are elegant in others.

The sense in which I include imaginations in the definition of *cogitatio* or thought differs from the sense in which I exclude them. *The forms or corporeal impressions which must be in the brain for us to imagine anything are not thoughts; but when the mind imagines or turns towards those impressions, its operation is a thought.*[5]

The earlier letter in which you wrote me objections about the *conarium*[6] must have been lost, unless you forgot to write them. I do not have any objections except your more recent ones, namely, that no nerve goes to the *conarium* and that it is too mobile to be the seat of the common sense. In fact, these two things tell entirely in my favour. Each nerve is designed for a particular sense or movement, some going to the eyes, others to the ears, arms, and so on. Consequently

---

[1] Latin words in a French context.
[2] *De Libertate Dei et Hominis* (Paris, 1630).
[3] AT vii. 111; HR ii. 16.      [4] Hobbes, the author of the *Third Objections*.
[5] Latin words in a French context.     [6] The pineal gland.

if the *conarium* was specially connected with one in particular, it could be deduced that it was not the seat of the common sense which must be connected to all of them in the same way. The only way in which they can all be connected with it is by means of the spirits, and that is how they are connected with the *conarium*. It is certain too that the seat of the common sense must be very mobile, to receive all the impressions which come from the senses; but it must also be of such a kind as to be movable only by the spirits which transmit these impressions. Only the *conarium* fits this description.

'*Anima*' in good Latin signifies *air*, or *breath*; it is in a transferred sense, I think, that it means *mind*. That is why I said that it is *often taken for a corporeal thing*.[1]

The axiom: *whatever can do the greater can do the lesser*[2] applies only *in the same order of operations, or in things which require a single power*.[2] For *among men*,[2] who doubts that a person who could not make a lantern may be able to make a good speech?

The controversy at Utrecht flared up again in 1641. Voetius had now become Rector of the university, and threatened to deprive Regius of his chair after a tumult during a public disputation at which one of his pupils had defended Cartesian theses. Descartes himself had some misgivings about the theses defended in his name, as the following letter shows.

## From the letter to Regius, May 1641[3]

Sir,

I certainly cannot complain that you and M. de Raey[4] have been so kind as to place my name at the head of your theses; but on the other hand I do not know how I can thank you for it. I see only that it means further work for me.

---

[1] AT vii. 27; HR i. 152.          [2] Latin words in a French context.

[3] AT iii. 370; AM iv. 346; in Latin; with omissions.

[4] A pupil of Regius who had defended Cartesian theses in a public disputation at Utrecht.

People will believe henceforth that my opinions are the same as yours and so I will have no excuse for not defending your propositions as best I can. So I shall have to examine with extreme care what you sent me to read, for fear of letting something pass which I would not wish to defend.

The first thing which I cannot approve is your saying that men have a threefold soul. In my religion this is a heretical thing to say; and quite apart from religion it goes against logic to regard the soul as a genus whose species would be the mind, the vegetative power, and the locomotive power of animals. When you speak of the sensitive soul you can only mean the locomotive power, unless you are confusing it with the rational soul; but the locomotive power does not differ even specifically from the vegetative power, while belonging to a totally different genus from the mind. But since we do not differ in substance, I will tell you how I would explain the matter.

There is only one soul in man, the rational soul; for no actions can be reckoned human unless they depend on reason. The vegetative power and the power of moving the body, which are called the vegetative and sensitive souls in plants and animals, exist also in man; but they should not in his case be called souls, because they are not the first principle of his actions, and they belong to a totally different genus from the rational soul.

The vegetative power in man is nothing but a certain arrangement of the parts of the body which, etc.

A little further on: The sensitive power, etc.

Then: So these two are simply, in the human body, etc.

Then: And since the mind, or rational soul, is distinct from the body, it is with good reason that it alone is called the soul.

Finally, where you say 'willing and understanding differ only as different ways of acting in regard to different objects' I would prefer 'they differ only as the activity and passivity of one and the same substance'. For strictly, understanding is the passivity of the mind and willing is its activity; but because we cannot will anything without understanding what we will, and we scarcely ever understand something without at the same time willing something, we do not easily distinguish in this matter passivity from activity.

Voetius' criticism on this point in no way tells against you. Theologians indeed say that no created substance is the immediate principle of its operation; but by this they mean that no creature can operate without the assistance of God, not that it needs some created faculty, distinct from itself, to operate by. It would be absurd to say that such a created faculty could be the immediate principle of an operation, while the substance itself could not.

In what you sent me I cannot find his other criticisms, and so I can make no judgement about them.

When you treat of colours, I cannot see why you exclude blackness, since the other colours too are only modes. I would simply say: 'blackness too is commonly counted as a colour, yet it is nothing but a certain arrangement etc.'

In treating of judgement, you say 'Unless it is accurate and exact, necessarily, in deciding, etc.'. I would put 'easily' rather than 'necessarily'. And shortly after, instead of 'so this can be suspended' I would put 'and this ...' for what comes after does not follow from what precedes, as the word 'so' suggests.

To say of the passions that their seat is in the brain is very paradoxical and even, I think, contrary to your own view. For although the spirits which move the muscles comes from the brain, the seat of the passions must be taken to be the part of the body which is most affected by them, which is undoubtedly the heart. So I would say: 'The principal seat of the passions in so far as they are corporeal, is the heart, since that is principally affected by them; but in so far as they affect also the mind, their seat is in the brain, since only the brain can directly act upon the mind.'

## Descartes to Mersenne, 16 June 1641[1]

I am not yet replying to the two little sheets of objections which you sent me, because you tell me that I can combine

[1] AT iii. 382; AM iv. 359; half in French, half in Latin; complete.

them with some others which I have not yet received, although you sent me them a week ago.[1] But the person who asked me what I meant by the word '*idea*' seems to promise more objections, and the way he begins makes me hope that the ones coming from him will be the best and strongest that can be made; so in case he is waiting for my reply to this before sending any others, you can tell him the gist of it, which is as follows. I use the word 'idea' to mean everything which can be in our thought, and I distinguish three kinds. *Some are adventitious,*[2] such as the idea we commonly have of the sun; *others are constructed or factitious,* in which class we can put the idea which the astronomers construct of the sun by their reasoning; and *others are innate, such as the idea of God, mind, body, triangle, and in general all those which represent true immutable and eternal essences. Now if from a constructed idea I were to conclude to what I explicitly put into it when I was constructing it, I would obviously be begging the question; but it is not the same if I draw out from an innate idea something which was implicitly contained in it but which I did not at first notice in it. Thus I can draw out from the idea of triangle that its three angles equal two right angles, and from the idea of God that He exists. So far from being a begging of the question, this method of argument, in which the true definition of a thing occurs as the middle term, is even according to Aristotle the most perfect of all.*

On 23 June 1641 Descartes sent to Mersenne Gassendi's *Fifth Objections* with his own *Replies.* They should be printed, he said, before Gassendi saw the replies in case he might be tempted to disown his objections. Some of the *Sixth Objections,* he complained, were held up in the post. Mersenne should hold the printer to the original division of the *Meditations* into paragraphs, but should give him a free hand with the punctuation.

The following letter deals with some objections from an unknown correspondent which had been forwarded by Mersenne (AT iii. 375).

---

[1] The *Sixth Objections*.          [2] The words in italics are in Latin.

## Descartes to Mersenne, July 1641[1]

... Is it possible that [your correspondent] could not understand, as he says, what I mean by the idea of God, the idea of the soul, and the ideas of imperceptible things? I mean only what he must himself have understood when he wrote to you that he did not know what they meant. For he did not say that he had no concept corresponding to the expressions 'God', 'soul', 'imperceptible things'; he just said that he did not know what I meant by the ideas of them. But if he had any concept corresponding to these expressions, as he doubtless had, he knew at the same time what was meant by the ideas of them, since it means simply the concept corresponding to the expressions. For by 'idea' I do not just mean the images depicted in the imagination, indeed, in so far as these images are in the corporeal fancy, I do not use that term for them at all. Instead, by the term 'idea' I mean in general everything which is in our mind when we conceive something, no matter how we conceive it.

But I realize that he is not a man to think he cannot conceive a thing when he cannot imagine it, as if this was the only way we have of thinking and conceiving. He clearly realized that was not my opinion, and he showed that it was not his either, since he said himself that God cannot be conceived by the imagination. But if He is not conceived by the imagination, then either one conceives nothing when one speaks of God (which would be a sign of terrible blindness) or one conceives Him in another manner; but whatever way we conceive Him, we have the idea of Him. For we cannot express anything by our words, when we understand what we are saying, without its being certain *eo ipso* that we have in us the idea of the thing which is signified by our words.

It will be easy then, for him to understand what I mean by the idea of God if he takes the word 'idea' in the way in

[1] AT iii. 391; AM iv. 305; in French; with omissions.

which I said explicitly that I took it, and is not confused by those who restrict it to the images of material things formed in the imagination. I mean by the idea of God nothing but what all men habitually understand when they speak of Him. This he must necessarily have understood himself; otherwise, how could he have said that God is infinite and incomprehensible and that He cannot be represented by our imagination? How could he affirm that these attributes belonged to Him, and countless others which express His greatness to us, unless he had the idea of Him? It must be agreed, then, that we have the idea of God, and that we cannot fail to know what this idea is, nor what must be meant by it; because without this we could not know anything at all about God. It would be no good saying that we believe that God exists, and that some attribute or perfection belongs to Him; this would say nothing because it would have no meaning to our mind. Nothing could be more impious or impertinent.

In the case of the soul the matter is even clearer. As I have shown, the soul is nothing but a thing which thinks, and so it is impossible for us ever to think of anything without at the same time having the idea of our soul as a thing capable of thinking of whatever we think of. It is true that a thing of such a nature cannot be imagined, that is, cannot be represented by a corporeal image. But that is not surprising, because our imagination is capable of representing only objects of sense-perception; and since our soul has no colour or smell or taste, nor anything which belongs to body, it is not possible to imagine it or form an image of it. But that does not make it any less conceivable; on the contrary, since it is by means of it that we conceive all other things it is itself more conceivable than all other things put together.

Next, I must tell you that your friend has altogether missed my meaning when, in order to mark the distinction between the ideas in the fancy and those in the mind, he says that the former are expressed by terms, and the latter by propositions. It is not whether they are expressed by terms or by propositions which makes them belong to the mind or the imagination; they can both be expressed in either way. It is the manner of conceiving them which makes the difference; whatever we conceive without an image is an idea of the pure mind, and whatever we conceive with an image is an idea of the imagination. As our imagination is tightly and narrowly limited, while our mind has hardly any limits, there are very few things, even corporeal things, which we can imagine, even though we are capable of conceiving them. One might perhaps think that a science which considers only sizes, shapes, and movements, would be most under the sway of imagination. But those who have studied it at all deeply know that it rests not at all on the phantoms of the fancy, but only on the clear and distinct notions of the mind.

He infers from my writings that the idea of God should be expressed by the proposition 'God exists' and concludes that the main argument I use to prove His existence is a simple begging of the question. How can he make such an inference? He must be very sharp-eyed to see something there which I never meant to say and which never entered my mind before I saw his letter. I based the proof of the existence of God on the idea which I find in myself of a supremely perfect Being, which is the customary notion we have of Him. It is true that the simple consideration of such a Being leads us so easily to the knowledge of His existence that it is almost the same thing to conceive God and to conceive that He exists; but nonetheless the idea we have of God as a supremely perfect Being is quite different from the proposition 'God exists', so that the one can serve as a means or premise to prove the other.

In the same way it is certain that after having come to know the nature of our soul by the steps I used, and after having thus learnt that it is a spiritual substance—because I see that all the attributes which belong to spiritual substances belong to it—a man does not have to be a great philosopher to conclude as I did that it is not corporeal. But a man certainly needs to have a very open mind, and rather an extraordinary one too, to see that the conclusion does not follow from the premises and to discover the flaw in the argument. It is this that I ask him to show me, and that I hope to learn from him if he is willing to take the trouble to teach me. I for my part will not refuse him my little clarifications, if he needs them and is willing to proceed in good faith.

I am, etc.

## From the letter to Mersenne, 22 July 1641[1]

Reverend Father,

I send you the *Sixth Objections* with my replies; and because the objections are made up of various papers which you sent me at different times, I have copied them out in my own writing in the way they seemed most conveniently combined. You sent me two new articles in one of your letters; I have added one of them to the end of the fifth point, after the words, 'cannot be found' as you told me.[2] You did not indicate any place to insert the other, so I thought best to divide it into two parts, and made the first into a seventh point, while adding the second to the end of the third. Finally, I found a new objection in the second copy which you sent me, and made it into an eighth point.

*      *      *

I do not understand your question whether our ideas are expressed by a simple term. Words are human inventions, so one can use one or more to express the same thing. But I explained in my reply to the *First Objections* how a triangle inscribed in a square can be taken as a single idea or as several.[3] Altogether, I think that all those which involve no affirmation or negation are innate; because the sense organs do not bring us anything which is like the idea which arises in us at their stimulus, and so this idea must have been in us before.

I am, etc.

---

[1] AT iii. 414; AM v. 30; in French; extracts.
[2] Cf. AT vii. 416; HR ii. 42.    [3] AT vii. 118; HR ii. 20.

## From the letter to [de Launay], 22 July 1641[1]

. . . The earliest judgements which we made in our child-hood, and the common philosophy later, have accustomed us to attribute to the body many things which belong only to the soul, and to attribute to the soul many things which belong only to the body. So people commonly mingle the two ideas of body and soul when they construct the ideas of real qualities and substantial forms, which I think should be altogether rejected. If you examine physics carefully, you can reduce all those things in it which fall under the province of intellectual knowledge to very few kinds, of which we have very clear and distinct notions. Once you have considered them I do not think you can fail to recognize whether, when we conceive one thing apart from another, this happens only by an abstraction of our mind or because the things are truly distinct. When things are separated only by a mental abstraction, you cannot help noticing their conjunction and union when you consider them together. But in the case of body and soul you cannot see any such connection, provided that you conceive them as they should be conceived, the one as that which fills space, the other as that which thinks. Indeed after the idea we have of God, which is very different from all those we have of created things, I do not know any other pair of ideas in nature which are as different from each other as these two . . .

I am, etc.

The following letter is a reply to a long series of objections to the *Fifth Replies* sent by a supporter of Gassendi. The letter containing the objections is extant, but its author is unknown; he is commonly given the name 'Hyper-aspistes', the Greek word for 'champion', which he used to refer to himself at the end of his letter. As will be seen, Descartes valued these objections sufficiently to want to print them, with his replies, in the first edition of the *Meditations*.

[1] AT iii. 419; AM v. 33; date and addressee uncertain; in French; extracts.

Descartes to Hyperaspistes, August 1641[1]

Sir,

Now that the objections I have so far received have been
sent to the printer, I had decided to keep any further
objections which might come for a second volume. But
since your objections claim to exhaust all the points that
remain, I gladly hasten to reply to them so that they can be
printed with the others.[2]

1. It would indeed be desirable to have as much certainty
in matters of conduct as is needed for the acquisition of
scientific knowledge; but it is easily shown that in such
matters so much is not to be sought nor hoped for.[3] This
can be shown *a priori* from the fact that a human being as a
whole is naturally corruptible, while the mind is incorrrupt-
ible and immortal. It can be shown more easily *a posteriori*
from the consequences that would follow. Suppose that a
man decided to abstain from all food to the point of starva-
tion, because he was not certain that it was not poisoned, and
thought that he was not bound to eat because it was not clearly
established that he had the means of keeping alive, and it
was better to wait for death by abstaining than to kill
himself by eating. Such a man would be rightly regarded as
insane and responsible for his own death. Suppose further
that he could not obtain any food that was not poisoned, and
that his nature was such that fasting was beneficial to him;
none the less, if the food appeared harmless and healthy, and
fasting appeared likely to have its usual harmful effects, he
would be bound to eat the food and thus follow the apparently beneficial course of action rather than the actually
beneficial one. This is so self-evident to all that I am
surprised that anyone could think otherwise.

[1] AT iii. 422; AM v. 38; in Latin; complete.
[2] In fact the objections and reply arrived too late to be included.
[3] Hyperaspistes had objected to Descartes' admission that less certainty was
needed for conduct than for speculation (AT vii. 350; HR ii. 206). It was more
important, he said, to avoid sin than to avoid error in metaphysics: 'why then do
you suppose or demand a lesser truth in morals than in science?' (AT iii. 398).

2. I nowhere said that because an infant's mind acts less perfectly than an adult's it follows that it is no less perfect; so I cannot be criticized on that account.[1] But because it does not follow either that it is more imperfect, I had the right to criticize someone who had assumed that to be the case. I had reason to assert that the human soul, wherever it be, even in the mother's womb, is always thinking. What more certain or evident reason could be wished for than the one I gave? I had proved that the nature or essence of soul consists in the fact that it is thinking, just as the essence of body consists in the fact that it is extended. Now nothing can ever be deprived of its own essence; so it seems to me that a man who denies that his soul was thinking at times when he does not remember noticing it thinking, deserves no more attention than a man who denied that his body was extended while he did not notice that it had extension. This does not mean that I believe that the mind of an infant meditates on metaphysics in its mother's womb; not at all. We know by experience that our minds are so closely joined to our bodies as to be almost always acted upon by them; and though in an adult and healthy body the mind enjoys some liberty to think of other things than those presented by the senses, we know there is not the same liberty in those who are sick or asleep or very young; and the younger they are the less liberty they have. So if one may conjecture on such an unexplored topic, it seems most reasonable to think that a mind newly united to an infant's body is wholly occupied in perceiving or feeling the ideas of pain, pleasure, heat, cold and other similar ideas which arise from its union and intermingling with the body. Nonetheless, it has in itself the ideas of God, itself, and all such truths as are called self-evident, in the same way as adult humans have when they are not attending to them; it does not acquire these ideas later on, as it grows older. I have no doubt that if it were taken out of the prison of the body it would find them within itself.

---

[1] In the *Fifth Replies* Descartes had said 'From the fact that the mind does not act as perfectly in the body of an infant as in that of an adult . . . it does not follow that it is made more or less perfect by the body'; AT vii. 354; HR ii. 209. Hyperaspistes had objected 'it does not follow that it is *not*.'

This view does not involve us in any difficulties.[1] The mind, though really distinct from the body, is none the less joined to it, and is affected by traces impressed on it, and is able to impress new traces on its own account. This is no harder for us to understand than it is for those who believe in accidents to understand how they act on corporeal substances while belonging to a wholly different category. It makes no difference that these accidents are called corporeal. If 'corporeal' is taken to mean anything which can in any way affect a body, then the mind too must be called corporeal in this sense; but if 'corporeal' is taken to mean whatever is made up of the sort of substance called body, then the mind cannot be called corporeal but neither can those accidents which are supposed to be really distinct from body. It is only in this latter sense that the mind is commonly said not to be corporeal. Thus, when a mind joined to a body thinks of a corporeal thing, certain particles in the brain are set in motion. Sometimes this results from the action of external objects on the sense organs, sometimes from the ascent of animal spirits from the heart to the brain, and sometimes from the mind's own action, when it is impelled of its own free will to a certain thought. The motion of these brain particles leaves behind traces on which memory depends. Purely intellectual things are not strictly remembered; they are no less thought of the first time they come to mind than the second. Of course, they are commonly associated with names, and these are corporeal, and so can be remembered. There are many other points to be noted on this topic which cannot now be explained in detail.

3. I did distinguish between what belongs to me, or to my nature, and what belongs only to my consciousness of myself (*meam notitiam*); but it cannot be deduced from this that my metaphysics reaches no conclusions about anything outside consciousness. Nor do the other objectionable conclusions follow. It is easy for the reader to tell when I was discussing mere consciousness, and when I was discussing the truth about the world.

---

[1] In his objection, Hyperaspistes had stressed the difficulty in conceiving the relation between incorporeal thoughts in the mind and corporeal traces in the brain.

I never used the word 'believe' when the topic was scientific knowledge; the word does not even occur in the passage here cited.[1] In the reply to the *Second Objections* I said 'enlightened by God, we trust that what is proposed for our belief has been revealed by him': but there I was speaking not of human scientific knowledge, but of faith.[2] And I did not assert that by the light of grace we clearly know the very mysteries of faith—though I would not deny that this too may happen—but only that we trust that they are to be believed. No one who really has the Catholic faith can doubt or be surprised that it is most evident that what God has revealed is to be believed and that the light of grace is to be preferred to the light of nature. The further questions on this topic do not concern me,[3] since I gave no occasion in my writings for them to be asked. Earlier, in the reply to the *Sixth Objections* I stated that I would not reply to such questions, and so I will say no more about them here.

4. The fourth objection rests on something I nowhere say: *viz.* 'that the highest point of my certainty is when we think we see something so clearly that the more we think about it the truer it seems.' So there is no need for me to answer what follows; though an answer could easily be given by anyone who distinguishes the light of faith from the natural light and prefers the former to the latter.[4]

5. The fifth objection too rests on something I nowhere say.[5] I utterly deny that we are ignorant what a thing is, or

---

[1] Hyperaspistes accused Descartes of teaching, in the *Second Replies,* that one should not believe anything unless one clearly saw that what was proposed for belief was true. This, he said, would erase the distinctions between knowledge and belief, and between faith and heresy.

[2] AT vii. 149; HR ii, 43.

[3] Hyperaspistes asked Descartes' opinion about non-Catholic martyrs. 'Do you think that you or anyone perceive the truth of the mystery of the Trinity more clearly than the contrary appears to a Jew or an Aryan?'

[4] Hyperaspistes had objected that Descartes had given no method by which a man may know whether he clearly perceives something or not. Turks think they see clearly that the doctrine of the Trinity is false, and claim that nothing in geometry or metaphysics is clearer.

[5] The fifth objection was against the *cogito, ergo sum.* 'Is it possible for you to understand a proposition without understanding its subject and predicate? But you do not know what is meant by 'thing', what is meant by 'exist', what is meant by 'thought'. Otherwise, you would say so clearly what they are that I too would

what thought is, or that I need to teach people this. It is so self-evident that there is nothing by which it could be explained more clearly. Finally I deny that we can think only of corporeal things.

6. It is true that we do not understand the infinite by the negation of limitation; and one cannot infer because limitation involves the negation of infinity, that the negation of limitation involves knowledge of infinity. What makes the infinite different from the finite is something real and positive; but limitation, which is what makes the finite different from the infinite, is a non-being or negation of being. That which is not cannot bring us to the knowledge of that which is; on the contrary, the negation of a thing has to be conceived on the basis of knowledge of the thing itself. When I said that it was enough for us to conceive of a thing bound by no limits in order to understand the infinite,[1] I was following a very common usage. Similarly, I kept the term 'infinite', when 'the greatest being' would be more correct, if we wanted all names to correspond to the nature of what they name. But usage demanded that I used the negation of a negation. If was as if, to refer to the largest thing, I had said it was not small, or had no smallness in it. But by this I did not mean that the positive nature of infinity was known through its negation, and so I did not contradict myself at all.

I did not deny that there is a power in the mind of amplifying its ideas[2]; but I frequently insisted that there could not be in the mind ideas thus amplified, or the power of so amplifying them, unless the mind came from God in whom there really exist all the perfections which can be reached by such amplification. I proved this from the principle that there can be nothing in an effect which is not pre-existent in the cause. And no one who deserves to be called a subtle philosopher in this field thinks that atoms exist of themselves.

---

clearly perceive the truth of that proposition. Moreover, you do not know whether it is you yourself who think or whether the world-soul in you does the thinking, as the Platonists believe' (AT iii. 403).

[1] AT vii. 368; HR ii. 218.

[2] Descartes had said (AT vii. 379; HR ii. 220) that the mind's power of amplifying human perfections must have come from God. Hyperaspistes asked 'Could it not come from the mind itself as an eternal and independent substance?'

For it is clear by the light of nature that there can be only one supreme being independent of everything else.

When it is said that a spinning top does not act upon itself, but is acted upon by the absent whip, I wonder how one body can be acted upon by another which is absent, and how activity and passivity are to be distinguished.[1] For I admit I am not subtle enough to grasp how something can be acted upon by something else that is not present—which may, indeed, be supposed not even existent, if the whip ceased to exist after whipping the top. Nor do I see why we could not as well say that there are now no activities in the world at all, but that all the things which happen are passivities of the activities there were when the world began. But I have always thought that it was one and the same thing which is called an activity in relation to a *terminus a quo* and a passivity in relation to a *terminus ad quem* or *in quo*. If so, it is inconceivable that there should be a passivity without an activity for even a single moment. Finally, I agree that the ideas of corporeal things—indeed of everything in the whole visible world, though not, as you say in your objection, of the visible world itself—could be produced by the human mind; but it does not follow that we do not know whether there is in reality anything corporeal. It is not my views, but conclusions wrongly deduced from them, that lead to difficulties. I proved the existence of material things not from the fact that we have ideas of them but from the fact that these ideas present themselves in such a way as to make us aware that they are not produced by ourselves but come from elsewhere.

7. I say first that in Bologna spar[2] the light of the sun is not preserved, but the sun's rays kindle a new light which can afterwards be seen in shadow. In any case, it would not follow that anything can be kept in being without the influence of God, since a true proposition may be illustrated by a false example. It is much more certain that nothing can

[1] Hyperaspistes had objected to Descartes' giving a spinning top as an example of an agent acting on itself (AT vii. 376; HR ii. 217).

[2] Descartes had said that creatures could not be kept in being without a continuous action of God, just as light would fail if the sun stopped shining (AT vii. 369; HR ii. 219). Hyperaspistes countered that phosphorescent substances, like Bologna spar, could shine in a closed room.

exist without the co-operation of God than that there is no sunlight without the sun. There is no doubt that if God withdrew his co-operation, everything which he has created would go to nothing; because all things were nothing until God created them and provided his co-operation. This does not mean that they should not be called substances, because when we call a created substance self-subsistent we do not rule out the divine co-operation which it needs in order to subsist. We mean only that it is a thing of a kind to exist without any other creature; and this is something that cannot be said about the modes of things, like shape and number. It is not the case that God would be showing the immensity of his power if he made things which could exist without him later on; on the contrary, he would thus be showing that his power was finite, since things once created would no longer depend on him. I agree that it is impossible that God should destroy anything except by withdrawing his co-operation, because otherwise he would be aiming at non-being by a positive action. But in admitting that I am not falling into any trap. For there is a great difference between what happens by God's positive action and what results from the cessation of his positive action: the former cannot be anything but excellent, the latter includes evils and sins and the destruction of beings, if any existent beings are ever destroyed.

There is no force in what you say about the nature of the triangle.[1] As I have insisted in several places, when God or infinity is in question, we must consider not what we can comprehend—we know that they are beyond our comprehension—but what conclusions we can reach by certain arguments. To find what kind of causal dependence these truths have on God, see my *Replies* to the *Sixth Objections*, article 8.[2]

8. I do not remember ever to have written, or even thought, what is here attributed to me.[3]

[1] Hyperaspistes had argued against Descartes' doctrine of the free creation of eternal truths. 'Let God do whatever he can; let us suppose *per impossibile*, that he never thought of a triangle: yet suppose you are in the world as you now are: would you not agree that it was true that the three angles of a triangle equal two right angles?'

[2] AT vii. 425; HR ii. 243.

[3] That an infinite series of subordinate causes is impossible.

9. I do not remember that I ever expressed surprise that not everybody experiences the idea of God in himself; for I have often observed that what men judge does not accord with what they understand. I do not doubt that everyone has within himself an implicit idea of God, that is to say, an aptitude to perceive it explicitly; but I am not surprised that not everyone feels that he has it or notices that he has it. Some people will perhaps not notice it even after reading my *Meditations* a thousand times. In the same way, people judge that so-called empty space is nothing; all the same they conceive it as a positive reality. In the same way, when people believe that accidents are real, they are representing them to themselves as substances, even though they do not judge them to be substances; and in many other matters men's judgements disagree with their perceptions. But if a man never makes a judgement except about things he clearly and distinctly perceives—a rule which I always keep as well as I can—then he cannot make different judgements at different times about the same thing. It is true that things which are clear and beyond doubt appear more certain to us the more often and the more attentively we think of them; but I do not remember that I ever made this the criterion of clear and indubitable certainty. I do not know where the word '*always*' occurs; but I know that when we say we *always* do something, we do not mean that we do it eternally, but whenever the occasion presents itself.[1]

10. It is self evident that we cannot know God's purposes unless God reveals them. From the human point of view adopted in ethics, it is true that everything was made for God's glory, in the sense that we must praise God for all that he has made; and it is true that the sun was made to give us light, in the sense that we see the sun does give us light. But it would be childish and absurd for a meta-physician to assert that God, like some vainglorious human being, had no other purpose in making the universe than to win men's praise; or that the sun, which is many times larger than the earth, was created for no other purpose than

---

[1] Hyperaspistes had asked why Descartes was certain he had the idea of God, since others denied having such an idea, and Descartes himself could not be sure, short of eternal experience, that he would *always* think as he now thought.

to give light to man, who occupies a very small part of the earth.

11. Here there is a confusion between the functions of the intellect and the will. The will does not understand, it only wills; and though, as I agreed before, we never will anything of which we have no understanding at all, yet experience shows clearly that about any given thing our will may extend further than our knowledge. Again, falsehood is never apprehended as truth, and those who deny that we have an idea of God do not really apprehend this even though perhaps they affirm it, believe it, and argue for it. As I remarked above, in answer to the ninth objection, men's judgements often differ from their conceptions or apprehensions.

12. I do not need to take great pains to answer here, since nothing is objected to me save the authority of Aristotle and his followers; and I do not pretend that I trust him more than I trust reason.[1]

It does not matter whether a man born blind has the ideas of colour or not, and it is pointless to cite the testimony of a blind philosopher.[2] For let us suppose that he has ideas exactly like our ideas of colours: he still cannot know that they are like ours, nor that they are called ideas of colours, because he does not know what ours are like. I do not see how I am in any worse position than you here, because even though the mind is indivisible it is none the less capable of acquiring various properties. It is not surprising that it does not construct in sleep proofs like Archimedes'[3]; because even in sleep it is still united to the body and is no freer than during waking life. Keeping long awake does not make the brain more fit to retain the traces impressed on it. In sleep and waking life alike, traces are better retained the more strongly they are impressed. And so sometimes we

[1] Hyperaspistes had quoted the Aristotelian dictum that nothing was in the intellect which was not first in the senses.

[2] Arguing for empiricism, Hyperaspistes had said 'Has anyone born blind ever perceived anything of light and colour? Of course not, as our three hundred blind men at Paris will testify, including a philosopher who when I asked him said he could not conceive colour or light.'

[3] Hyperaspistes had said it should do this if the senses were a hindrance rather than a help.

remember even dreams, but we remember better what we have thought of in waking life. The reasons for this will be clear in my *Physics*.

13. When I said that God was his own being,[1] I was using the regular theological idiom to express that it belongs to God's essence to exist. The same cannot be said of a triangle, whose whole essence can be correctly conceived even if it be supposed that in reality there is no such thing.

I said that the sceptics would not have doubted the truths of geometry if they had duly recognized God because since those geometrical truths are very clear they would have had no occasion to doubt them if they had known that whatever is clearly conceived is true. The knowledge of this is contained in a sufficient knowledge of God, and that is the premiss missing in their argument.

The question whether a line consists of points or segments is irrelevant and need not be answered here.[2] I must remark however that in the place cited, p. 543,[3] I was not talking about any and every geometrical topic, but only about those proofs which the sceptics doubted even though they clearly understood them. You cannot have a sceptic saying 'Let the evil genius deceive me as much as he can . . .'[4] because anyone who says this is *eo ipso* not a sceptic since he does not doubt everything. Certainly I have never denied that the sceptics themselves, as long as they clearly perceive some truth, spontaneously assent to it. It is only in name, and perhaps in intention and resolve, that they adhere to their heresy of doubting everything. But I was discussing only the things which we remember having clearly perceived earlier, not the things which we clearly perceive at the present moment, as can be seen on pp. 84 and 344.[5]

14. The mind is co-extensive with an extended body even though it has itself no real extension in the sense of

---

[1] AT vii. 383; HR ii. 228.
[2] Hyperaspistes had tried to show that either supposition led to absurdity, and thus to generate sceptical doubts about geometry.
[3] AT vii. 384; HR ii. 229.
[4] Hyperaspistes had said that a sceptic could say 'Let the evil genius deceive me as much as he can, he will never deceive me about this geometrical proposition'—a parody of the *Second Meditation*.
[5] AT vii. 69, 245; HR i. 183; ii. 114.

occupying a place and excluding other things from it. How this can be, I explained above by the illustration of gravity conceived as a real quality. I also showed above that when Ecclesiastes says that man has no advantage over a beast of burden he is speaking only of the body; for immediately afterwards he goes on to deal separately with the soul saying 'Who knows if the spirit of the sons of Adam', etc.[1]

You ask how to tell which way of conceiving things is more imperfect and more revealing of the weakness of our minds: being unable to conceive one thing without another (e.g. mind without body) or conceiving one thing completely apart from another. You must see which of these proceeds from a positive faculty and which from the privation of the same faculty. Then it is easy to see that the real faculty of the mind is its ability to conceive two things apart; and it is the lack of this faculty which makes it apprehend two things in a confused manner as a single thing. In the same way eyesight is more perfect when it distinguishes accurately between the different parts of an object than when it perceives them all together as a single thing. Of course a man whose eyes are unsteady may take one thing for two, as men often do when drunk; and philosophers may do the like, not when they distinguish essence from existence—because normally they do not suppose any greater distinction between them than there really is—but when in the same body they make a distinction between matter, form and various accidents as if they were so many different things. In such cases the obscurity and confused nature of the conception makes it easy for them to realize that it arises not only from a positive faculty but also from a defect of some faculty; if they paid careful attention they could notice that they do not have completely distinct ideas of the things they thus suppose to be distinct.

If all the places insufficiently explained above have been commented on in these objections, I am much indebted to their author for giving me grounds to hope that no more objections will be forthcoming.

---

[1] Ecclesiastes 3: 19–21.

The *Meditations* were published on 28 August 1641 by Michel Soly at Paris. In September Descartes wrote to Mersenne 'As for my *Metaphysics* I have not given it a thought since I sent you my reply to Hyperaspistes.' But two months later he told him that he was dissatisfied with Soly as a publisher, and was arranging for the Elzevirs to bring out a second edition of the *Meditations* in Holland.

Meanwhile, the controversy at Utrecht grew more bitter. In December Regius defended a number of theses which gave offence to orthodox scholastics, and sent copies to Descartes for his comments. Descartes' immediate reply was favourable, though he had reservations concerning Regius' psychological terminology: volition, he said, was the only activity of the soul, while intellection and vision was a passivity; perception could only be called an activity if one took 'activity' to mean any positive power. But in a second letter, Descartes was much more sharply critical of Regius' tactics, and counselled a partial recantation.

## Descartes to Regius, December 1641[1]

Sir,

In your theses you say that a human being is an *ens per accidens*.[2] You could scarcely have said anything more objectionable and provocative. The best way I can see to remedy this is to say that in your ninth thesis you considered the whole human being in relation to the parts of which he is made up, and in your tenth thesis you considered the parts in relation to the whole. Say too that in your ninth you said that a human being came into being *per accidens* out of body and soul in order to express that it can in a sense be said to be inessential (*accidentarium*) for the body to be joined to a soul, and for the soul to be joined to a body, since the body can exist without a soul and the soul can exist without a body. For the term 'accident' means anything which can be present or absent without its possessor ceasing to exist; some accidents, considered in themselves, may be substances; as clothing is an accident of a human being. Tell them that in spite of this you did not say that a human being was an *ens per accidens*, and you showed sufficiently, in your tenth thesis, that you thought it to be an

[1] AT iii. 459; AM v. 84; in Latin; complete.      [2] Not an essential unity.

*ens per se.*[1] For there you said that body and soul, in relation
to the whole human being, are incomplete substances; and
it follows from their being incomplete that what they
constitute is an *ens per se.* Something which comes into
being *per accidens* may yet be an *ens per se*: for mice are
generated, or come into being, *per accidens* from dirt, and
yet they are *entia per se.* It may be objected that for a human
body to be joined to a soul, is not inessential but its very
nature; because if a body has all the dispositions required to
receive a soul, which it must have if it is to be strictly a
human body, then short of a miracle it must be united to a
soul. Moreover, it may be objected that it is not the soul's
being joined to the body, but its being separated from it
after death, which is inessential to it. You should not
altogether deny this, for fear of giving further offence to
the theologians; but you should reply that these things can
still be called inessential because when we consider the body
alone we perceive nothing in it demanding union with the
soul, and nothing in the soul obliging it to be united to the
body; which is why I said above that it was inessential in a
sense, not that it was absolutely inessential.

A simple alteration is a process which does not change the
form of a substance, such as the heating of wood; generation
is a process which changes the form, such as setting fire to
something. Although both kinds of process come about in
the same way, there is a great difference in the way of
conceiving them and also in reality. For forms, at least the
more perfect ones, are collections of a number of qualities
with a power of mutual preservation. In wood there is only
moderate heat, to which after being heated it returns of its
own accord; but in fire there is strong heat, which it always
preserves as long as it is fire.

You should not be angry with the colleague who advised
you to add a corollary to explain your thesis: it seems to me
that it was a friendly piece of advice.

You left out a word in the tenth of your handwritten
theses. You say 'all the other', and you do not say what:
you mean: 'all the other qualities'.

I have nothing to say about the rest. There is hardly any-

[1] An essential unity.

thing in them which you have not said elsewhere; that is something I am glad to see. It would be a great task to want always to find something new.

If you come here, I will always be very pleased to see you.

## From the letter to Gibieuf, 19 January 1642[1]

... You inquire about the principle by which I claim to know that the idea I have of something is not *an idea made inadequate by the abstraction of my intellect*.[2] I derive this knowledge purely from my own thought or consciousness. I am certain that I can have no knowledge of what is outside me except by means of the ideas I have within me; and so I take great care not to relate my judgements immediately to things in the world, and not to attribute to such things anything positive which I do not first perceive in the ideas of them. But I think also that whatever is to be found in these ideas is necessarily also in the things themselves. So, to tell whether my idea has been made incomplete or inadequate by the abstraction of my mind, I merely look to see whether I have derived it, not from some more complete object outside myself, but by abstraction from some more rich or more complete idea which I have in myself. Intellectual abstraction would consist in my turning my thought away from one part of the contents of the richer idea the better to apply it to another part with greater attention. Thus, when I consider a shape without thinking of the substance or the extension whose shape it is, I make a mental abstraction. I can easily recognize this abstraction afterwards when I look to see whether I have derived the idea of pure shape from some richer idea within myself, to which it is joined in such a way that although one can think of the one without paying any attention to the other, it is impossible to deny one of the other when one thinks of both together.

---

[1] AT iii. 472; AM v. 103; in French; with omissions.
[2] Latin words in a French context.

For I see clearly that the idea of shape is joined in this way to the idea of extension and substance, since it is impossible to conceive a shape while denying that it has an extension, or to conceive an extension while denying that it is the extension of a substance. But the idea of a substance with its extension and shape is a complete idea, because I can conceive it alone, and deny of it everything else of which I have an idea. Now it seems to me very clear that the idea which I have of a thinking substance is complete in this sense, and that I have in my mind no other idea which is prior to it and joined to it in such a way that I cannot think of the two together while denying the one of the other; for if there was any such within me, I must necessarily know it. You will say perhaps that the difficulty remains, because although I conceive the soul and the body as two substances which I can conceive separately, and which I can even deny of each other, I am not certain that they are in reality such as I conceive them to be. Here we have to recall the principle already stated, that we cannot have any knowledge of things except by the ideas we conceive of them; and consequently, that we must not judge of them except in accordance with these ideas, and we must even think that whatever conflicts with these ideas is absolutely impossible and involves a contradiction. Thus we have no reason to affirm that there is no mountain without a valley, except that we see that the ideas of the two things cannot be complete when we consider them apart; though of course by abstraction we can obtain the idea of a mountain, or of an upward slope, without considering that the same slope can be travelled downhill. In the same way we can say that the existence of atoms, or parts of matter which have extension and yet are indivisible, involves a contradiction, because it is impossible to have the idea of an extended thing without also having the idea of half of it, or a third of it, and so conceiving it as being divisible by two or three. From the simple fact that I consider the two halves of a part of matter, however small it may be, as two complete substances, *whose ideas are not made inadequate by the abstraction of my intellect*, I conclude with certainty that they really are divisible. Someone may tell me that though I can conceive them apart I have no

reason to deny their inseparability because I do not know
that God has not united or joined them so tightly that they
are entirely inseparable. I would reply that however he
may have joined them, I am sure that he can also disjoin
them; so that absolutely speaking I have reason to call
them divisible, since he has given me the faculty of conceiving them as such. I say the same about the soul and the
body and in general all the things of which we have distinct
and complete ideas; that is, I say that their being inseparable
involves a contradiction. But I do not deny that there can
be in the soul or the body many properties of which I have
no ideas; I only deny that there are any which are incon-
sistent with the ideas that I do have, including the idea that
I have of their distinctness; for otherwise God would be a
deceiver and we would have no rule to make us certain of
the truth.

I believe that the soul is always thinking for the same
reason as I believe that light is always shining, even though
there are not always eyes looking at it, and that heat is
always warm though no one is being warmed by it, and that
body, or extended substance always has extension, and in
general that whatever constitutes the nature of a thing
always belongs to it as long as it exists. So it would be
easier for me to believe that the soul ceased to exist at the
times when it is supposed to cease to think than to conceive
that it could exist without thought. And I do not see any
difficulty here, except that people think it superfluous to
believe that it thinks at times when no memory of the
thought remains with us afterwards. But consider that every
night we have a thousand thoughts, and even while awake
we had a thousand thoughts within the hour of which no
trace remains in our memory, and which seem no more use
than thoughts we may have had before we were born. Then
you will find it easier to be convinced of my theory than to
judge that a substance whose nature is to think can exist
while not thinking at all.

I do not see any difficulty in allowing on the one hand that
the faculties of imagination and sensation belong to the soul,
because they are species of thoughts, and on the other hand
that they belong to the soul only as joined to the body,

because they are kinds of thoughts without which one can conceive the soul entirely pure.

We observe in animals movements similar to those which result from our imaginations and sensations; but that does not mean that we observe imaginations and sensations in them. These movements can take place without imagination, and we have arguments to prove that they do so take place in animals, as I hope to show clearly by describing in detail the architecture of their members and the causes of their movements. . . .

In January 1642 Descartes learnt of developments at Utrecht. Voetius had attempted to have Regius condemned for heresy and deprived of his chair. This had been thwarted by a burgomaster favourable to Regius, but the partisans of Voetius held a public disputation at Christmas in which they attacked three propositions: that a human being was an *ens per accidens*, that the earth moved round the sun, and that substantial forms were to be rejected. Regius, afraid of heckling, decided to reply in writing rather than by a counter-disputation, and sent his reply for Descartes' approval.

## From the letter to Regius, January 1642[1]

Sir,

I have had here all afternoon a distinguished visitor, M. Alphonse,[2] who discussed the Utrecht affair at length in a friendly and prudent manner. I agree with him entirely that you should refrain from public disputations for some time, and should be extremely careful not to annoy people by hard words. I should like it best if you never put forward any new opinions, but retained all the old ones in name, and merely brought forward new arguments. This is a course of action to which nobody could take exception, and yet those who understood your arguments would spontaneously draw

---

[1] AT iii. 491; AM v. 111; in Latin; extracts.          [2] Pollot.

from them the conclusions you had in mind. For instance, why did you openly reject substantial forms and real qualities? Do you not remember that on p. 164 of the French edition of my *Meteors*,[1] I expressly said that I did not at all reject or deny them, but simply found them unnecessary in setting out my explanations. If you had taken this course, everybody in your audience would have rejected them as soon as they saw they were useless, but you would not have become so unpopular with your colleagues.

But what is done cannot be undone. Now you must try to defend as moderately as possible the true things you said, and to correct without any obstinacy the untrue, or improper things you said. Remind yourself that there is nothing more praiseworthy in a philosopher than a candid acknowledgment of his errors.

For instance, when you said that a human being was an *ens per accidens*,[2] I know that you meant only what everyone else admits, that a human being is made up of two things which are really distinct; but the expressions *ens per accidens* is not used in that sense by scholastics. If you cannot use the explanation which I suggested in a previous letter—and I see that in your latest paper you have departed from it to some degree, and not altogether avoided the hazards—then it is much better to admit openly that you misunderstood the scholastic expression than to try unsuccessfully to cover the matter up. You should say that fundamentally you agree with the others and that your disagreement with them was merely verbal. And whenever the occasion arises, in public and in private, you should give out that you believe that a human being is a true *ens per se*, and not an *ens per accidens*, and that the mind and the body are united in a real and substantial manner. You must say that they are united not by position or disposition, as you say in your last paper— for this too is open to objection and, in my opinion, quite untrue—but by a true mode of union, as everyone agrees, though nobody explains what this means and so you need not do so either. You could do so, however, as I did in my *Metaphysics*, by saying that we perceive that sensations such as pain are not pure thoughts of a mind distinct from a body,

[1] AT vi. 239; Olscamp 268.      [2] See above, p. 121.

but confused perceptions of a mind really united to one. For if an angel were in a human body, he would not have sensations as we do, but would simply perceive the motions which are caused by external objects, and in this way would differ from a real man.

\*          \*          \*

[Descartes then rejects Regius' proposed reply, and suggests alternative answers to each of Voetius' criticisms. *Inter alia*, he says:]

In his first point, [Voetius] asks whether the denial of substantial forms can be reconciled with Sacred Scripture. No one can doubt this who knows that these philosophical entities, which are unknown outside the schools, never crossed the minds of the prophets and apostles who composed the sacred scriptures at the dictation of the Holy Ghost. To prevent any ambiguity of expression, it must be observed that when we deny substantial forms, we mean by the expression a certain substance joined to matter, making up with it a merely corporeal whole, and which, no less than matter and even more than matter—since it is called an actuality and matter only a potentiality—is a true substance, or self-subsistent thing. Such a substance, or substantial form, present in purely corporeal things but distinct from matter, is nowhere, we think, mentioned in Holy Writ. . . . Nor can it be said that the words '*genus*' or '*species*' denote substantial differences, since there are genera and species of accidents and modes, as shape is a genus in relation to circles and squares, which no one supposes to have substantial forms etc.

\*          \*          \*

It would certainly be absurd for those who believe in substantial forms to say that these forms are themselves the immediate principles of their actions; but it is not absurd to say this if one does not regard such forms as distinct from active qualities. Now we do not deny active qualities, but we say that they should not be regarded as having any degree of reality greater than that of modes; for to regard them so is to conceive them as substances. Nor do we deny dispositions (*habitus*), but we divide them into two kinds. Some are purely material and depend only on the shape or other state of the parts. Others are immaterial or spiritual, like the states of faith, grace and so on which theologians talk of; these do not depend on anything bodily, but are spiritual modes inhering in the mind, just as movement and shape are corporeal modes inhering in the body.

*              *              *

All the arguments to prove substantial forms could be applied to the form of a clock, which nobody says is a substantial form. The arguments, or physical proofs, which we think would force a truth-loving mind to abandon substantial forms, are mainly the following *a priori* metaphysical or theological ones. It is inconceivable that a substance should come into existence without a new creation by God; but we see that every day many so-called substantial forms come into existence; and yet the people who think they are substances do not believe that they are created by God; so their view is mistaken.

*              *              *

The second proof is drawn from the purpose or use of substantial forms. They were introduced by philosophers solely to account for the proper actions of natural things, of which they were supposed to be the principles and bases, as was said in an earlier thesis. But no natural action can be explained by these substantial forms, since their defenders admit that they are occult and that they do not understand them themselves. If they say that some action proceeds from a substantial form it is as if they said that it proceeds from something they do not understand; which explains nothing. So these forms are not to be introduced to explain the causes of natural actions. Essential forms explained in our fashion on the other hand, give manifest and mathematical reasons for natural actions, as can be seen with regard to the form of common salt in my *Meteors*.[1]

\*       \*       \*

We affirm that a human being is made up of body and soul, not by the mere presence or proximity of one to the other, but by a true substantial union. For this there is, indeed, required a natural disposition of the body and the appropriate configuration of its parts; but the union differs from position and shape and other purely corporeal modes, because it reaches the incorporeal soul as well as the body. The idiom which we used was perhaps unusual, but we think it is sufficiently apt to express what we meant. When we said that a human being was an *ens per accidens*[2] we meant this only in relation to its parts, the soul and the body; we meant that to each of these parts it was in a manner inessential to be joined to the other, because each could subsist apart, and what can be present or absent without its possessor ceasing to exist is called an accident. But if a human being is considered in himself as a whole, I say of course that he is a single *ens per se*, and not *per accidens*; because the union which joins a human body and soul to each other is not inessential to a human being, but essential, since a man without it is not a man. But many more people make the mistake of thinking that the soul is not really distinct from the body than make the mistake of admitting their distinction and denying their substantial union, and in order to refute those who believe souls to be mortal it is more important to teach the distinction of parts in man than to teach their union. And so I thought I would please the theologians more by saying that a human being was an *ens per accidens*, in order to make the distinction, than if I said that he was an *ens per se*, in reference to the union of the parts.

---

[1] AT vi. 249; Olscamp 275.       [2] See above, p. 121.

# From the letter to Huygens, 31 January 1642[1]

... Four or five days ago I received the paper of the Jesuits.[2] It is now a prisoner in my hands, and I want to treat it as courteously as I can; but I find it so guilty that I see no way of saving it. Every day I call my council of war about it, and I hope that in a short time you will be able to see the account of the trial.

Perhaps these scholastic wars will result in my *World* being brought into the world. It would be out already, I think, were it not that I want to teach it to speak Latin first.[3] I shall call it *Summa Philosophiae* to make it more welcome to the scholastics, who are now persecuting it and trying to smother it before its birth. The ministers are as hostile as the Jesuits.

# From the letter to Mersenne, March 1642[4]

... I send you the first three sheets of Father Bourdin's objections[5]; I cannot send you the whole yet owing to the negligence of the publisher. Please keep the manuscript copy which you have, so that he cannot say that I have changed anything in his copy, which I was careful to have printed as accurately as possible without changing a single letter. You will perhaps be surprised that I accuse him of such duplicity; but you will see worse to come. I have treated him as courteously as possible, but I have never seen a paper so full of faults. I hope however to keep his cause separate from that of his colleagues, so that they cannot bear me any

---

[1] AT iii. 520; AM v. 146; in French; extract.
[2] The *Seventh Objections*, of Father Bourdin S.J.
[3] The allusion is to the *Principles of Philosophy*.
[4] AT iii. 542; AM v. 169; in French; extract.     [5] The *Seventh Objections*.

ill will unless they want openly to declare themselves enemies of truth and partisans of calumny.

I have looked in S. Augustine for the passages you mentioned about the fourteenth Psalm; but I have not been able to find them, nor anything on that Psalm. I have also looked for the errors of Pelagius, to discover why people say that I share his opinions, with which I have never hitherto been acquainted. I am surprised that those who want to slander me should seek such false and far-fetched pretexts. Pelagius said that it was possible without grace to do good works and merit eternal life, and this was condemned by the church; I say that it is possible to know by natural reason that God exists, but I do not say that this natural knowledge by itself, without grace, merits the supernatural glory which we hope for in heaven. On the contrary, it is evident that since this glory is supernatural, more than natural powers are needed to merit it. I have said nothing about the knowledge of God except what all the theologians say too. By natural reason it may be known that He is all good, all powerful, and all truthful. Knowledge of such truths may prepare infidels to receive the faith, but cannot suffice to enable them to reach heaven. For that it is necessary to believe in Jesus Christ and other revealed matters, and that depends upon grace.

I see that people find it very easy to misunderstand what I write. Truth is indivisible, so the slightest thing which is added or taken away falsifies it. Thus, you quote as an axiom of mine: whatever we clearly conceive is or exists. That is not at all what I think, but only that whatever we perceive clearly is true, and so it exists, if we perceive that it cannot not exist; or that it can exist, if we perceive that its existence is possible. For although the objective being of an idea must have a real cause, it is not always necessary that this cause should contain it formally, but only eminently.

Thank you for what you tell me of the Council of Constance's condemnation of Wycliffe[1]; but I do not see that this tells at all against me. He would have been condemned no less if all the fathers of the council had followed my opinion. When they denied that the substance of bread and wine

[1] Wycliffe was condemned in 1418 for denying transubstantiation.

remained to be the subject of the accidents, they did not define that the accidents were real, and that is what I said I had never read in the Councils. But I am very obliged to you for the great care you take of everything which concerns me.

Regius' reply to Voetius, based partly on Descartes' letter of January 1642, was published on 16 February of that year. At Voetius' instance, the magistrates of Utrecht ordered the book to be suppressed, and forbade Regius to teach anything except physics and medicine. Throughout the spring and summer of the year Descartes wrote Regius frequent letters of encouragement, congratulating him on 'suffering persecution for truth's sake' but counselling obedience to the magistrates' decrees. Descartes described the events at Utrecht, along with his controversy with the Jesuit Bourdin, in the *Letter to Father Dinet,*[1] which he completed in April. This letter was printed in the second edition of the *Meditations*, which appeared this year at Amsterdam and contained, as additions to the first edition, also the *Seventh Objections* and the discussion on transubstantiation which had earlier been excised by Mersenne from the end of the *Fourth Objections.*

Of all the controversial correspondence of the year 1642 only occasional fragments are of philosophical interest.

## From the letter to Regius, June 1642[2]

... On p. 66 you seem to make a greater difference between living and lifeless things than there is between a clock or other automaton on the one hand, and a key or sword or other non-self-moving appliance on the other. I do not agree.

\*     \*     \*

To solve your objection about the idea of God, you must observe that the argument is based not on the essence of the idea, by which it is only a mode existing in the human mind and therefore no more perfect than a human being,

---

[1] AT vii. 563–603; HR ii. 347–76.
[2] AT iii. 565; AM v. 201; in Latin; extract.

but on its objective perfection, which the principles of metaphysics teach must be contained formally or eminently in its cause. Suppose someone said that anyone can paint pictures as well as Apelles, because they consist only of patterns of paint and anyone can make all kinds of patterns with paint. To such a suggestion we should have to reply that when we are talking about Apelles' pictures we are not considering just a pattern of colours, but a pattern skilfully made to resemble reality, such as can only be produced by those very practised in this art.

## From the letter to Huygens, 10 October 1642[1]

. . . I am doubly obliged to you, Sir, because neither your affliction nor the many occupations which I am sure it brought have prevented you from thinking of me and taking the trouble to send me this book.[2] I know that you have a great affection for your family and that the loss of any member of it cannot but be very painful to you. I know also that you have great strength of mind and are well acquainted with all the remedies which can lessen your sorrow. But I cannot refrain from telling you one which I have always found most powerful, not only to enable me to bear the death of those I have most loved, but also to prevent me from fearing my own, though I love life as much as anyone.

It consists in the consideration of the nature of our souls. I think I know very clearly that they last longer than our bodies, and are destined by nature for pleasures and felicities much greater than those we enjoy in this world. Those who die pass to a sweeter and more tranquil life than ours; I cannot imagine otherwise. We shall go to find them some day, and we shall still remember the past; because we have, on my view, an intellectual memory which is certainly independent of the body. And although religion teaches us

---

[1] AT iii. 578; AM v. 220; in French; extract.

[2] Thomas White's *De Mundo dialogi tres*, which Descartes had reviewed in the earlier part of the letter.

much on this topic, I must confess a weakness in myself
which is, I think, common to the majority of men. However
much we wish to believe, and however much we think we
do firmly believe all that religion teaches, we are not
commonly so moved by it as when we are convinced by
very evident natural reasons.

I am, etc.

Descartes' correspondence with Mersenne in the winter of 1642–3 ranged
as usual over many topics: the civil war in England, the manufacture of
eyeglasses, how to stop a chimney smoking, how to discover the relative weight
of air and water, why a cherry stone shoots out when pressed between the
fingers. Mersenne was also informed of the publication, in 1643, of Descartes' *Letter to Voetius* in reply to Voetius' *Philosophia Cartesiana*. The
following letter contains a philosophical account of Descartes' principle of
inertia.

# From the letter to Mersenne, 26 April 1643[1]

My view on your questions depends on two principles of
Physics, which I must first establish.[2]
The first is that I do not believe there are in nature any
real qualities, attached to substances and separable from
them by divine power like so many little souls in their bodies.
Motion, and all the other modifications of substance which
are called qualities, have no greater reality, on my view, than
is commonly attributed by philosophers to shape, which
they call only a mode and not a real quality. My principal
reason for rejecting these real qualities is that I do not see
that the human mind has any notion, or particular idea, to
conceive them by; so that when we talk about them and
assert their existence we are asserting something we do not
conceive, and doing something we do not understand. The

[1] AT iii. 648; AM v. 278; in French; extract.
[2] Mersenne had asked, *inter alia*, whether two missiles of equal matter, size, and
shape must travel the same distance if projected at the same speed in the same
direction through the same medium.

second reason is that the philosophers invented these real qualities only because they did not think they could otherwise explain all the phenomena of nature; but I find on the contrary that these phenomena are better explained without them.

The other principle is that whatever is or exists remains always in the state in which it is, unless some exterior cause changes it; so that I do not think there can be any quality or mode which perishes of itself. If a body has a certain shape it does not lose it unless it is altered by collision with some other body; similarly if it has some motion, it should continue to keep it, unless prevented by some exterior cause. I prove this by metaphysics; for God, who is the author of all things, is entirely perfect and unchangeable; and so it seems to me absurd that any simple thing that exists, and so has God for its author, should have in itself the principle of its destruction. Heat, sound, and other such qualities present no difficulty; for they are only motions in the air which there encounter various obstacles which make them stop.

Since movement is not a real quality but only a mode, it can only be conceived as the change by which a body leaves the vicinity of some others; and there are only two properties of it to consider: its greater or less velocity, and its direction. This change may be brought about by various causes; none the less it is impossible, if these causes impel it in the same direction with the same velocity, that they should impart to it any difference of nature.

So I think that if two missiles equal in matter, size, and shape, set off with the same speed in the same medium and the same direction, neither could go further than the other . . .

In October 1642 Descartes had learnt that Princess Elizabeth of Bohemia, in exile at the Hague, had read his *Meditations* with enthusiasm. He offered to visit her to explain any difficulties she encountered; but she put her questions in writing in a letter of 6 May 1643. 'How can the soul of man', she asked, 'being only a thinking substance, determine his bodily spirits to perform voluntary actions?' Descartes' reply began a correspondence which lasted until his death.

## Descartes to Elizabeth, 21 May 1643[1]

Madame,

The honour your Highness does me in sending her commandments in writing is greater than I ever dared hope; and it is more consoling to my unworthiness than the other favour which I had hoped for passionately, which was to receive them by word of mouth. If I had been permitted to pay homage to you[2] and offer you my very humble services when I was last at the Hague, I would have had too many wonders to admire at the same time. Seeing superhuman sentiments flowing from a body such as painters give to angels, I would have been ravished like a man coming fresh from earth to heaven. Thus I would hardly have been able to reply to your Highness, as she doubtless noticed when once before I had the honour of speaking with her. Your clemency has willed to comfort me by committing the traces of your thoughts to paper, so that I can read them many times, and grow accustomed to consider them. Thus I am less overwhelmed, but no less full of admiration, observing that it is not only at first sight that they seem perceptive, but that the more they are examined, the more judicious and solid they appear.

I may truly say that the question you ask is the one which may most properly be put to me in view of my published writings. There are two facts about the human soul on which depend all the things we can know of its nature. The first is that it thinks, the second is that it is united to the body and can act and be acted upon along with it. About the second I have said hardly anything; I have tried only to make the first well understood. For my principal aim was to prove the distinction between soul and body, and to this end only the first was useful, and the second might have been harmful. But because your Highness' vision is so

---

[1] AT iii. 663; AM v. 289; in French; complete.
[2] The frequent awkward changes from third to second person are in the original.

clear that nothing can be concealed from her, I will try now to explain how I conceive the union of the soul and the body and how the soul has the power to move the body.

First I observe that there are in us certain primitive notions which are as it were models on which all our other knowledge is patterned. There are very few such notions. First, there are the most general ones, such as being, number, and duration, which apply to everything we can conceive. Then, as regards body in particular, we have only the notion of extension which entails the notions of shape and motion; and as regards soul in particular we have only the notion of thought, which includes the conceptions of the intellect and the inclinations of the will. Finally, as regards soul and body together, we have only the notion of their union, on which depends our notion of the soul's power to move the body, and the body's power to act on the soul and cause sensations and passions.

I observe next that all human scientific knowledge consists solely in clearly distinguishing these notions and attaching each of them only to the things to which it applies. For if we try to solve a problem by means of a notion that does not apply, we cannot help going wrong. Similarly we go wrong if we try to explain one of these notions by another, for since they are primitive notions, each of them can only be understood by itself. The use of our senses has made the notions of extension, shape, and movement more familiar to us than the others; and the main cause of our errors is that we commonly want to use these notions to explain matters to which they do not apply. For instance, we try to use our imagination to conceive the nature of the soul, or to conceive the way in which the soul moves the body after the manner in which one body is moved by another.

In the *Meditations* that your Highness condescended to read, I tried to give a conception of the notions which belong to the soul alone by distinguishing them from those that apply to the body alone. Accordingly, the next thing I must explain is how to conceive those that apply to the union of the soul with the body, and how to distinguish them from those which belong to the body alone or those which belong to the soul alone. At this point what I wrote at the end of my reply to the *Sixth Objections* may be useful. It is in our own soul that we must look for these simple notions. It possesses them all by nature, but it does not always sufficiently distinguish them from each other, or attach them to the objects to which they ought to be attached.

So I think that we have hitherto confounded the notion of the soul's power to act on the body with the power one body has to act on another. We have attributed both powers not to the soul, whose nature we did not yet know, but to the various qualities of bodies such as weight, heat etc. We imagined these qualities to be real, that is to say to have an existence distinct from that of bodies, and so to be substances, although we called them qualities. In order to conceive them we sometimes used notions we have for the purpose of knowing bodies, and sometimes used notions we have for the purpose of knowing the soul, depending on whether we were attributing to them something material or something immaterial. For instance, when we suppose that heaviness is a real quality of which all we know is that it has the power to move the body that possesses it towards the centre of the earth, we find no difficulty in conceiving how it moves the body nor how it is united to it. We do not suppose that the production of this motion takes place by a real contact between two surfaces, because we find by introspection that we have a specific notion to conceive it by. I think that we misuse this notion when we apply it to heaviness, which as I hope to show in my *Physics*, is not anything really distinct from body; but it was given us for the purpose of conceiving the manner in which the soul moves the body.

If I used more words to explain myself I would show that I had not realized the incomparable quality of your Highness' mind; but I would be too presumptuous if I dared to think that my reply should entirely satisfy her. I will try to avoid both errors by adding nothing for the present except that if I am capable of writing or saying anything which may give her pleasure, I will always count it a great privilege to take up my pen or to visit the Hague for that purpose; and that nothing in the world is so dear to me as the power of obeying her commands. I cannot here find any reason for observing the Hippocratic oath she enjoined on me,[1] since she has written nothing which does not deserve to be seen and admired by all. I will only say that as I prize infinitely your letter, I will treat it as misers treat their treasures. The more they prize them, the more they hide them, grudging the sight of them to the rest of the world and placing their supreme happiness in looking at them. So I will be glad to enjoy in solitude the benefit of looking at your letter; and my greatest ambition is to be able to call myself and to be your, etc.

Elizabeth replied, on 20 June, that she was too stupid to understand how the discarded idea of a falsely attributed quality could help us to understand how an immaterial substance could move a body; especially as Descartes was about to refute the notion of heaviness in his forthcoming *Physics*. 'I must admit', she wrote, 'that it would be easier for me to attribute matter and extension to the soul, than to attribute to an immaterial being the capacity to move and be moved by a body.'

## Descartes to Elizabeth, 28 June 1643[2]

Madame,

I am very obliged to your Highness because although she saw how badly I explained myself in my last letter about the question she was good enough to put me, she still has enough patience to listen to me on the same topic and to give me the opportunity to mention the things I left out. The principal omissions seem to me as follows. First of all I distinguished three kinds of primitive ideas or notions each of which is known in its own proper manner and not by comparison with any other: i.e. the notion of soul, the notion of body, and the notion of union between soul and body. After that I should have explained the difference between these three kinds of notion and between the opera-

[1] Elizabeth had called Descartes her doctor, and had claimed that he was bound by the Hippocratic oath not to reveal the weakness of her mind.

[2] AT iii. 690; AM v. 322; in French; complete.

tions of the soul by which we take possession of them. I should have explained also how to make each of them familiar and easy to us, and why I used the analogy of heaviness. Finally I should have shown how it is possible to conceive the soul as material (which is what it is to conceive its union with the body), while still being able to discover that it is separable from the body. I think this covers the topics which your Highness proposed for me in her letter.

First of all then, I observe one great difference between these three kinds of notions. The soul can be conceived only by pure intellect; the body (i.e. extension, shape, and movement) can likewise be known by pure intellect, but much better by intellect aided by imagination; and finally what belongs to the union of the soul and the body can be known only obscurely by pure intellect or by intellect aided by imagination, but it can be known very clearly by the senses. That is why people who never philosophize and use only their senses have no doubt that the soul moves the body and that the body acts on the soul. They regard both of them as a single thing, that is to say, they conceive their union; because to conceive the union between two things is to conceive them as  one single thing. Metaphysical thoughts, which exercise the pure intellect, help to familiarize us with the notion of the soul; and the study of mathematics, which exercises mainly the imagination in the consideration of shapes and movements, accustoms us to form distinct notions of bodies. But it is the ordinary course of life and conversation, and abstention from meditation and from the study of the things which exercise the imagination, that teaches us how to conceive the union of the soul and the body.

I am almost afraid that your Highness will think that I am not now speaking seriously; but that would go against the respect which I owe you and which I will never cease to show you. I can say with truth that the chief rule I have always observed in my studies, which I think has been the most useful to me in acquiring what knowledge I have, has been never to spend more than a few hours a day in the thoughts which occupy the imagination and a few hours a year on those which occupy the pure intellect. I have given all the rest of my time to the relaxation of the senses and the repose of the mind. And I include among the exercise of the imagination all serious conversations and anything which needs to be done with attention. This is why I have retired to the country. In the busiest city in the world I could still have as many hours to myself as I now employ in study, but I could not spend them so usefully if my mind was tired by the attention required by the bustle of life. I take the liberty of writing this to your Highness, so that she may see how genuine is my admiration for her devoting time to the meditations needed to appreciate the distinction between the mind and the body, despite all the business and care which attend people who combine great minds with high birth.

I think it is those meditations rather than thoughts requiring less attention that have made your Highness find obscurity in our notion of their union. It does not seem to me that the human mind is capable of conceiving at the same time the distinction and the union between body and soul, because for this it is necessary to conceive them as a single thing and at the same time to conceive them as two things; and this is absurd. This is why I made use earlier of an analogy with heaviness and other qualities which we commonly imagine to be united to certain bodies in the way that thought is united to ours. I supposed that your Highness still had in mind the arguments proving the distinction between the soul and the body, and I did not want to ask her to put them away in order to represent to herself the notion of the union which everyone has in himself without philosophizing. Everyone feels that he is a single person with both body and thought so related by nature that the thought can move the body and feel the things which happen to it. I did not worry about the fact that the analogy with heaviness was lame because such qualities are not real as people imagine them to be. This was because I thought that your Highness was already completely convinced that the soul is a substance distinct from the body.

Your Highness observes that it is easier to attribute matter and extension to the soul than to attribute to it the capacity to move and to be moved by the body without having matter. I beg her to feel free to attribute matter and extension to the soul because that is simply to conceive it as united to the body. And once she has formed a proper conception of this and experienced it in herself, it will be easy for her to consider that the matter attributed to the thought is not thought itself, and that the extension of the matter is of different nature from the extension of the thought, because the former is determined to a definite place, from which it excludes all other bodily extension, which is not the case with the latter. And so your Highness will easily be able to return to the knowledge of the distinction of soul and body in spite of having conceived their union.

I think that it is very necessary to have understood, once in a lifetime, the principles of metaphysics, since it is by them that we come to the knowledge of God and of our soul. But I think also that it would be very harmful to occupy one's intellect frequently in meditating upon them, since this would impede it from devoting itself to the functions of the imagination and the senses. I think the best thing is to content oneself with keeping in one's memory and one's belief the conclusions which one has once drawn from them, and then employ the rest of one's study time to thoughts in which the intellect co-operates with the imagination and the senses.

The great devotion which I feel to your Highness's service gives me hope that my frankness will not be disagreeable to her. I would have written at greater length, and tried to clarify on this occasion all difficulties on this topic, but I am forced to stop by a piece of bad news. I learn from Utrecht that I am summoned before the Magistrates to justify what I have written about one of their ministers.[1] This despite the fact that he has calumniated me very unworthily, and that everything that I wrote about him for my just defence was only too well known to everyone. I must go to find ways of freeing myself from their quibblings as soon as I can.

I am, etc.

---

[1] The *Letter to Voetius.*

'The senses teach me *that* the soul moves the body', insisted Elizabeth, 'but neither they nor the intellect nor the imagination teaches me *how*. Perhaps there are properties of the soul unknown to us which will overturn the conviction of the soul's non-extension which I acquired from the excellent arguments of your *Meditations*.' Descartes did not reply. Almost all his letters which survive from June 1643 until May 1644 concern the proceedings against him at Utrecht. The only letters to Elizabeth in this period, in November 1643, concern a geometrical puzzle she raised. One undated letter, which perhaps belongs to this period, concerns the theological implications of Cartesian doubt.

## Descartes to Buitendijck, 1643[1]

In the letter which you were good enough to write to me, I find three questions which clearly indicate the candour of your desire for information. Nothing could give me greater pleasure than to answer them.

Your first question was, whether it is ever permissible to doubt about God, that is, whether, in the order of nature, one can doubt of the existence of God. I think that a distinction is called for here between the aspect of doubt which concerns the intellect and that which concerns the will. As to the intellect, since it is not a faculty of choice, we must not ask whether something is permissible to it or not; we can only ask whether something is possible to it. Now it is certain that there are many people whose intellect can doubt of God. This includes all those who cannot give an evident proof of his existence, even though they may have the true faith; because faith belongs to the will, and leaving that aside, a man with faith can examine by his natural reason whether there be any God, and thus doubt about God. As for the will, once again we must make a distinction, between doubt as an end, and doubt as a means. For if someone sets out to doubt about God with the intention of persisting in the doubt, then he sins gravely, since he wishes to remain in doubt on a matter of such importance. But if someone sets out to doubt as a means of acquiring a clearer knowledge of the truth, then he is doing something altogether pious and

[1] AT iv. 62; AM v. 82; in Latin; complete.

honourable, because nobody can will the end without willing
also the means, and in Scripture itself men are often invited
to seek this knowledge of God by natural reason. Nor is
there any sin if a man, for the same purpose, temporarily
puts out of his mind all the knowledge which he can have
of God; for we are not bound to think unceasingly that God
exists, otherwise we would never be allowed to sleep or to do
anything else; because as often as we do something else, we
put away for that time all the knowledge which we can have
of the Godhead.

Your second question is, whether it is permissible to
suppose anything false in matters concerning God. Here
we must distinguish between the true God, clearly known,
and false gods. Once the true God is clearly known, not only
is it not permissible, it is not possible for the human  mind
to attribute anything false to him, as I have explained in my
*Meditations* on pp. 152, 159, 269, and elsewhere.[1] But the
case is not the same with false divinities, i.e. evil spirits,
or idols, or other such gods invented by the error of the
human mind—all these are called gods in the Bible—nor
with the true God, so long as he is known only confusedly.
To attribute to these something false as a hypothesis can be
either good or bad, depending on whether the purpose of
framing such a hypothesis is good or bad. For what is thus
imagined and attributed hypothetically is not *eo ipso*
affirmed by the will as true, but is merely proposed for examination to the intellect; and so it is neither good nor bad in
itself,[2] but takes its moral quality from the purpose for
which it is framed. Thus, take the case of a man who
imagines God to be a deceiver—even the true God, but not
yet clearly enough known to himself nor to the others for
whose sake he frames this hypothesis. Let us suppose that
he does not make use of this fiction for any evil purpose of
persuading others to believe falsehood of the Godhead, but
only to enlighten the intellect, and bring greater knowledge
of God's nature to himself and others. Such a man is in no
way sinning that good may come. There is no malice at all
in his action; he does something which is good in itself and
no one can rebuke him for it except calumniously.

[1] AT vii. 68; HR i. 182.    [2] Nullam includit boni aut mali rationem formalem.

Your third question is about the motion which you think I regard as the soul of brute beasts. I do not remember ever having written that motion is the soul of brutes; indeed I have not publicly expressed an opinion on the topic. But because, by the word 'soul', we usually mean a substance, and because I think that motion is a mode of bodies, I would not wish to say that motion is the soul of brutes. (By the way, I do not admit various kinds of motion, but only local motion from place to place, which is common to all bodies, animate and inanimate alike.) I would prefer to say with the Bible (Deuteronomy 12, 23) that blood is their soul; for blood is a fluid body in rapid movement, and its more rarefied parts are called spirits. It is these which move the whole machine of the body as they flow from the arteries through the brain into the nerves and muscles. Farewell.

## Descartes to [Mesland], 2 May 1644[1]

Reverend Father,

I know that it is very difficult to enter into another man's thoughts, and experience has taught me how difficult many people find mine. I am the more grateful to you for the trouble which you have taken to examine them; and I cannot but think highly of you when I see that you have taken such full possession of them that they are now more yours than mine. The difficulties which you put me come rather from the matter in hand, and the defects of my expression, than from any lack of understanding on your part. You have in fact provided the solution of the principal ones. But none the less I will tell you my views on all of them.

I agree that in the case of particular and limited causes, whether physical or moral, it is often found that those which produce a certain effect are incapable of producing many others which appear to us less remarkable. Thus one human being can produce another human being, but no human

[1] AT iv. 110; AM vi. 140; in French; complete.

being can produce an ant; and a King, who makes a whole
people obey him, cannot always get obedience from a horse.
But in the case of a universal and indeterminate cause, it
seems to me a common notion of the most evident kind that
*whatever can do the greater can also do the lesser*; it is like the
maxim that *the whole is greater than the part*.[1] Rightly
understood, this notion applies also to all particular causes,
moral as well as physical: for it would be a greater thing for
a human being to be able to produce human beings and ants,
than to be able only to produce human beings; and a King
who could command horses as well would be more powerful
than one who could command only his people. Just so,
when they want to attribute great power to the music of
Orpheus, they say that it could move even the beasts.

It does not make much difference whether my second
proof, the one based on our own existence, is regarded as
different from the first proof, or merely as an explanation
of it.[2] Just as it is an effect of God to have created me, so
it is an effect of His to have put the idea of himself in me;
and there is no effect coming from him, from which one
cannot prove his existence. None the less, it seems to me
that all these proofs based on his effects are reducible to a
single one; and also that they are incomplete, if the effects
are not evident to us (that is why I considered my own
existence rather than that of heaven and earth, of which I
am not equally certain) and if we do not add to them the idea
which we have of God. For since my soul is finite, I cannot
know that the order of causes is not infinite, except in so
far as I have in myself that idea of the First Cause; and even
if there be admitted a First Cause who keeps me in existence,
I cannot say that it is God unless I truly have the idea of
God. I hinted at this in my reply to the First Objections;
but I did so very briefly, so as not to bring into contempt
the arguments of others, who commonly accept the principle that a series cannot go on for ever. I do not accept that
principle; on the contrary, I think that in the division of the
parts of matter there really is an endless series, as you will
see in my treatise on Philosophy, which is almost printed.

[1] Here and below, the italics represent Latin words in a French context.
[2] *Third Meditation*, AT vii. 47–52; HR i. 165–71.

I do not know that I laid it down that God always does what he knows to be the most perfect, and it does not seem to me that a finite mind can judge of that. But I tried to solve the difficulty in question, about the cause of error, on the assumption that God had made the world most perfect; since if one makes the opposite assumption the difficulty disappears altogether.

I am grateful to you for pointing out the places in Saint Augustine which can be used to give authority to my views. Some other friends of mine had already done so, and I am pleased that my thoughts agree with those of such a great and holy man. I am not the kind of person who wants his views to appear novel; on the contrary, I conform my views to those of others so far as truth permits me.

I regard the difference between the soul and its ideas as the same as that between a piece of wax and the various shapes it can take. Just as it is not an activity but a passivity in the wax, to take various shapes, so, it seems to me, it is a passivity in the soul to receive one or other idea and only its volitions are activities. It receives its ideas partly from objects in contact with the senses, partly from impressions in the brain, and partly from precedent dispositions in the soul and motions of the will. Similarly, a piece of wax owes its shapes partly to the pressure of other bodies, partly to its own earlier shape or other qualities such as heaviness or softness, and partly also to its own movement, when, having been pushed it has in itself the power to continue moving.

The difficulty we feel in learning the sciences, and in clearly setting before ourselves the ideas which are naturally known to us arises from the false prejudices of our childhood, and other causes of error, as I have tried to explain at length in the treatise I am having printed.

As for memory, I think that the memory of material things depends on the traces which remain in the brain, after any image has been imprinted on it; and that the memory of intellectual things depends on some other traces which remain in thought itself. But the latter are of a wholly different kind from the former, and I cannot explain them by any illustration drawn from corporeal things without a great deal of qualification. The traces in the brain, on the other hand, dispose it to move the soul in the same way as it moved it before, and thus to make it remember something. It is rather as the folds in a piece of paper or cloth make it easier to fold in that way than if it had never been so folded before.

The moral error which occurs when a man believes something false with good reason—for instance, because authority has told him—involves no privation provided that it is affirmed only as a rule for practical action, in a case where there is no moral possibility of knowing better. Accordingly it is not strictly an error; it would be one if it were asserted as a truth of physics, because the testimony of an authority is not sufficient in such a case.

As to free will, I have not seen what Fr. Petavius has written about it; but from what you say in explaining your opinion on the topic it does not appear that my views are very different. For first, I beg you to observe that I did not say that a man was indifferent only if he lacked knowledge; but rather, that he is more indifferent the less reasons he knows in favour of choosing one side rather than another; and this, I think, cannot be denied by anybody. I agree with you when you say that a man can suspend his judgement; but I tried to explain in what manner this can be done. For it seems to me certain that *a great light in the intellect is followed by a strong inclination in the will*[1]; so that if we see very clearly that a thing is good for us it is very difficult— and, on my view, impossible, as long as one continues in the same thought—to stop the course of our desire. But the nature of the soul is such that it hardly attends for more than a moment to a single thing; and so, as soon as our attention turns from the reasons which show us that the thing is good for us, and we merely keep in our memory that it seemed desirable to us, we can call up before our mind some other reason to make us doubt of it, and so suspend our judgement, and perhaps even form a contrary judgement. And so, since you regard freedom not simply as indifference but rather as a real and positive power to determine oneself, and since I agree that the will has such a power, the difference between us is a merely verbal one.

[1] *Fourth Meditation*, AT vii. 59; HR i. 176.

However, I do not see that it makes any difference to that power whether it is accompanied by indifference, which you agree is an imperfection, or whether it is not so accompanied, when there is nothing in the understanding except light, as in the case of the blessed who are confirmed in grace. And so I call free whatever is voluntary, whereas you wish to restrict the name to the power to determine oneself only if accompanied by indifference. But so far as concerns names, I wish above all to follow usage and precedent.

As for irrational animals, it is obvious that they are not free, since they do not have this positive power to determine themselves; what they have is a pure negation, namely, the not being forced or constrained.

The only thing which prevented me from speaking of the freedom which we have to follow good or evil was the fact that I wanted to avoid as far as possible all theological controversies and stay within the limits of natural philosophy. But I agree with you that wherever there is an occasion for sinning, there is indifference; and I do not think that in order to do wrong it is necessary to see clearly that what we are doing is evil. It is sufficient to see it confusedly, or without in any way seeing it or attending to the reasons which prove it simply to remember that one has hitherto judged it so. For if we saw it clearly it would be impossible to sin, as long as we saw it in that fashion; that is why they say that *whoever sins, does so in ignorance.*[1] And a man may earn merit even though, seeing very clearly what he must do, he does it infallibly, and without any indifference, as Jesus Christ did during his earthly life. Since a man has the power not always to attend perfectly to what he ought to do, it is a good action to pay attention and thus to ensure that our will follows so promptly the light of our understanding that there is no longer in any way indifference. In any case, I did not write that grace entirely prevents indifference; but simply that it makes us incline to one side rather than to another, and so diminishes indifference without diminishing freedom; from which it follows, on my view, that this freedom does not consist in indifference.

I turn to the difficulty of conceiving how it was free and

[1] Aristotle, *Nicomachean Ethics* iii. 1110b28.

indifferent for God to make it not be true that the three angles of a triangle were equal to two right angles, or in general that contradictories could not be true together. It is easy to dispel this difficulty by considering that the power of God cannot have any limits, and that our mind is finite and so created as to be able to conceive as possible things which God has wished to be in fact possible, but not to be able to conceive as possible things which God could have made possible, but which he has in fact wished to make impossible. The first consideration shows us that God cannot have been determined to make it true that contradictories cannot be true together, and therefore that he could have done the opposite. The second consideration shows us that even if this be true, we should not try to comprehend it since our nature is incapable of doing so. And even if God has willed that some truths should be necessary, this does not mean that he willed them necessarily; for it is one thing to will that they be necessary, and quite another to will them necessarily, or to be necessitated to will them. I agree that there are contradictions which are so evident, that we cannot put them before our minds without judging them entirely impossible, like the one which you suggest: *that God might have made creatures independent of him.* But if we would know the immensity of his power we should not put these thoughts before our minds, nor should we conceive any precedence or priority between his understanding and his will; for the idea which we have of God teaches us that there is in him only a single activity, entirely simple and entirely pure. This is well expressed by the words of St. Augustine: *They are so because you see them to be so*[1]; because in God *seeing and willing* are one and the same thing.

I distinguish lines from surfaces, and points from lines, as modes from modes but I distinguish a body from the surfaces, lines, and points belonging to it as a substance from its modes. And there is no doubt that at least one mode which belongs to bread remains in the Blessed Sacrament, since its outward shape, which is a mode, remains. As for the extension of Jesus Christ in that Sacrament, I gave no

---

[1] *Confessions* xiii. 30.

explanation of it, because I was not obliged to, and I keep away, as far as possible, from questions of theology, especially as the Council of Trent has said that He is present in a manner which we can scarcely express in words. I quoted that phrase, towards the end of my reply to the *Fourth Objections*, precisely to excuse myself from giving an explanation. But I am prepared to say that if men were a little more used to my kind of philosophy, they could be shown a way of explaining this mystery which would stop the mouths of the enemies of our religion so that they could say nothing against it.

There is a great difference between abstraction and exclusion. If I said simply that the idea which I have of my soul does not represent it to me as being dependent on a body and identified with it, this would be merely an abstraction, from which I could form only a negative argument, which would be unsound. But I say that this idea represents it to me as a substance which can exist even though everything belonging to body be excluded from it; from which I form a positive argument, and conclude that it can exist without the body. And this exclusion of extension can be clearly seen in the nature of the soul, as you have very well observed, from the fact that one cannot think of a half of a thinking thing.

I do not want to give you the trouble of sending me what you have written about my *Meditations* because I hope to go to France soon, and there, I hope, I shall have the honour of seeing you. Meanwhile believe me, etc.

In the spring of 1644 Descartes was called to France on family business. In the course of his travels he took the opportunity to supervise the translations of his works. At Amsterdam the *Discourse* and *Essays* were being translated into Latin by de Courcelles; in Paris the Duc de Luynes was translating the *Meditations*, and Clerselier the *Objections* and *Replies*, from Latin into French. The *Principles of Philosophy*, dedicated to Princess Elizabeth, were published at Amsterdam on 10 July; copies reached Paris in August and were distributed by Descartes to his friends. A translation was immediately produced by the Abbé Picot and read over by Descartes during his return journey in November. Few letters survive from this period; those that do are, like the following, of only marginal philosophical interest.

## Descartes to Elizabeth, July 1644[1]

Madame,

My journey could not be accompanied by any misfortune, since I have been so happy during it as to be in your Highness' mind.[2] The very flattering letter which tells me this is the most precious gift I could receive in this country. It would have made me altogether happy if it had not told me also that the sickness which troubled your Highness before I left the Hague had left some traces of indisposition in the stomach. The remedies which your Highness has chosen, diet and exercise, are in my opinion the best of all. But I except psychological remedies, because there is no doubt that the soul has great power over the body, as is shown by the great bodily changes produced by anger, fear, and the other passions. The soul guides the spirits into the places where they can be useful or harmful; however, it does not do this by a direct volition, but only by willing or thinking about something else. For our body is so constructed that certain of its motions follow naturally upon certain thoughts: as we see that blushes accompany shame, tears compassion, and laughter joy. I know no thought more proper to preserve health than a strong conviction and firm belief that the architecture of our bodies is thoroughly sound. Once one is well one cannot easily fall ill except through extraordinary excess, or injury by the air or other exterior cause; and once one is ill, one can easily recover by the unaided force of nature, especially when one is still young. This conviction is beyond doubt more true and more reasonable than that of some people who are convinced by an astrologer or doctor that they must die at a certain time, and for this reason alone fall ill, and frequently even die. I have seen that happen to several people. But I could not help being extremely sad, if I thought that your Highness'

[1] AT v. 64; AM vi. 152; in French; complete.
[2] Descartes was in Paris, about to visit Poitou on family business.

indisposition still continued. I prefer to hope that it is already quite over. But the desire to be certain makes me want very much to return to Holland.

I propose to leave here in five or six days for Poitou and Brittany, where I must do the business which brought me here. As soon as I have put my affairs in order I am very anxious to return to the region where I have been so happy as to have the honour of speaking with your Highness. Although there are many people here whom I honour and esteem, I have not yet seen anything to make me stay permanently. And I am, more than I can say, etc.

In 1645–6 Descartes wrote a number of letters to the Jesuit Father Mesland on the topic of transubstantiation, the doctrine that in the Eucharist the bread and wine is turned into the body and blood of Jesus Christ so that only the appearances of bread and wine remain without their substance. The first of these letters is of great philosophical interest because it develops a theory of the criterion of identity of an individual human body.


## Descartes to Mesland, 9 February 1645[1]

Reverend Father,

Your letter of 22 October reached me only eight days ago, which is why I have not been able earlier to assure you of my great obligation to you. It is not because you took the trouble to read and examine my *Meditations* that I am obliged to you, for since we were not acquainted beforehand I presume that it was the matter alone which attracted you; and it is not because you have made such a good abstract of it that I am obliged to you, for I am not so vain as to think that you did it for my sake, and I have a sufficiently good opinion of my arguments to believe that you thought them worth making intelligible to many, to which end the new form you have given them will be very useful. I am obliged to you rather because in explaining them, you have been very careful to

[1] AT iv. 161; AM vi. 189; in French; complete.

make them appear in their full strength, and to interpret to
my advantage many things which might have been distorted
or concealed by others. It is this in particular which makes
me recognize your candour and your desire to do me favour.
I have not found a single word, in the manuscript that
you were good enough to send me, with which I do not
entirely agree; and though it contains many thoughts which
are not in my *Meditations*, or are not proved there in the same
manner, none the less there is not one which I would not be
willing to accept as my own. When, in the *Discourse on
Method*, I said that I did not recognize the thoughts which
people attributed to me, I was not thinking of people who
have examined my writings as carefully as you; I was thinking of people who had tried to gather my opinions from
what I said in familiar conversation.

In discussing the Blessed Sacrament I spoke of the surface which is intermediate between two bodies, that is to
say between the bread (or the body of Jesus Christ after the
consecration) and the air surrounding it.[1] By 'surface' I do
not mean any substance or real nature which could be
destroyed by the omnipotence of God, but only a mode, or
manner of being, which cannot be changed without a
change in that in which or by which it exists; just as it
involves a contradiction for the square shape of a piece of
wax to be taken away from it without any of the parts of the
wax changing their place. This surface intermediate
between the air and the bread does not differ in reality from
the surface of the bread, nor from the surface of the air
touching the bread; these three surfaces are in fact a single
thing and differ only in relation to our thought. That is to
say: when we call it the surface of the bread we mean that
although the air which surrounds the bread is changed, the
surface remains always *numerically the same*,[2] provided that
the bread does not change, but changes with it if it does.
And when we call it the surface of the air surrounding the
bread, we mean that it changes with the air and not with
the bread. And finally, when we call it the surface intermediate between the air and the bread, we mean that it

[1] The *Fourth Replies*, AT vii. 251; HR ii. 118.
[2] Here and below, italics represent Latin words in a French context.

does not change with either, but only with the shape of the dimensions which separate one from the other; so that in that sense it is simply by that shape that it exists, and by that alone that it can change. For if the body of Jesus Christ is put in the place of the bread, and other air comes in place of that which surrounded the bread, the surface which is between that air and the body of Jesus Christ is still *numerically the same* as that which was between the other air and the bread, because its numerical identity does not depend on the identity of the bodies between which it exists, but only on the identity or similarity of the dimension. Similarly, we can say that the Loire is the same river as it was ten years ago, although it is not the same water, and perhaps there is no longer a single part left of the earth which surrounded that water.

As for the manner in which one can conceive the body of Jesus Christ to be in the Blessed Sacrament, I do not think it is for me to explain, since the Council of Trent teaches that he is there *in a manner of existence which can scarcely be expressed in words*. I quoted these words on purpose at the end of my answer to the *Fourth Objections* to excuse myself from speaking further on the topic, especially because not being a theologian by profession I was afraid that anything I might write might be less well taken from me than from another. All the same, since the Council does not say that it *cannot be expressed in words*, but only that it *can scarcely be expressed in words*, I will venture to tell you here in confidence a manner of explanation which seems to me very elegant and useful for avoiding the calumny of heretics who object that our belief on this topic is entirely incomprehensible and involves a contradiction. I do so on condition that if you communicate it to anyone else you will please not attribute its authorship to me; and on condition that you do not communicate it to anyone at all unless you judge it to be altogether in accord with what has been laid down by the Church.

First of all, I consider what exactly is the body of a man, and I find that this word 'body' is very ambiguous. When we speak in general of a body, we mean a determinate part of matter, a part of the quantity of which the universe is composed. In this sense, if the smallest amount of that quantity were removed we would *eo ipso* judge that the body was smaller and no longer complete; and if any particle of the matter were changed we would at once think that the body was no longer quite the same, no longer *numerically the same*. But when we speak of the body of a man, we do not mean a determinate part of matter with a determinate size; we mean simply the whole of the matter joined to the soul of that man. And so, even though that matter changes, and its quantity increases or decreases, we still believe that it is the same body, *numerically the same* body, provided that it remains joined in substantial union with the same soul; and we think that this body is whole and entire provided that it has in itself all the dispositions required to preserve that union. Nobody denies that we have the same bodies as we had in our infancy, although their quantity has much increased, and according to the common opinion of doctors, which is doubtless true, there is no longer in them any part of the matter which then belonged to them, and even though they do not have the same shape any longer; so that they are only *numerically the same* because they are informed by the same soul. Personally, I go further. I have examined the circulation of the blood, and I believe that nutrition takes place by a continual expulsion of parts of our body, which are driven from their place by the arrival of others. Consequently I do not think that there is any part of our bodies which remains *numerically* the same for a single moment, although our body, *qua* human body, remains always *numerically* the same provided that it is united with the same soul. In that sense, it can even be called indivisible; because if an arm or a leg of a man is amputated, we think that it is only in the first sense of 'body' that his body is divided—we do not think that a man who has lost an arm or a leg is less a man than any other. Altogether then, provided that a body is united with the same rational soul, we always take it as the body of the same man whatever matter it may be and whatever quantity or shape it may have; and we count it as an entire body, provided that it needs no additional matter in order to remain joined to the same soul.

Moreover, I observe that when we eat bread and drink

wine, the small parts of the bread and wine dissolve in our stomach, and pass at once into our veins; so that they transubstantiate themselves naturally and become parts of our bodies simply by mixing with the blood. However, if we had sharp enough eyesight to distinguish them from the other particles of blood, we would see that they are still numerically the same as those which previously made up the bread and the wine. So that if we did not consider their union with the soul, we could still call them bread and wine as before.

Now this transubstantiation takes place without any miracle. But using it as an illustration, I see no difficulty in thinking that the miracle of transubstantiation which takes place in the Blessed Sacrament consists in nothing but the fact that the particles of bread and wine, which in order for the soul of Jesus Christ to inform them naturally would have had to mingle with his blood and dispose themselves in certain specific ways, are informed by his soul simply by the power of the words of consecration. The soul of Jesus Christ could not have remained naturally united to each of these particles of bread and wine unless they were united with many others to make up all the organs of a human body necessary for life; but in the Sacrament it remains supernaturally conjoined with each of them even when they are separated. In this way it is easy to understand how the body of Jesus Christ is present only once in the whole host, when it is undivided, and yet is entire in each of its parts, when it is divided; because all the matter which is together informed by the same human soul, large or small as it may be, is taken for an entire human body.

No doubt this explanation will be shocking at first to those who are accustomed to believe that for the body of Jesus Christ to be in the Eucharist all its members must be there with the same quantity and shape and *numerically* the same matter as they had when he ascended into heaven. But they will easily free themselves from these difficulties if they bear in mind that nothing of the kind has been decided by the Church. It is not necessary for the integrity of a human body that it should possess all the exterior members with their quantity and matter; and such things are in no way useful or fitting in this sacrament, in which the soul of Jesus Christ informs the matter of the host, so as to be received by men and to unite himself more closely with them. This does not in any way diminish the veneration due to the sacrament. Moreover, people should bear in mind that it is impossible, and seems manifestly to involve a contradiction, that these members should be present; because what we call the arm or hand of a man is what has the exterior shape, size, and use of one; so that whatever one might imagine in the host as the hand or the arm of Jesus Christ, it goes against all the dictionaries and entirely changes the use of the words to call it an arm or a hand, since it has neither extension, nor exterior shape, nor use.

I would be most grateful if you would tell me your opinion of this explanation, and I would be glad also to know Father Vatier's opinion, but time does not allow me to write to him.

## Descartes to [Mesland], 9 February 1645[1]

As for the freedom of the will, I entirely agree with what the Reverend Father here wrote. Let me explain my opinion more fully. I would like you to notice that 'indifference' seems to me to mean here the state of the will when it is not impelled one way rather than another by any perception of truth or goodness. This was the sense in which I took it when I said that the lowest degree of liberty was that by which we determine ourselves to things to which we are indifferent. But perhaps others mean by 'indifference' a positive faculty of determining oneself to one or other of two contraries, that is to say to pursue or avoid, to affirm or deny. I do not deny that the will has this positive faculty. Indeed, I think it has it not only with respect to those actions to which it is not pushed by any evident reasons on one side rather than on the other, but also with respect to all

---

[1] AT iv. 218; AM vi. 237; in Latin; complete. The date and addressee of this letter are very doubtful.

other actions; so that when a very evident reason moves us in one direction, although, morally speaking, we can hardly move in the contrary direction, absolutely we can. For it is always open to us to hold back from pursuing a clearly known good, or from admitting a clearly perceived truth, provided we consider it a good thing to demonstrate the freedom of our will by so doing.

It must be noted also that liberty can be considered in the actions of the will before they are elicited, or after they are elicited.

Considered with respect to the time before they are elicited, it entails indifference in the second sense but not in the first. Although, when we contrast our own judgement with the commandments of others, we say that we are freer to do those things which have not been prescribed to us by others and in which we are allowed to follow our own judgement, we cannot similarly make a contrast within the field of our own judgements and thoughts and say that we are freer to do those things which seem neither good nor evil, or in which there are many reasons *pro* but as many reasons *contra*, than in those in which we see much more good than evil. For a greater liberty consists either in a greater facility in determining oneself, or of a greater use of the positive power which we have of following the worse although we see the better. If we follow the course which appears to have the most reasons in its favour, we determine ourselves more easily; if we follow the opposite, we make more use of that positive power; and thus we can always act more freely in those cases in which we see much more good than evil than in those cases which are called *adiaphora* or indifferent. In this sense too the things which are commanded us by others, and which we would not otherwise do spontaneously, we do less freely than the things which are not commanded; because the judgement that these things are difficult to do is opposed to the judgement that it is good to do what is commanded; and the more equally these two judgements move us the more indifference, in the first sense, they confer on us.

But liberty considered in the acts of the will at the moment when they are elicited does not entail any indifference either in the first or second sense; because what is done cannot remain undone once it is being done. But it consists simply in ease of operation; and at that point freedom, spontaneity, and voluntariness are the same thing. It was in this sense that I wrote that I took a course more freely the more reasons drove me towards it; because it is certain that in that case our will moves itself with greater facility and force.

In the spring of 1645 Princess Elizabeth suffered from 'a slow fever and a dry cough'. Descartes informed her, on 18 May, that the commonest cause of slow fever was sadness, and its sovereign cure was the mastery of reason over the passions. Elizabeth, in reply, agreed that she was very depressed; her family troubles had left her no time to read any philosophy except the works of Sir Kenelm Digby. Her doctors had prescribed a course of the waters of Spa: what did Descartes recommend?

# Descartes to Elizabeth, May or June 1645[1]

Madame,

I have read the letter which your Highness did me the honour to write me, and I could not help being very distressed that a virtue so rare and so perfect is not accompanied by the health and prosperity which it deserves. I can easily understand how many things must continually displease your Highness, and I know that they are more difficult to overcome when they are of such a kind that true reason does not command us to oppose them directly or try to remove them. They are domestic enemies with whom one is forced to keep company, and one has to be perpetually on guard lest they injure one. I know only one remedy for this: so far as possible to distract one's imagination and senses from them, and when obliged by prudence to consider them, to do so with one's intellect alone.

In this matter it is easy, I think, to observe the difference between the intellect on the one hand and the imagination

[1] AT iv. 218; AM vi. 237; in French; complete.

and senses on the other. Consider a person who had every reason to be happy but who saw continually enacted before him tragedies full of disastrous events, and who spent all his time in consideration of sad and pitiful objects. Let us suppose that he knew they were imaginary fables so that though they drew tears from his eyes and moved his imagination they did not touch his intellect at all. I think that this by itself would be enough gradually to close up his heart and make him sigh in such a way that the circulation of his blood would be delayed and slowed down. The grosser parts of his blood, sticking together, could easily block the spleen, by getting caught and stopping in its pores; while the more rarefied parts, being continually agitated, could affect his lungs and cause a cough which in time could be very dangerous. On the other hand, there might be a person who had many genuine reasons for distress but who took such pains to direct his imagination that he never thought of them except under compulsion by some practical necessity, and who spent the rest of his time in the consideration of objects which could furnish contentment and joy. This would help him by enabling him to judge more soberly about the things which mattered because he would look on them without passion. Moreover I do not doubt that this by itself would be capable of restoring him to health, even if his spleen and lungs were already in a poor condition because of the bad temperament of blood produced by sadness. This would be especially likely if he used also medical remedies to thin out the obstructing part of the blood. I think that the waters of Spa are very good for this purpose, above all if your Highness while taking them observes the customary recommendation of doctors, and frees her mind from all sad thoughts, and even from all serious meditations on scientific subjects. She should be like people who convince themselves they are thinking of nothing because they are observing the greenness of a wood, the colours of a flower, the flight of a bird, or something else requiring no attention. This is not a waste of time but a good use of it, and one may hope thus to recover perfect health, which is the foundation of all the other goods of this life.

I know that everything I write is better known to your

Highness than to me, and that it is not the theory but the practice which is difficult; but the great favour which your Highness does me in showing that she finds it not unpleasant to learn my sentiments, makes me take the liberty to write them as they are. I take the further liberty of adding that I found by experience in my own case that the remedy I suggested cured an illness almost exactly similar, and perhaps even more dangerous. I was born of a mother who died, a few days after my birth,[1] from a disease of the lung, caused by distress. From her I inherited a dry cough and a pale colour which stayed with me until I was more than twenty, so that all the doctors who saw me up to that time condemned me to die young. But I have always had an inclination to look at things from the most favourable angle and to make my principal happiness depend upon myself alone, and I think that this inclination caused the indisposition, which was almost part of my nature, gradually to disappear.

I am very obliged to your Highness for sending me her opinion of the book of M. le Chevalier Digby, which I will not be able to read until they have translated it into Latin. M. Jonsson, who was here yesterday, informed me that some people wish to do this; he told me also that I may send my letters to your Highness by the ordinary post, which I would not have dared to do without his suggestion. I was putting off writing this because I was waiting for one of my friends to go to the Hague to give it to your Highness. I greatly regret the absence of M. de Pollot, because I could learn from him how your indisposition progresses. However, the letters which are sent for me to the Alkmaar postman are always delivered to me; and just as there is nothing in the world which I so passionately desire as to be able to serve your Highness, so there is nothing which can make me more happy than to have the honour to receive her commandments.

I am, etc.

---

[1] Descartes' mother died on 13 May 1597, thirteen months after his birth.

In summer 1645 Descartes quarrelled with his disciple Regius, whose views were diverging more and more from his own. 'Formerly you treated the mind as a substance distinct from the body and described man as an *ens per accidens*; now you go to the opposite extreme, and because of the close union of mind and body in a single man you say that the mind is only a mode of the body. This last error is much worse than your earlier one.'[1]

In July Descartes suggested to Elizabeth that they should read and discuss together Seneca's *De Vita Beata*.

## Descartes to Elizabeth, 4 August 1645[2]

Madame,

When I chose Seneca's *de vita beata* to suggest to your Highness as an agreeable topic of discussion, I took account only of the reputation of the author and the importance of his topic, without thinking of his manner of treating it. I have since given some thought to this and find it not sufficiently accurate to deserve to be followed. To assist your Highness to make a judgement on the topic, I will try to explain how I think the topic should have been treated by such a philosopher, unenlightened by faith, with only natural reason to guide him.

At the beginning he says very well that all men want to live happily (*vivere beate*), but not all see clearly what makes a life happy. But first we must know what '*vivere beate*' means; I would translate it into French '*vivre heureusement*', if there were not a difference between '*heur*' and '*beatitude*'. The former depends only on outward things: a man is thought more fortunate (*heureux*) than wise if some good happens to him without his own effort; but happiness (*beatitude*) consists, it seems to me, in a perfect contentment of mind and inner satisfaction, which is not commonly possessed by those who are most favoured by fortune, and which is acquired by the wise without fortune's favour. So *vivere beate*, to live happily, is to have a perfectly content and satisfied mind.

Next we must consider what makes a life happy, i.e. what

---

[1] AT iv. 248; AM vi. 265.    [2] AT iv. 262; AM vi. 279; in French; complete.

are the things which can give us this supreme contentment. Such things, I observe, can be divided into two classes: those which depend on us, like virtue and wisdom, and those which do not, like honours, riches, and health. For it is certain that a man of good birth who is not ill, and who lacks nothing can enjoy a more perfect contentment than another who is poor, unhealthy and deformed provided that the two are equally wise and virtuous. None the less a small vessel may be just as full as a large one, although it contains less liquid; and similarly if we regard each man's contentment as the full satisfaction of all his reasonable desires, I do not doubt that the poorest man, least blest by nature and fortune, can be entirely content and satisfied just as much as every one else, although he does not enjoy as many good things. It is only this sort of contentment which is here in question; to seek the other sort would be a waste of time, since it is not in our own power.

It seems to me that every man can make himself content without any external assistance, provided that he respects three conditions, which are related to the three rules of morality which I put in the *Discourse on Method*.[1]

The first is always to employ his mind as well as he can to discover what he should or should not do in all the circumstances of life.

The second is to have a firm and constant resolution to carry out whatever reason recommends without being diverted by passion or appetite. Virtue, I believe, consists precisely in firmness in this resolution; though I do not know that anyone has ever so described it. Instead, they have divided it into different species to which they have given various names, because of the various objects to which it applies.

The third is to bear in mind that while one thus guides oneself, as far as one can, by reason, all the good things which one does not possess are all equally outside one's power. In this way one will accustom oneself not to desire them. Nothing can impede our contentment except desire, regret, and repentance; but if we always do what reason tells us, even if events show us afterwards that we were mistaken,

[1] AT vi. 23–8; HR i. 95–8.

we will never have any grounds for repentance, because it was not our own fault. We do not desire to have more arms or more tongues than we have, and yet we do desire to have more health or more riches. The reason is simply that we imagine that the latter, unlike the former, can be acquired by our exertions, or are due to our nature. We can rid ourselves of that opinion by bearing in mind that since we have always followed the advice of our reason, we have left undone nothing that was in our power; and that sickness and misfortune are no less natural to man than prosperity and health.

Of course not every kind of desire is incompatible with happiness: only those which are accompanied with impatience and sadness. It is also not necessary that our reason should be free from error; it is sufficient if our conscience testifies that we have never lacked resolution and virtue to carry out whatever we judge the best course. So virtue by itself is sufficient to make us happy in this life. But virtue unenlightened by intellect can be false: that is to say, the will and resolution to do well can carry us to evil courses, if we think them good; and in such a case the contentment which virtue brings is not solid. Moreover, such virtue is commonly set in opposition to pleasure, appetite and passion, and is accordingly very difficult to practise. The right use of reason on the other hand, by giving a true knowledge of good, prevents virtue from being false; by accommodating it to licit pleasures makes it easy to practise; and by making us realize the condition of our nature sets bounds to our desires. So we must conclude that the greatest felicity of man depends on the right use of reason; and consequently the study which leads to its acquisition is the most useful occupation one can take up. Certainly it is the most agreeable and delightful.

After this, it seems to me, Seneca should have taught us all the principal truths whose knowledge is necessary to facilitate the practice of virtue and to regulate our desires and passions, and thus to enjoy natural happiness. That would have made his book the finest and most useful that a pagan philosopher could have written. But this is only my opinion, which I submit to the judgement of your Highness; and if she is good enough to tell me where I go wrong, I will be most grateful, and I will show, by correcting my error, that I am, etc.

Descartes' next letter, on 18 August, makes a number of detailed criticisms of the text of the *De Vita Beata*. This letter crossed with one from Elizabeth expressing disappointment with Seneca.

## Descartes to Elizabeth, 1 September 1645

Madame,

When last I wrote I was uncertain whether your Highness was at the Hague or at Rhenen, so I addressed my letter via Leyden; and the one you condescended to write me was only delivered to me after the departure of the messenger who had brought it to Alkmaar. So I have been unable to tell you earlier how proud I am that my judgement of the book you read is no different from yours, and that my manner of reasoning seems natural to you. I am sure that if you had had as much leisure as I have had to think about these topics, I could not write anything which you would not have observed better than I; but because your Highness' age, birth, and business have not permitted this, perhaps what I write can save you time.

Even my faults will give you opportunities for observing the truth. For instance, I spoke of a happiness which depends entirely on our free will, which all men can acquire without assistance from without. You observe very truly that there are diseases which take away the power of reasoning and with it the power of enjoying the satisfaction proper to a rational mind. This shows me that what I said about all men without exception applies only to those who have the free use of their reason, and in addition know the way to reach such happiness. For everybody wants to make himself happy; but most people do not know how to, and often a bodily indisposition prevents their will from being free. This happens too when we are asleep; because nobody, however philosophical, can prevent himself having bad dreams when his temperament so disposes him. However, experience shows that if one has often had a certain thought while one's mind was at liberty, it returns again however indisposed one's body may be. Thus I can boast that my own dreams never portray anything distressing, and there is no doubt that it is a great advantage to have long accustomed oneself to drive away sad thoughts. But we cannot altogether answer for ourselves except when we are in our own power. It is better to lose one's life than to lose the use of reason, because even without the teachings of faith, natural philosophy by itself makes us hope that our soul will be in a happier state after death than now; and makes us fear nothing more than being attached to a body which altogether takes away its liberty.

There are other indispositions which do no harm to one's reason but which merely alter the humours, and make a man unusually inclined to sadness, or anger, or some other passion. These certainly cause distress, but they can be overcome; and the harder they are to conquer, the more satisfaction the soul can take in doing so. The same is true of all exterior handicaps, such as the splendour of high birth, the flatteries of courts, the adversities of fortune, and also great prosperity, which commonly does more than misfortune to hamper the would-be philosopher. When everything goes according to our wishes we forget to think of ourselves; when fortune changes we are the more surprised the more we trusted it. Altogether, we can say, nothing can completely take away our power of making ourselves happy provided that it does not trouble our reason. It is not always the things which seem the most distressing which do the most harm.

But in order to discover what contribution each thing can make to our contentment, we must consider what are its possible causes. This information is also most valuable in making it easy to practise virtue; because all actions of our soul that acquire us some perfection are virtuous, and all our contentment consists in our interior awareness of possessing some perfection. Thus whenever we practise any virtue—

that is to say, do what reason tells us we should do—we automatically receive satisfaction and pleasure from so doing. But pleasures are of two kinds: those that belong to the mind by itself, and those that belong to the whole human being, that is to say to the mind as joined to the body. These last present themselves in a confused manner to the imagination and often appear much greater than they are, especially before we possess them; and this is the source of all the evils and all the errors of life. For according to the rule of reason, each pleasure should be measured by the size of the perfection which produces it; it is thus that we measure those whose causes are clearly known to us. But often passion makes us believe certain things to be much better and more desirable than they are; then, when we have taken much trouble to acquire them, and in the process lost the chance of possessing other more genuine goods, possession of them brings home to us their defects; and thence arises dissatisfaction, regret, and remorse. And so the true function of reason is to examine the just value of all the goods whose acquisition seems to depend in some way on our conduct, so that we always devote our efforts to obtaining those which are in truth the most desirable. If, in such cases, fortune opposes our plans and makes them fail, we shall at least have the satisfaction that our loss was not our fault; and despite our failure we shall enjoy all the natural happiness whose acquisition was really within our power.

Anger, for instance, can sometimes excite in us such violent desires for vengeance that it makes us imagine more pleasure in chastizing our enemy than in preserving our honour or our life, and makes us risk both imprudently in the attempt. Whereas, if reason examines what is the good or perfection on which the pleasure derived from vengeance is based, it will find—unless the vengeance serves to prevent future offences—that there is nothing except our imagination that we have some superiority and advantage over the person on whom we are taking vengeance. And this is often only a vain imagination, which is worthless in comparison with honour or life, or even the satisfaction to be had from seeing one's own mastery of one's anger when one abstains from revenge.

The same is true of the other passions. They all represent the goods to which they tend with greater splendour than they deserve, and before we experience pleasures they make them seem greater than experience shows them to be. This is why pleasure is commonly dispraised, because the word is used to mean only the pleasures which frequently deceive us by their appearance, and make us neglect other much solider pleasures, such as the pleasures of the mind commonly are, which are not so impressive in anticipation. I say 'commonly' because not all pleasures of the mind are praiseworthy: they can be founded on some false opinion. An instance is the pleasure we take in slander, which is based only on the belief that the worse others are esteemed, the better esteemed we shall be ourselves. Also, they can deceive us by their appearance, when some strong passion accompanies them, as can be seen in the pleasure arising from ambition.

But the main difference between the pleasures of the body and those of the mind is the following. The body is subject to perpetual change, and indeed its preservation and well-being depend on change; so the pleasures proper to it last a very short time, since they arise from the acquisition of something useful to the body at the moment of reception, and cease as soon as it stops being useful. The pleasures of the soul, on the other hand, can be as immortal as the soul itself, provided they are so solidly founded that neither the knowledge of truth nor any false persuasion can destroy them.

The true function of reason, then, in the conduct of life is to examine and consider without passion the value of all perfections of body and soul that can be acquired by our conduct, so that since we are commonly obliged to deprive ourselves of some goods in order to acquire others, we shall always choose the better. Because the pleasures of the body are minor, it can be said in general that it is possible to make oneself happy without them. However, I do not think that they should be altogether despised, nor even that one should free oneself altogether from passion. It is enough to subject one's passions to reason; and once they are thus tamed they are sometimes useful precisely to the degree that they tend to excess. I will never have a more

excessive passion than that which impels me to the respect
and veneration which I owe you and makes me, etc.

## Descartes to Elizabeth, 15 September 1645[1]

Madame,

Your Highness has so accurately observed all the reasons
which prevented Seneca from expounding clearly his opinion
on the supreme good, and you have read his book so carefully, that I would fear to be tedious if I continued examining
his chapters one by one. Moreover, I do not want to put off
replying to your question how to fortify one's understanding
so as to discern what is the best in all the actions of life. And
so, without following Seneca any further, I will try simply
to explain my own opinion on the topic.

In order to be always disposed to judge well only two things
seem to me necessary. One is the knowledge of truth, the
other is practice in remembering and assenting to this
knowledge whenever the occasion demands. But because
nobody except God knows everything perfectly, we have to
content ourselves with knowing the truths most useful to
us.

The first and chief of these is that there is a God on whom
all things depend, whose perfections are infinite, whose
power is immense, and whose decrees are infallible. This
teaches us to accept calmly all the things which happen to
us as expressly sent by God. Moreover, since the true
object of love is perfection, when we lift up our minds to
consider Him as He is, we find ourselves naturally so inclined to love Him, that we even rejoice in our afflictions at
the thought that they are an expression of His will.

The second thing we must know is the nature of our soul.
We must know that it is a substance independent of, and
nobler than, the body, and that it is capable of enjoying many
satisfactions not to be found in this life. This prevents us
from fearing death, and so detaches our affections from the

[1] AT iv. 287; AM vi. 297; in French; complete.

things of this world that we scorn whatever is in the power of fortune.

Here it is important to judge worthily of the works of God and to have a vast idea of the extent of the universe, such as I tried to convey in the third book of my *Principles.* For if we imagine that beyond the heavens there is nothing but imaginary spaces, and that all the heavens are made only for the service of the earth, and the earth only for man, we will be inclined to think that this earth is our principal abode and this life our best. Instead of discovering the perfections that are truly within us, we will attribute to other creatures imperfections which they do not have, so as to raise ourselves above them. We will be so absurdly presumptuous as to wish to belong to God's council and assist Him in the government of the world; and this will bring us a mass of vain anxiety and distress.

After acknowledging the goodness of God, the immortality of our souls, and the immensity of the universe, there is yet another truth that is, in my opinion, most useful to know. That is, that though each of us is a person distinct from others, whose interests are accordingly in some way different from those of the rest of the world, we must still think that none of us could subsist alone and each one of us is really one of the many parts of the universe, and more particularly a part of the earth, the State, the society, and the family to which we belong by our domicile, our oath of allegiance, and our birth. And the interests of the whole, of which each of us is a part, must always be preferred to those of our individual personality—with measure, of course, and discretion, because it would be wrong to expose ourselves to a great evil to procure only a slight benefit to our kinsfolk or our country. (Indeed if a man were worth more, by himself, than all his fellow citizens he would have no reason to destroy himself to save his city.) But if a man saw everything in relation to himself, he would not hesitate to injure others greatly when he thought he could draw some slight advantage; and he would have no true friendship, no fidelity, no virtue at all. On the other hand, if a man considers himself a part of the community he delights in doing good to everyone, and does not hesitate even to risk his life in the service of others, when the occasion demands. If he could, he would even be willing to lose his soul to save others. So that this consideration is the source and origin of all the most heroic actions done by men. A man seems to me more pitiful than admirable if he risks death from vanity, in the hope of praise, or through stupidity, because he does not apprehend the danger. But when a man risks death because he believes it to be his duty, or when he suffers some other evil to bring good to others, then he acts in virtue of the consideration that he owes more to the community of which he is a part than to himself as an individual, though this thought may be only confusedly in his mind without his reflecting upon it. Once a man knows and loves God as he should he has a natural impulse to think in this way; because, abandoning himself altogether to God's will, he strips himself of his own interests, and has no other passion than to do what he thinks pleasing to Him. Thus he acquires a mental satisfaction and contentment incomparably more valuable than all the passing joys which depend upon the senses.

In addition to these truths which concern all our actions in general, others must be known which concern more particularly each individual action. The chief of these, in my view, are those I mentioned in my last letter: namely, that all our passions represent to us the goods to whose pursuit they impel us as being much greater than they really are; and that the pleasures of the body are never as lasting as those of the soul, nor as great in possession as they appear in anticipation. We must pay great attention to this, so that when we feel ourselves moved by some passion we should suspend our judgement until it is calmed, and not let ourselves easily be deceived by the false appearance of the goods of this world.

I have only this to add, that one must also examine minutely all the customs of one's place of abode to see how far they should be followed. Though we cannot have certain proofs of everything, still we must take sides, and in matters of custom embrace the opinions that seem the most probable, so that we may never be irresolute when we need to act. For nothing causes regret and remorse except irresolution.

173

I said above that besides the knowledge of truth, practice also is required if one is to be always disposed to judge well. We cannot continually pay attention to the same thing; and so however clear and evident the reasons may have been that persuaded us of some truth in the past, we can later be turned away from believing it by some false appearances unless we have so imprinted it on our mind by long and frequent meditation that it has become a settled disposition with us. In this sense the scholastics are right when they say that virtues are *habitus*; because our failings are rarely due to the lack of theoretical knowledge of what one should do, but to lack of knowledge in practice, that is for lack of a firm habit of belief. And since in examining these truths I am also increasing in myself the corresponding habit, I am particularly obliged to your Highness for allowing me to correspond with her about them. There is no activity in which I think my leisure better spent than one in which I can prove that I am, etc.

## Descartes to Elizabeth, 6 October 1645[1]

Madame,

I have sometimes asked myself the following question. Is it better to be cheerful and content, imagining the goods one possesses to be greater and more valuable than they are, and not knowing or caring to consider those one lacks; or is it better to have more consideration and knowledge, so as to know the just value of both, and thus grow sad. If I thought joy the supreme good, I should not doubt that one should try to make oneself joyful at any price, and I should approve the brutishness of those who drown their sorrows in wine, or assuage them with tobacco. But I make a distinction between the supreme good—which consists in the exercise of virtue, or, what comes to the same, the possession of all those goods

---

[1] AT iv. 304; AM vi. 312; in French; complete.

whose acquisition depends upon our free will—and the satisfaction of mind which results from that acquisition. Consequently, seeing that it is a greater perfection to know the truth than to be ignorant of it, even when it is to our disadvantage, I must conclude that it is better to have less cheer and more knowledge. So it is not necessarily the most cheerful person who has the most satisfied mind; on the contrary, great joys are commonly sober and serious, and only slight and passing joys are accompanied by laughter. So I cannot approve of trying to deceive oneself by feeding on false imaginations; because the resulting pleasure can only touch the surface of the soul, leaving it to feel interior bitterness at the realisation of that falsehood. It could indeed happen that the soul was so continually diverted that it never achieved such realization; but that would not amount to the enjoyment of the happiness we are discussing, since the latter must depend on our behaviour, whereas the former could only come from luck.

But the case is different when we can turn our minds to different considerations which are equally true, and some of them incline to contentment and others incline the other way. In such a case it seems to me that prudence demands that we dwell mainly in those which give us satisfaction. Indeed, since almost everything in the world can be looked at from one point of view which makes it appear good, and from another which brings out its defects, I think that one way in which we should display skill is in looking at things from the point of view which makes them seem most to our advantage, provided that this does not involve self-deception.

So, when your Highness considers the circumstances which have given her more leisure to cultivate her reason than many others of her age, if she will please also consider how much more she has profited from them than others, I am sure that she will have reason to be contented. And I do not see why she should prefer to compare herself to other women in a matter for regret than in a matter which could give her satisfaction. Our nature is such that our mind needs much relaxation if it is to be able to spend usefully a few moments in the search for truth. Too great application to study does not refine the mind but wears it down. Consequently, we should not reckon the time which we have spent on instructing ourselves by comparison with the number of hours we have had at our disposition but rather, I think, by comparison with what we see commonly happens to others, as an indication of the normal scope of the human mind.

I think also that there is nothing to repent of when we have done what we judged best at the time for deciding to act, even though later, thinking it over at our leisure, we judge that we made a mistake. There would be more ground for repentance if we had acted against our conscience, even though we realised afterwards that we had done better than we thought. For we are responsible only for our thoughts and it does not belong to human nature, to be omniscient, nor always to judge on the spur of the moment as well as when there is plenty of time to deliberate.

The vanity which makes a man think better of himself than he deserves is a vice which displays a weak and base soul; but this does not mean that the strongest and most noble souls have a duty to despise themselves. We must do ourselves justice, and recognize our perfections as well as our faults. Propriety forbids us to boast of our good qualities, but it does not forbid us to be aware of them.

Finally, it is true that we lack the infinite knowledge which would be necessary for a perfect acquaintance with all the goods between which we have to choose in the various situations of our lives. We must, I think, be contented with a modest knowledge of the most necessary truths such as those I listed in my last letter.

In that letter I have already given my opinion on your Highness' question whether it is more correct to see everything in relation to oneself or put oneself to great anxiety for others. If we thought only of ourselves, we could enjoy only the goods which are peculiar to ourselves; whereas, if we consider ourselves as part of some larger body, we share also in the goods which belong to it in common, without losing any of those which belong to ourselves. With evils, the case is not the same, because philosophy teaches that evil is nothing real, but only a privation. When we are sad on account of some evil which has happened to our friends, we do not share in the defect in which this evil consists; and whatever sadness or distress we feel on such occasions cannot be as great as the interior satisfaction which always accompanies good actions, and especially actions which proceed from a pure affection for others which has no reference to self, that is, from the Christian virtue called charity. And so, while weeping and deeply troubled it is possible to have more pleasure than while laughing at one's ease.

It is easy to show that the pleasure of the soul which constitutes happiness is not inseparable from cheerfulness and bodily comfort. This is shown by tragedies, which please us more the sadder they make us, and by bodily exercises like hunting and tennis which are pleasant in spite of being arduous—indeed we see that often the fatigue and exertion involved increases the pleasure. The soul derives contentment from such exercise because it observes the strength, or skill, or some other perfection of the body to which it is joined; but the contentment which it finds in weeping at some pitiable and tragic episode in the theatre arises chiefly from its impression that it is performing a virtuous action in having compassion on the afflicted. Indeed in general the soul is pleased to feel passions arise in itself, no matter what they are, provided that it remains in control of them.

But I must examine these passions in more detail so as to be able to define them. It will be easier for me to do so in this letter than if I were writing to anyone else, because your Highness has read the treatise which I once drafted on the nature of animals.[1] You know already how I think various impressions are formed in their brain: some by the external objects which act upon the senses, and others by the internal dispositions of the body, either by the traces of previous impressions left in the memory, or by the agitation of the spirits which come from the heart. In man the brain is also acted on by the soul which has some power to change cerebral impressions just as those impressions in their turn

[1] Since the publication of the *Principles*, Descartes had been working on a treatise on animal physiology; it was never completed.

have the power to arouse thoughts which do not depend on the will. Consequently, the term 'passion' can be applied in general to all the thoughts which are thus aroused in the soul by cerebral impressions alone, without the concurrence of the will, and therefore without any action of the soul itself; for whatever is not an action is a passion. Commonly however, the term is restricted to thoughts which are caused by some extraordinary agitation of the spirits. For thoughts that come from external objects, or from the interior dispositions of the body—such as the perception of colours, sounds, and smells, hunger, thirst, pain and so on— are called external or internal sensations. Those that depend on the traces left by previous impressions in the memory and the ordinary motion of the spirits are dreams, whether they are real dreams in sleep or day dreams in waking life when the soul does not determine itself to anything of itself, but idly follows the impressions in the brain. When the soul, on the other hand, uses the will to determine itself to some thought which is not just intelligible, but also imaginable, this thought makes a new impression on the brain, which is not, from the soul's point of view, a passion, but an action; and this is what is properly called imagination. Finally, when the normal behaviour of the spirits is such that it commonly arouses sad or cheerful thoughts or the like, this is not attributed to passion, but to the nature or humour of the man in whom they are aroused; and so we say that one man has a sad nature, another is of a cheerful humour, and so on. So there remain only the thoughts that come from some special agitation of the spirits, whose effects are felt as in the soul itself. It is these that are passions properly so called.

Of course almost all our thoughts depend on more than one of the causes I have just listed; but each thought is called after its chief or most notable cause. This makes many people confuse the sensation of pain with the passion of sadness, and the sensation of titillation with the passion of joy, which they also call pleasure or delight. People also confuse the sensations of thirst and hunger with the desire to drink and eat, which is a passion. This is because the causes that give rise to pain commonly also agitate the spirits in such a way as to arouse sadness, and those that produce a feeling of titillation agitate them in such a way as to excite joy, and so in other cases.

Sometimes also people confuse the inclinations or habits which dispose to a certain passion with the passion itself, though the two are easy to distinguish. For instance when it is announced in a town that enemies are coming to besiege it, the inhabitants at once make a judgement about the evil which may result to them: this judgement is an action of their soul and not a passion. And though this judgement is to be found in many alike, they are not all equally affected by it; some are more affected than others in proportion to the greater or less habit or inclination they have towards fear. Their souls can receive the emotion that constitutes the passion only after they have made the judgement, or else at least conceived the danger without making a judgement, and then imprinted an image of it in the brain, by another action, namely imagination. When a soul does this it acts upon the spirits, which travel from the brain through the nerves into the muscles, and makes them enter the muscles which close the openings of the heart. This retards the circulation of the blood so that the whole body becomes pale, cold, and trembling, and the spirits returning from the heart to the brain are agitated in such a way that they are useless for forming any images except those which excite in the soul the passion of fear. All these things happen so quickly one after the other that the whole thing seems like a single operation. Similarly, in all the other passions there occurs some special agitation in the spirits leaving the heart.

I planned to write thus much to your Highness eight days ago, and to add a detailed explanation of all the passions. But I found it difficult to list them, and so I had to let the postman leave without my letter, and in the meanwhile I have received the one your Highness was kind enough to write me. Now I have more points to answer, and so I must postpone the examination of the passions.[1]

---

[1] Elizabeth's letter was a reply to Descartes' of 15 September, p. 171. It objected that resignation to God's will did not reconcile one to the ill will of men; that belief in immortality might make one seek death; and that consideration of the vast extent of the universe might make us doubt of God's providence.

I must say at once that all the reasons that prove that God exists and is the first and unchangeable cause of all effects that do not depend on human free will prove similarly, I think, that He is also the cause of all those that do so depend. For the only way to prove that He exists, is to consider Him as a supremely perfect being; and he would not be supremely perfect if anything could happen without coming entirely from Him. It is true that faith alone tells us about the nature of the grace by which God raises us to a supernatural happiness; but philosophy by itself is able to discover that the slightest thought could not enter into a man's mind without God's willing, and having willed from all eternity, that it should so enter. The scholastic distinction between universal and particular causes is out of place here. The sun, although the universal cause of all flowers, is not the cause of the difference between tulips and roses; but that is because their production depends also on some other particular causes which are not subordinated to the sun. But God is the universal cause of everything in such a way as to be also the total cause of everything; and so nothing can happen without His will.

It is true also that knowledge of the immortality of the soul, and of the felicity of which it will be capable after this life, might give occasion to those who are tired of this life to leave it, if they were certain that they would afterwards enjoy that felicity. But no reason guarantees this, and there is nothing to show that the present life is bad except the false philosophy of Hegesias, whose book was forbidden by Ptolemy because many of its readers killed themselves.[1] True philosophy, on the contrary, teaches that even amid the saddest disasters and most bitter pains a man can always be content, provided that he knows how to use his reason.

As for the extent of the universe, I do not see how the consideration of it tempts one to separate particular providence from the idea we have of God. God is quite different from finite powers. They can be used up, so when we see that they are employed in great effects we have reason to judge it unlikely that they also extend to slight ones. But the greater we esteem the works of God to be, the better we

---

[1] See Cicero, *Tusculana* i. 34.

observe the infinity of His power; and the better known this infinity is to us, the more certain we are that it extends even to the most particular actions of human beings.

When your Highness speaks of the particular providence of God as being the foundation of theology, I do not think that you have in mind some change in God's decrees occasioned by actions that depend on our free will. No such change is theologically tenable; and when we are told to pray to God, that is not so that we should inform Him of our needs, nor that we should try to change the order established from all eternity by His providence—either of these aims would be blameworthy—but simply to obtain whatever He has, from all eternity, willed to be obtained by our prayers. I think that all theologians agree on this, including the Arminians, who seem the most jealous of the rights of free will.

I agree that it is difficult to determine exactly how far reason ordains that we should devote ourselves to the community. However, it is not a matter on which it is necessary to be very precise; it is enough to satisfy one's conscience, and then leave a lot of room for one's inclination. For God has so established the order of things, and has joined men together in so close a community, that even if everyone were to relate everything to himself, and had no charity for others, he would still commonly work for them as much as was in his power, provided that he was prudent, especially if he lived in an age in which morals were not corrupted. Moreover, as it is a nobler and more glorious thing to do good to others than to oneself it is the noblest souls who have the greatest inclination thereto and who make least account of the goods they possess. Only weak and base souls value themselves above their true value, and are like small vessels that a few drops of water can fill. I know that your Highness is not at all like that. Base souls cannot be persuaded to take trouble for others unless you can show them that they will reap some profit for themselves; but in order to persuade your Highness to look after her health it is necessary to point out to her that she cannot long be useful to those she loves if she neglects herself.

## Descartes to [the Marquess of Newcastle], October 1645[1]

... The treatise on animals, on which I began work more than fifteen years ago, cannot be finished until I have made many experiments which I have not yet been able to make and do not foresee the possibility of making. Consequently I dare not promise to publish it for a long time yet. None the less, I will obey you in all you may command me, and I regard it as a very great favour that you take pleasure in learning my opinions on philosophical problems.

I am convinced that hunger and thirst are felt in the same manner as colours, sound, smells, and all the other objects of the external senses, that is, by means of nerves stretched like fine threads from the brain to all the other parts of the body. They are so disposed that whenever one of these parts is moved, the place in the brain where the nerves originate moves also, and its movement arouses in the soul the sensation attributed to that part. I have tried to explain this at length in my *Dioptrics*. I said there that the different motions of the optic nerve make the soul feel all the diversities of colours and light; and similarly, I believe that the sensation of hunger is caused by a motion of the nerves which go to the base of the stomach and that the sensation of thirst is caused by a different motion of the same nerves and the nerves which go to the throat. To explain the cause of the motion of these nerves, I observe that just as one's mouth waters when one has a good appetite and sees food on the table, so normally a great quantity of water comes into the stomach in the same circumstances. It is carried thither by the arteries, whose ends have narrow openings of such a shape as to permit the passage of water but not of the other parts of the blood. It is like a kind of *aqua fortis* which mingles with the small parts of the food one has eaten and dissolves them into chyle, and then returns with them

[1] AT iv. 325; AM vi. 326; in French; with omissions.

through the veins into the blood. But if this liquid finds no food to dissolve when it enters the stomach, it uses its force on the wall of the stomach and stimulates the nerves attached to it in such a way as to make the soul have the sensation of hunger. And so if there is no food in the stomach, one cannot but have that sensation, unless there are obstructions preventing the liquid from entering, or cold and sticky humours to blunt its force, or unless the temperament of the blood is corrupted so that the liquid which it sends into the stomach is in some way unusual. It is always one of these causes which takes away the appetite in sickness. Another possibility is that the blood, though not corrupted, may contain little or none of that liquid: I think this is what happens to those who have gone a long time without eating. It is said that after some days they stop being hungry. The reason for this is that during that time all the liquid may have left the pure blood and been exhaled in sweat, or lost by insensible perspiration or through urination. This is confirmed by the story of a man who is said to have survived three weeks underground without eating, simply by drinking his urine. Since he was shut up underground, his blood did not diminish so much by insensible transpiration as it would have done in the open air.

Moreover, I think thirst is caused in the following manner. The blood serum which usually goes through the arteries to the stomach and the throat in liquid form and thus wets them, sometimes travels thither in the form of vapour which dries them up and thus agitates their nerves in the manner needed to arouse in the soul the desire to drink. Thus there is no more difference between this vapour which arouses thirst, and the liquid which causes hunger, than there is between actual sweat and the insensible perspiration of the whole body.

I think the only general cause of the movements in the world is God. At the first instant of His creation of matter, He began to move its various parts in different ways; and now, by the same action as He conserves matter He conserves also as much movement as He then put into it. I have tried to explain this in the second part of my *Principles*.[1]

[1] Article 36, AT viii. 61; HR i. 267.

And in the third part I have described in detail the matter of which I take the sun to be composed[1]; and in the fourth I described the nature of fire.[2] And so I could not add anything now which would not be more difficult to understand than what I then wrote. I also said expressly in the eighteenth article of the second part,[3] that I think the existence of a vacuum involves a contradiction, because we have the same idea of matter as we have of space. Because this idea represents a real thing to us, we would contradict ourselves, and assert the contrary of what we think, if we said that that space was void, that is, that something we conceive as a real thing is not real.

The preservation of health has always been the principal end of my studies, and I do not doubt that it is possible to acquire much information about medicine which has hitherto been unknown. But the treatise on animals which I plan and which I have not yet been able to complete is only a prolegomenon to the acquisition of this information, and so I am careful not to boast that I already possess it. All I can say at present is that I share the opinion of Tiberius who thought everyone over thirty had enough experience of what was harmful or beneficial to be his own doctor.[4] Indeed it seems to me that anybody who has any intelligence, and who is willing to pay a little attention to his health, can better observe what is beneficial to it than the most learned doctors. I pray God with all my heart for the preservation of yours, and that of your brother.[5]

I am, etc.

## Descartes to Elizabeth, 3 November 1645[6]

Madame,

... I agree that the sadness of tragedies would not please as it does if we feared that it might become so excessive as to

---

[1] Article 54, AT viii. 107; HR i. 274.
[2] Article 80, AT viii. 249; HR i. 284.
[3] AT viii. 50; HR i. 263.          [4] Suetonius, *Life of Tiberius*, article 69.
[5] Sir Charles Cavendish.
[6] AT iv. 330; AM vi. 330; in French; with omissions.

make us uncomfortable. But when I said that there are passions which are the more useful the more they tend to excess, I only meant to speak of those which are altogether good; as I indicated when I added that they should be subject to reason. There are, indeed, two kinds of excess. There is one which changes the nature of a thing, and turns it from good to bad, and prevents it from remaining subject to reason; and there is another which only increases its quantity, and turns it from good to better. Thus excess of courage is only temerity when it passes the limits of reason; but as long as it remains within them, it can consist simply in the absence of irresolution and fear.

These last few days I have been thinking about the number and order of all the passions, so as to examine their nature in detail. But I have not yet sufficiently digested my opinions on this topic to dare to tell them to your Highness. I will not fail to do so as soon as I can.

As for free will, I agree that if we think only of ourselves we cannot help regarding ourselves as independent; but when we think of the infinite power of God we cannot help believing that all things—including our free will—depend on Him. For it involves a contradiction to say that God has created men of such a nature that the actions of their will do not depend on His. It is the same as saying that His power is both finite and infinite: finite since there is some-thing which does not depend on it; infinite, since it was able to create that independent thing. But just as the knowledge of the existence of God should not take away our certainty of the free will which we experience and feel in ourselves, so also the knowledge of our free will should not make us doubt of the existence of God. The independence which we experience and feel in ourselves, and which suffices to make our actions praiseworthy or blameworthy, is not incompatible with the dependence of quite another kind which all things share in relation to God.

As for the state of the soul after this life, I am not as well informed as M. Digby. Leaving aside what faith tells us, I agree that by natural reason alone we can make favourable conjectures and indulge in fine hopes, but we cannot have any certainty. But natural reason teaches us also that we have always more good than evil in this life, and that we should never leave what is certain for what is uncertain. Consequently, in my opinion, it teaches that though we should not seriously fear death, we should equally never seek it.

I do not need to reply to any objection which theologians may make about the vast extent which I have attributed to the universe, since your Highness has already replied on my behalf. I will only add that if such an extent could make the mysteries of our faith less credible, the same is true of the dimensions that the astronomers have always attributed to the heavens. They have always thought them so large as to make the earth, by comparison, to be only a point, yet the objection is never made against them.

If prudence were mistress of events I do not doubt that your Highness would succeed in everything she undertakes; but all men would have to be perfectly wise before one could infer from what they ought to do what they will in fact do. At least it would be necessary to know in detail the humour of all those with whom one was to have any dealings. Even that would not be enough, because they have in addition their own free will, whose motions are known only to God. . . .

## Descartes to ***, 1645 or 1646[1]

I do not remember where I spoke of the distinction between essence and existence. However, I make a distinction between modes, strictly so called, and attributes, without which the things whose attributes they are cannot be; or between the modes of things themselves and the modes of thought. (Forgive me if I here change into another language to express myself better.[2]) Thus shape and motion are modes, in the strict sense, of corporeal substance; because the same body can exist at one time with

---

[1] AT iv. 348; AM vi. 345; complete.
[2] At this point the original changes from French into Latin.

one shape and at another with another, now in motion and now at rest; whereas, on the other hand, neither this shape nor this motion can be without this body. Thus love, hatred, affirmation, doubt and so on are true modes in the mind. But existence, duration, size, number and all universals are not, it seems to me, modes in the strict sense; nor are justice, mercy and so on in God. They are referred to by a broader term and called attributes, or modes of thought, because we do indeed think of the essence of a thing in one way when we abstract from whether it exists or not, and in a different way when we consider it as existing; but the thing itself cannot be outside our thought without its existence, nor without its duration or size and so on. Therefore I say that shape and other similar modes are strictly speaking modally distinct from the substances whose modes they are; but there is a lesser distinction between the other attributes. This latter can be called modal—as I did at the end of my replies to the *First Objections*—but only in a broad sense of the term, and it is perhaps better called Formal. But to avoid confusion, in the first part of my *Treatise on Philosophy*, in article 60,[1] where I discuss it explicitly, I call it a distinction of reason (*rationis ratiocinatae*). I do not recognize any distinction of reason *rationis ratiocinantis*— that is one which has no foundation in reality—because we cannot have any thought without a foundation; and consequently in that article, I did not add the word *ratiocinatae*.[2] It seems to me that the only thing which causes difficulty in this area is the fact that we do not sufficiently distinguish between things existing outside our thought and the ideas of things in our thought. Thus, when I think of the essence of a triangle, and of the existence of the same triangle, these two thoughts, as thoughts, even taken objectively, differ modally in the strict sense of the term 'mode'; but the case is not the same with the triangle existing outside thought, in which it seems to me manifest that essence and existence

[1] *Principles* i. 60; AT viii. 28; HR i. 243.

[2] This untranslatable pair of terms was thus explained by Scholastics. A distinction made by reason was *rationis ratiocinantis* if made by the mind without foundation in reality (as between *definiens* and *defininendum*: man and rational animal), and *rationis ratiocinatae* if made with foundation in reality (as between rational and animal in man).

187

are in no way distinct. The same is the case with all universals. Thus, when I say Peter is a man, the thought by which I think of *Peter* differs modally from the thought by which I think of *man*, but in Peter himself being a man is nothing other than being Peter. So, then, I postulate three kinds of distinction: first, real distinction between two substances; and then modal and formal distinctions which are *rationis ratiocinatae*. All these three can be called real in contrast to the distinction of reason *rationis ratiocinantis*; and in this sense it can be said that essence is really distinct from existence. Again, if by essence we mean a thing as it is objectively in the intellect, and by existence the same thing in so far as it is outside the intellect, it is manifest that the two are really distinct.

Thus, almost all the controversies of philosophy arise only from misunderstandings between philosophers.[1] Forgive me if this discussion is too confused; the postman is about to leave, and I have only time to add here that I am very obliged to you for your remembrance of me, and that I am, etc.

In November 1645 Elizabeth's brother Prince Edward became a Catholic in order to marry the Princess of Mantua. Elizabeth wrote to Descartes expressing her distress at his conversion. Descartes replied rather sharply that he could not be expected to sympathize. Those who were not Catholics, he said, should remember that if they or their ancestors had not left the Roman faith they would not hold their present religion. He went on, in the passages printed below, to discuss the freedom of the will.

## From the letter to Elizabeth, January 1646[2]

I turn to your Highness' problem about free will. I will try to give an illustration to explain how this is both dependent and free. Suppose that a King has forbidden duels, and knows with certainty that two gentlemen of his kingdom who live in different towns have a quarrel, and are so

[1] This last paragraph is in French.
[2] AT iv. 351; AM vii. 1; in French; extracts.

hostile to each other that if they meet nothing will stop them from fighting. If this King orders one of them to go on a certain day to the town where the other lives, and orders the other to go on the same day to the place where the first is, he knows with certainty that they will meet, and fight, and thus disobey his prohibition; but none the less he does not compel them, and his knowledge, and even his will to make them act thus, does not prevent their combat when they meet being as voluntary and as free as if they had met on some other occasion and he had known nothing about it. And they can be no less justly punished for disobeying the prohibition. Now what a King can do in such a case, concerning certain free actions of his subjects, God, with His infinite foresight and power does infallibly in regard to all the free actions of all men. Before He sent us into the world He knew exactly what all the inclinations of our will would be; it is He who gave us them, it is He who has disposed all the other things outside us so that such and such objects would present themselves to our senses at such and such times, on the occasion of which he knew that our freewill would determine us to such or such an action; and He so willed, but without using any compulsion. In the King of my story it is possible to distinguish two different types of volition, one according to which he willed that these gentlemen should fight, since he caused them to meet; and the other according to which he willed that they should not, since he forbade duels. In the same way the theologians make a distinction in God's willing: He has an absolute and independent will, according to which He wills all things to come about as they do, and another relative will which concerns the merit and demerit of men, according to which He wants them to obey His laws.

I must also make a distinction between two sorts of goods, in order to defend what I wrote earlier—namely that in this life we have always more good than evil—against your Highness' objection concerning all the inconveniences of life.[1] When we consider the idea of goodness as a rule for our actions, we take it as a maximum of perfection, which is

---

[1] 'Human beings', Elizabeth had written, 'have more occasions for distress than delight, and there are a thousand errors for one truth.'

contrasted with an infinite number of evils, as a single straight line can be contrasted with an infinite number of curves. This is the sense in which philosophers commonly say that *good needs a faultless cause while evil comes from any single defect.*[1] But when we consider the good and evil in a single thing, to discover what value to put on it, as I did when I spoke of the value we should put on this life, we must take 'good' as meaning whatever is advantageous and 'evil' as meaning whatever is disadvantageous; the other defects the thing may have are not taken into account. Thus, if a man is offered a post, he considers on the credit side the honour and profit he may expect from it, and on the debit side the trouble, the danger, the loss of time, and other such things. Having compared the evils and the good, he accepts or refuses according as he finds the latter greater or less than the former. It was in this latter sense that I said that there are always more good things than evil in this life; and I said this because I think we should make little account of all things outside us that do not depend on our free will in comparison with those that do depend on it. Provided we know how to use our will well, we can make everything which depends on it good and thus prevent the evils that come from elsewhere, however great they may be, from penetrating any further into our souls than the sadness which actors arouse when they enact before us some tragic history. But I agree that to reach such a point a man has to be very philosophical indeed. None the less, I think that even those who most give rein to their passions, really judge deep down, even if they do not themselves perceive it, that there is more good than evil in this life. Sometimes they may call death to help them when they feel great pain, but it is only to help them bear their burden, as in the fable, and for all that they do not want to lose their life. And if there are some who do want to lose it, and who kill themselves, it is due to an intellectual error and not to a well reasoned judgement, nor to an opinion imprinted on them by nature, like the one which makes a man prefer the goods of this life to its evils.

[1] Latin words in a French context.

For the greater part of 1645 Mersenne had been absent from Paris on travels abroad. Descartes' correspondence with him recommenced in 1646. The two men discussed *inter alia* Roberval's book *Aristarchii Samii de mundi systemata*, which proposed a theory of universal attraction between particles.

## From the letter to Mersenne, 20 April 1646[1]

... Finally, it is a most absurd suggestion that in all the particles of the matter of the universe there resides some property in virtue of which they are drawn towards each other and attract each other in their turn; and that in each particle of terrestrial matter in particular there is a similar property in respect to other terrestrial particles which does not interfere with the former property. For in order to make sense of this one would have to suppose not only that each particle of matter had a soul, and indeed several different souls, which did not impede each other, but also that these souls were conscious, and indeed divine, to be able to know without any intermediary what was happening in those distant places, and to exercise their powers there. . . .

Out of Descartes' correspondence with Princess Elizabeth there grew the *Treatise on the Passions*, his last major work. A draft of the treatise was ready to be sent to Elizabeth in the spring of 1646; she commented on it in a letter of 25 April.

## Descartes to Elizabeth, May 1646[2]

Madame,

I discover by experience that I was right to include vain-glory among the passions; because when I see the favourable judgement which your Highness has made of my little

[1] AT iv. 316; AM vii. 45; in French; extract.
[2] AT iv. 406; AM vii. 58; in French; complete.

treatise about them I cannot prevent myself from feeling it. I am not at all surprised that you have also noticed faults in it, since I had no doubt there must be many. It is a topic that I have never before studied, and I have only made a sketch without adding the colours and decorations which would be needed for it to be presented to eyes less clear than those of your Highness.

Moreover, I did not mention all the principles of physics which I used to work out the particular movements of blood accompanying each passion. This was because I could not properly prove them without explaining the formation of all the parts of the human body; and that is something so difficult that I would not yet dare to undertake it, though I am more or less convinced in my own mind of the truth of the principles presupposed in the treatise. The chief ones are as follows. The function of the liver and the spleen is to contain reserve blood, less purified than the blood in the veins; and the fire in the heart needs constantly to be fed either by the juices of food coming directly from the stomach, or in their absence by this reserve blood (the other blood in the veins expands too easily). Our soul and our body are so linked that the thoughts which have ever accompanied some movements of our body since our life began still accompany them at present; so that if the same movements are aroused afresh by some external cause, they arouse in the soul the same thoughts; and contrariwise, if we have the same thoughts they produce the same movements. Finally, the machine of our body is constructed in such a way that a single thought of joy or love or the like is sufficient to send the animal spirits through the nerves into all the muscles needed to cause the different movements of the blood which, as I said, accompany the passions. It is true that I found difficulty in working out what was peculiar to each passion, because they never occur singly; none the less, since they occur in different combinations I tried to discover the changes that occur in the body when they change company. Thus, for instance, if love were always united with joy I would not know which of the two was responsible for the feeling of heat and dilatation that they cause around the heart; but since love is sometimes also united with sadness, and in that case the heat is still felt but not the dilatation, I decided that the heat belonged to love and the dilatation to joy. Again, although desire almost always goes with love, they are not always together in the same degree, because when there is no hope a man may have much love and little desire. In such a case the subject does not have the diligence and promptitude he would have if his desire were greater, and consequently it can be deduced that these characteristics arise from desire and not from love.

I quite believe that sadness takes away many people's appetite; but because I have always found in my own case that it increases it, I based my account on that. I think that the difference between people in this matter arises thus: some people's first cause of sadness in their life was that they did not receive enough food, while for others it was that the food they received was bad for them. In the latter case, the movement of animal spirits which takes away the appetite has ever afterwards remained joined with the passion of sadness. We see also that the movements which accompany other passions differ slightly from person to person, and this can be attributed to some similar cause.

It is true that admiration has its origin in the brain, and cannot be caused solely by the temperament of the blood as joy and sadness can. But by means of the impression it makes in the brain it can act on the body just like any other passion, and in a way more effectively because the surprise which it involves causes the promptest of all movements. We can move our hands or our feet more or less at the same instant as the thought of moving them occurs, because the idea of this movement formed in the brain sends the spirits into the muscles appropriate for the purpose. In the same way the idea of a pleasant thing, if it takes the mind by surprise, immediately sends the spirits into the nerves that open the orifices of the heart; and thus admiration, by the surprise it involves, increases the force of the movement caused by joy. The immediate dilatation of the orifices of the heart causes the blood entering by the vena cava and exiting by the arterial vein to inflate the lungs suddenly.

The exterior symptoms that commonly accompany the passions may also sometimes be due to other causes. Thus, a red face is not always the result of shame; it may come from the heat of a fire or from exercise. A sardonic grin may be due to a convulsion of the nerves of the face. Similarly a man may sigh sometimes out of habit, or out of sickness, but this does not mean that sighs are not symptoms of sadness and desire when they are in fact caused by these passions. I have never heard or noticed that sighs may also be caused by a full stomach; but if so I think it is a movement which nature uses to make the food juices pass more rapidly through the heart and thus speed the emptying of the stomach. For sighs, by exercising the lungs, make the blood they contain descend more quickly through the venous artery into the left side of the heart. This facilitates the reception into the lungs of the new blood, made up of food juices, which travels thither from the stomach through the liver and the heart.

I agree that the remedies against excessive passions are difficult to practise, and also that they are insufficient to prevent bodily disorders; but they suffice to prevent the soul being troubled by them and losing its free judgement. For this purpose I do not consider it necessary to have an exact knowledge of the truth on every topic, nor even to have foreseen in detail all possible eventualities, which would doubtless be impossible. It is enough to have imagined in general circumstances more distressing than one's own and to be prepared to bear them. Moreover, I do not think that it is easy to sin by excess in desiring the necessities of life; it is only desires for evil or superflous things that need controlling. As for those which tend only to good, it seems to me that the greater they are the better. To palliate my own faults I listed a certain langour as an excusable passion, but none the less I esteem much more highly the diligence of those who are swift and ardent in performing what they conceive to be their duty even when they do not expect much profit from it.

I lead such a retired life, and have always been so far from the conduct of affairs, that I would be no less impudent than the philosopher who wanted to lecture on the duties of a general in the presence of Hannibal if I took it on me to enumerate here the maxims one should observe in a life of public service. I do not doubt that your Highness' maxim is the best of all, namely that it is better to guide oneself by experience in these matters than by reason. It is rarely that we have to do with people who are as perfectly reasonable as men ought to be, so that one cannot judge what they will do simply by considering what they ought to do; and often the soundest advice is not the most successful. That is why one has to take risks and put oneself in the power of fortune, which I hope will always be as obedient to your desires as I am, etc.

Descartes' translator Clerselier introduced him to his brother-in-law Chanut, an official in government service. In 1646 Chanut went to Sweden as ambassador for the King of France. The following is the first of a series of letters Descartes wrote to him in Stockholm.

## Descartes to Chanut, 15 June 1646[1]

Sir,

I was very glad to learn from your letters that Sweden is not so far from here that one cannot have news from it in a few weeks. So I shall sometimes have the happiness of corresponding with you and sharing in the results of the studies you plan to make. Since you are good enough to look at my *Principles* and examine them, I am sure that you will notice in them many obscurities and faults. It will be very valuable for me to discover them, and I know no one who can inform me of them better than you. I only fear that you will soon grow tired of reading the book since what I have written is only distantly connected with moral philosophy, which you have chosen as your principal study.

Of course, I agree with you entirely that the safest way to find out how we should live is to discover first what we are, what kind of world we live in, and who is the Creator of this world, or the Master of the house we live in. But I cannot

[1] AT iv. 440; AM vii. 82; in French; complete.

at all claim or promise that all I have written is true, and further there is a very great distance between the general notion of Heaven and Earth, which I have tried to convey in my *Principles*, and the detailed knowledge of the nature of man, which I have not yet discussed. However, I do not want you to think I wish to dissuade you from your plan, and so I must say in confidence that what little knowledge of physics I have tried to acquire has been a great help to me in establishing sure foundations in moral philosophy. Indeed I have found it easier to reach satisfactory conclusions on this topic than on many others concerning medicine on which I have spent much more time. So that instead of finding ways to preserve life, I have found another, much easier and surer way, which is not to fear death. But this does not depress me, as it commonly depresses those whose wisdom is drawn entirely from the teaching of others, and rests on foundations which depend only on human prudence and authority.

I will say no more except that while I am waiting for the plants to grow in my garden which I need for some experiments to continue my physics, I am spending some time also on thinking about particular moral problems. Last winter, for instance, I sketched a little treatise on the nature of the Passions of the Soul, without any idea of publication; and I would now feel inclined to write something more on the topic, if I were not made indolent by seeing how depressingly few people condescend to read what I write. But in your service I will never be indolent; because I am, etc.

## Descartes to Clerselier, June 1646[1]

Sir,

My hope of soon being at Paris makes me lazy about writing to those whom I hope to have the honour to see there. So it is already some time since I received your letter;

[1] AT iv. 442; AM vii. 84; in French; complete.

but I thought that you could not be very anxious for an answer to your question as to what should be taken as the first principle, since you replied to it yourself in the same letter better than I could do.

I will only add that the word '*principle*' can be taken in several senses. It is one thing to look for a common notion so clear and so general that it can serve as a principle to prove the existence of all the beings (*entia*) to be discovered later; and another to look for a being whose existence is known to us better than that of any other, so that it can serve as a principle to discover them.

In the first sense, it can be said that '*the same thing cannot both be and not be at the same time*'[1] is a principle which can serve in general, not to make known the existence of anything else, but simply to confirm its truth once known, by the following reasoning: 'It is impossible that that which is, is not; I know that such a thing is; so I know that it is impossible that it is not.' This is of no importance, and makes us no wiser.

In the second sense, the first principle is that our soul exists, because there is nothing whose existence is more manifest to us.

I will also add that one should not require the first principle to be such that all other propositions can be reduced to it and proved by it. It is enough if it is useful for the discovery of many, and if there is no other proposition on which it depends, and none which is easier to discover. It may be that there is no principle at all to which alone all things can be reduced. They do indeed reduce other propositions to the principle that *the same thing cannot both be and not be at the same time*, but their procedure is superfluous and useless. On the other hand it is very useful indeed to convince oneself first of the existence of God, and then of the existence of all creatures, through the consideration of one's own existence.

Father Mersenne had told me that M. le Conte had composed some objections against my philosophy; but I have not yet seen them. Please assure him that I am

---

[1] Latin words in a French context.

waiting for them and that I take it as a favour that he has taken the trouble to write them.

The Achilles of Zeno is not difficult to solve if you bear in mind what follows. If you add to the tenth part of a certain quantity the tenth of that tenth, which is a hundredth, and then the tenth of this latter, which is a thousandth of the first, and so on *ad infinitum*, all these tenths, though supposed to be really infinite, add up only to a finite quantity, namely a ninth of the first quantity, as can easily be shown. For example, if from the line AB you take away the tenth part

```
              G
A─────────────────────────────────────────────────B
        C E F    D
```

of the side towards A, namely AC, and at the same time you take away eight times as much from the other side, namely BD, there will remain between them only CD which is equal to AC; then in turn if you take away from CD the tenth on the side towards A, that is CE, and eight times as much from the other side, that is DF, there will remain between them only EF which is the tenth of the whole CD; and if you continue indefinitely to take away from the side marked A a tenth of what you took away beforehand, and eight times as much from the other side, you will always find that there will remain, between the two last lines that you have taken away, a tenth of the whole line from which they have been taken away; and from that tenth you will always be able to take away further lines in the same way. But if you suppose that this has been done an actually infinite number of times, then nothing at all will remain between the two last lines which have thus been taken away; and from each side you will have arrived exactly at the point G, supposing that AG is a ninth of the whole AB and consequently that BG is eight times AG. For since what you have taken away from the side towards B will always have been eight times what you took away from the side towards A, it follows that the aggregate or total of all these lines taken away from the side towards B, which together make up the line BG, will also be eight times AG, which is the aggregate of all those which have been taken away from the side of A.

Consequently, if to the line AC you add CE, which is a tenth of it, and then a tenth of that tenth, and so on *ad infinitum*, all these lines together will only make up the line AG which is a ninth of the whole AB, which is what I set out to prove.

Once we realise this we have an answer to anyone who says that a tortoise who has ten leagues start can never be overtaken by a horse which goes ten times as fast as it, because while the horse travels these ten leagues, the tortoise travels one more, and while the horse travels the league the tortoise goes ahead another tenth of a league and so on for ever. The answer is that it is true that the horse will never overtake it while travelling that league and that tenth of a league and that hundredth and thousandth and so on of a league; but that does not mean that it will never overtake it, because that tenth and hundredth and thousandth only mount up to a ninth of a league, at the end of which the horse will start to be in the lead. The catch is that people imagine this ninth of a league to be an infinite quantity, because they divide it in their imagination into infinite parts. I am infinitely etc.

During the summer of 1646 Descartes met Elizabeth for the last time. She asked him to read Macchiavelli's *Prince* and send her his opinion of it. He did so in the following letter.

## Descartes to Elizabeth, September 1646[1]

Madame,

I have read the book which your Highness asked me to discuss, and I find in it many maxims which seem excellent: for instance, in the nineteenth and twentieth chapters, that a prince should always avoid the hatred and contempt of his subjects, and that the love of the people is worth more than fortresses. But there are also many others which I cannot approve. I think that the author's greatest fault is that he

[1] AT iv. 485; AM vii. 163; in French; complete.

does not sufficiently distinguish between princes who have come to power by just means, and those who have usurped it by illegitimate methods; and that he recommends indiscriminately maxims that are only suitable for the latter. If you are building a house on foundations insufficient to support high thick walls, the walls will have to be low and insubstantial; and similarly, those who have gained power by crime are commonly compelled to continue their course of crime, and would be unable to defend themselves if they took to virtue.

It is of such princes that what he says in chapter three is true: that they cannot help being hated by many, and that it is often more advantageous for them to do great harm than to do slight harm because slight offences merely arouse a desire for revenge, whereas great ones take away the power to exact it. And similarly in chapter 15 he says that if they decided to be good they could not but be ruined being in the midst of the great number of wicked people throughout the world. And in chapter 19 he says that one can be hated for good actions no less than for bad ones.

On these foundations he erects some very tyrannical maxims: for instance, he urges princes to be willing to ruin a whole country in order to remain master of it; to use great cruelty, provided it is soon over and done with; to try to appear good rather than to be good in reality; to keep their word only as long as it is useful; to dissimulate and to betray. Finally, he says that in order to rule one must strip oneself of all humanity and become as ferocious as any animal.

It is a sorry thing to make a book full of maxims which cannot even give any security to those to whom they are offered. He agrees himself that princes cannot protect themselves from the first fellow who is willing to risk his own life to take revenge on them.

It seems to me that quite contrary maxims should be proposed for the instruction of good princes, however newly they may have come to power; and it should be presupposed that the means which they have used to gain power have been just. Almost always, I think, they are just, provided the princes who use them think them to be; because justice between sovereigns does not have the same bounds as justice between individuals. It seems to me that in these cases God gives right to those to whom He gives power. But of course the most just actions become unjust when those who do them think them so.

A distinction must also be made between subjects, friends, and enemies. With regard to these last it is permitted to do almost anything, provided that some advantage to oneself or one's subjects ensues; and I do not think it wrong in such a case to join the fox with the lion and use artifice as well as force. And I include among enemies all those who are neither friends nor allies, because one has a right to make war on such people when it is to one's advantage and when their power is increasing in a suspicious and alarming manner. But I rule out one type of deception which is so directly hostile to society that I do not think it is ever permissible to use it, although our author approves it in several places; and that is pretending to be a friend of those one wishes to destroy, in order to take them by surprise. Friendship is too sacred a thing to be abused in this way; and someone who has once feigned love for someone in order to betray him deserves to be disbelieved and hated by those whom he afterwards wishes genuinely to love.

As for allies, a prince should keep his word to them strictly, even when it is to his own disadvantage; because no disadvantage can outweigh the utility of a reputation for keeping one's promises; and a prince can only acquire this reputation on occasions where it involves him in some loss. But in cases where he would be altogether ruined, the law of nations dispenses him from his promise. It is necessary to use much circumspection in promising if one is to be able always to keep faith.

It is a good thing to be on friendly terms with the majority of one's neighbours, but I think it best not to have strict alliances except with sovereigns less powerful than oneself. Because however loyal one intends to be oneself, one should not expect the same from others; one should count on being cheated whenever one's allies find it to their advantage. Those who are more powerful may find it to their advantage to do so whenever they wish; not so those who are less powerful.

As for subjects, there are two kinds: great people and common people. I mean by the expression 'great people' all those who can form parties against the Prince. Of their fidelity he must be very certain; if he is not he should employ all his efforts to bring them low. If they show any tendency to disturb the peace, he should treat them as he would foreign enemies. On this all politicians agree. As for his other subjects, he should above all avoid their hatred and contempt. This, I think, he can always do provided that he dispenses justice strictly according to their custom—that is, in accordance with the laws with which they are familiar—without excessive rigour in punishment or excessive indulgence in pardoning.

The prince must not hand over everything to his ministers; he should leave them to pronounce the most odious condemnations and display his own concern with everything else. He should also guard his dignity; he should not relax anything of the honour and deference the people think due to him, but should not ask for more. He should perform in public only important or universally commendable actions, taking his pleasures in private and never at anyone else's expense. Finally he should be immovable and inflexible. I do not mean that he should hold fast to his own first notions; he cannot have his eye everywhere and so he must ask advice, and hear many people's reasons, before coming to a decision. But once he has announced his decision, he must be inflexible in holding to it even if this does him harm; for it can hardly be as harmful to him as the reputation of being light and inconstant.

Consequently, I disapprove the maxims of chapter 15, that since the world is very corrupt a man who tries always to be good is bound to come off badly, and that a prince, for his own defence, must learn to be wicked when the occasion demands. Unless, by a good man, he means a superstitious and simple man who would not dare to give battle on the sabbath, and whose conscience could never rest unless he changed the religion of his people. But if we consider that a good man is one who does all that true reason tells him, it is certain that the best thing is to try always to be good.

Again, I do not believe what is said in chapter 19, that a

man may be hated for good actions no less than for bad ones. It is true that envy is a species of hatred, but that is not what the author means; princes are not commonly envied by the majority of their subjects but only by grandees or by their neighbours, to whom the same virtues which cause fear cause envy. No prince should ever abstain from well doing in order to avoid that sort of hatred; and the only kind which can harm him is hatred arising from the injustice or arrogance which the people judge him to have. For we see that even people condemned to death do not commonly hate their judges, if they think they have deserved the sentence; and even undeserved evils are borne if it is thought that the prince from whom they come is in some way forced to inflict them and does so with regret; because it is thought to be just that he should prefer the general utility to that of individuals. The only difficulty is when there are two parties to be satisfied who judge differently what is just, as when the Roman Emperors had to satisfy both citizens and soldiers. In such a case it is reasonable to accord something to both sides without trying to bring instantly to reason people unaccustomed to listen to it. They must be gradually made acquainted with it by the publication of pamphlets or the preaching of sermons or other means. Altogether, the common people will put up with whatever it can be persuaded is just, and is offended by whatever it imagines to be unjust. The arrogance of princes, that is the usurpation of authority or rights or honours thought undue, is odious to the common people only because it is regarded as a species of injustice.

Moreover, I do not share the opinion this author expressed in his preface that as a man who wants to sketch mountains must be in the plain to see their shape so also one must be a private citizen in order to discover the office of a prince. Because the pencil represents only what is seen from afar; but the chief motives of the actions of princes often depend on circumstances so unique that one cannot imagine them if one is not oneself a prince or has not been long privy to a prince's secrets.

For this reason I would be ridiculous if I thought I could teach anything to your Highness on this topic. That is not my purpose; I only wish my letters to provide variety upon her journey, which I pray may be prosperous,[1] as doubtless it will be if your Highness resolves to follow the maxims that everyone's felicity depends on himself, and that one must not let oneself be ruled by Fortune. We must take every advantage that Fortune offers but we must not be unhappy over those she refuses. In all the affairs of the world there are many reasons pro and many reasons contra; and so we must dwell principally on those which make us approve what we cannot avoid. The most unavoidable evils, I think, are the diseases of the body, from which I pray God preserve you; and I am, etc.

In 1646 Regius published his *Fundamenta Physicae* containing many more or less Cartesian ideas. Descartes disowned the book in the Preface to the French edition of the *Principles*.

# From the letter to Mersenne, 5 October 1646[2]

... A few days ago I saw a book which will make me henceforth much less free in communicating my thoughts than I have been hitherto; it is a book by a Professor of Utrecht, Regius, entitled *Foundations of Physics*. In it he repeats most of the things I put in my *Principles of Philosophy*, my *Dioptrics*, and my *Meteors* and piles up whatever he has had from me in private, and even things he could only have had by indirect routes and which I did not want him to be told. He retails all this in such a confused manner, and provides so few arguments, that his book can only make my opinions look ridiculous, and give a handle to my critics in two ways. Those who know that he hitherto made great profession of friendship with me, and followed blindly all my opinions, will blame all his faults on me. And if I ever decide to publish the doctrines I have not yet published,

1 Elizabeth's family were moving from the Hague to Berlin.
2 AT iv. 508; AM vii. 171; in French; extract.

since they will have some resemblance to what he has
written, it will be said that I have borrowed them from him.
But the worst is that while in matters of physics he has
followed closely whatever he thought to be my opinion
(though in some places he has made serious mistakes even
about this) he has done just the opposite in matters of
metaphysics; and in four or five places where he treats of
them he takes exactly the contrary position to the one in my
*Meditations*. I wanted to warn you of this so that if the book
should fall into your hands, you will have my opinion of it,
and will know that it has been published against my wishes
and without my knowledge, and that I do not regard its
compiler as my friend. If you have not yet got it, you can
save the price of it.


## From the letter to [the Marquess of Newcastle], 23 November 1646[1]


...I agree entirely with your Lordship's judgement of
Chemists. I think they use words in an uncommon sense
only to give the appearance of knowing what they do not. I
think also that what they say about reviving flowers by their
salts is only a baseless imagination, and that the powers of
their extracts are quite different from the powers of the plants
from which they are taken. This is clear empirically because
wine, vinegar, and brandy, three extracts made from the
same grapes, have such different tastes and powers. In my
view, the chemists' salt, sulphur, and mercury are no more
different from each other than the four elements of the
philosophers, and not much more different than water is
from ice, foam, and snow. I think that all these bodies are
made of the same matter, and that the only thing which
makes a difference between them is that the tiny parts of
matter which constitute some of them do not have the same
shape or arrangement as the parts which constitute the
others. I hope that your Lordship will soon be able to see

[1] AT iv. 569; AM vii. 222; in French; extracts.

this explained at some length in my *Principles of Philosophy*, which are about to be printed in French.

\*   \*   \*

I cannot share the opinion of Montaigne and others who attribute understanding or thought to animals. I am not worried that people say that men have an absolute empire over all the other animals; because I agree that some of them are stronger than us, and believe that there may also be some who have an instinctive cunning capable of deceiving the shrewdest human beings. But I observe that they only imitate or surpass us in those of our actions which are not guided by our thoughts. It often happens that we walk or eat without thinking at all about what we are doing; and similarly, without using our reason, we reject things which are harmful for us, and parry the blows aimed at us. Indeed, even if we expressly willed not to put our hands in front of our head when we fall, we could not prevent ourselves. I think also that if we had no thought we would eat, as the animals do, without having to learn to; and it is said that those who walk in their sleep sometimes swim across streams in which they would drown if they were awake. As for the movements of our passions, even though in us they are accompanied with thought because we have the faculty of thinking, it is none the less very clear that they do not depend on thought, because they often occur in spite of us. Consequently they can also occur in animals, even more violently than they do in human beings, without our being able to conclude from that that they have thoughts.

In fact, none of our external actions can show anyone who examines them that our body is not just a self-moving machine but contains a soul with thoughts, with the exception of words, or other signs that are relevant to particular topics without expressing any passion. I say words or other signs, because deaf-mutes use signs as we use spoken words; and I say that these signs must be relevant, to exclude the speech of parrots, without excluding the speech of madmen, which is relevant to particular topics even though it does not follow reason. I add also that these words or signs must not express any passion, to rule out not only cries of joy or sadness and the like, but also whatever can be taught by training to animals. If you teach a magpie to say good-day to its mistress, when it sees her approach, this can only be by making the utterance of this word the expression of one of its passions. For instance it will be an expression of the hope of eating, if it has always been given a titbit when it says it. Similarly, all the things which dogs, horses, and monkeys are taught to perform are only expressions of their fear, their hope, or their joy; and consequently they can be performed without any thought. Now it seems to me very striking that the use of words, so defined, is something peculiar to human beings. Montaigne and Charron may have said that there is more difference between one human being and another than between a human being and an animal; but there has never been known an animal so perfect as to use a sign to make other animals understand something which expressed no passion; and there is no human being so imperfect as not to do so, since even deaf-mutes invent special signs to express their thoughts. This seems to me a very strong argument to prove that the reason why animals do not speak as we do is not that they lack the organs but that they have no thoughts. It cannot be said that they speak to each other and that we cannot understand them; because since dogs and some other animals express their passions to us, they would express their thoughts also if they had any.

I know that animals do many things better than we do, but this does not surprise me. It can even be used to prove they act naturally and mechanically, like a clock which tells the time better than our judgement does. Doubtless when the swallows come in spring, they operate like clocks. The actions of honeybees are of the same nature, and the discipline of cranes in flight, and of apes in fighting, if it is true that they keep discipline. Their instinct to bury their dead is no stranger than that of dogs and cats who scratch the earth for the purpose of burying their excrement; they hardly ever actually bury it, which shows that they act only by instinct and without thinking. The most that one can say is that though the animals do not perform any action which shows us that they think, still, since the organs of their body are not very different from ours, it may be conjectured that there is attached to those organs some thoughts such as we experience in ourselves, but of a very much less perfect kind. To which I have nothing to reply except that if they thought as we do, they would have an immortal soul like us. This is unlikely, because there is no reason to believe it of some animals without believing it of all, and many of them such as oysters and sponges are too imperfect for this to be credible. But I am afraid of boring you with this discussion, and my only desire is to show you that I am, etc.

## Descartes to Chanut, 1 February 1647[1]

Sir,

I cannot rest until I have replied to the most welcome letter I have just received from you. The problems you set would be difficult for wiser men than I to discuss in a short time, but I know that however long I spent I could not solve them fully. Consequently, I prefer to write at once what my zeal dictates than to take longer thought and after all to write no better.

You ask my opinion about three things.[2] 1. What is love? 2. Does the light of nature by itself teach us to love God? 3. Which is worse if uncontrolled and abused, love or hatred?

In answer to the first question, I make a distinction between love which is purely intellectual or rational and love which is a passion. The first, in my view, consists simply in the fact that when our soul perceives some present or absent good, which it judges to be fitting for itself, it unites itself to it in volition, that is to say, it considers itself and the good in question as forming two parts of a single whole. Then, if the good is present, that is, if the soul possesses it, or is possessed by it, or is united to it not only in volition but also in fact and reality in the appropriate manner, in that case the

1 AT iv. 600; AM vii. 287; in French; complete.
2 Chanut had asked the questions on behalf of Queen Christine of Sweden.

movement of the will which accompanies the knowledge
that this is good for it, is joy; if on the other hand the good
is absent, then the movement of the will which accompanies
the knowledge of its lack is sadness; while the movement
which accompanies the knowledge that it would be a good
thing to acquire it, is desire. All these motions of the will
which constitute love, joy, sadness, and desire, in so far as
they are rational thoughts and not passions, could exist in
our soul even if it had no body. For instance, if the soul
perceived that there are many very fine things to be known
about Nature, its will would be infallibly impelled to love
the knowledge of those things, that is, to consider it as
belonging to itself. And if it was aware of having that
knowledge, it would have joy; if it observed that it lacked
the knowledge, it would have sadness; and if it thought it
would be a good thing to acquire it, it would have desire.
There is nothing in all these motions of its will which would
be obscure to it, nor of which it could fail to be perfectly
aware, provided that it reflected on its own thoughts.

   But while our soul is joined to our body, this rational love
is commonly accompanied by the other kind of love, which
can be called sensual or sensuous. This (as I said briefly of
all passions, appetites, and sensations on p. 461 of the French
edition of my *Principles*[1]) is nothing but a confused thought,
aroused in the soul by some motion of the nerves, which
disposes it to the other, clearer, thought which constitutes
rational love. Just as in thirst the sensation of the dryness of
the throat is a confused thought which disposes to the desire
for drink, but is not identical with that desire; so, in love a
mysterious heat is felt around the heart, and a great abundance of blood in the lungs, which make us open our arms
as if to embrace something, and this makes the soul join to
itself in volition the object presented to it. But the thought
by which the soul feels the heat is different from the thought
which joins it to the object; and sometimes it happens that
the sensation of love occurs in us without our will being
impelled to love anything, because we do not discover any
object we think worthy of it. It can also happen on the other
hand that we are aware of a most worth-while good, and join

[1] AT viii. 321; HR i. 294.

ourselves to it in volition, without having any corresponding passion, because the body is not appropriately disposed.

Commonly, however, these two loves occur together; because the two are so linked that when the soul judges an object to be worthy of it, this immediately disposes the heart to the motions which excite the passion of love; and when the heart is similarly disposed by other causes, that makes the soul imagine lovable qualities in objects in which, at another time, it would see nothing but faults. There is no reason to be surprised that certain motions of the heart should be naturally connected in this way with certain thoughts, which they in no way resemble. The soul's natural capacity for union with a body brings with it the possibility of an association between thoughts and bodily motions or conditions so that when the same conditions recur in the body they impel the soul to the same thought; and conversely when the same thought recurs, it disposes the body to return to the same condition. In the same way when we learn a language, we connect the letters or the pronunciation of certain words, which are material things, with their meanings, which are thoughts; and then when we later hear the same words we conceive the same things, and when we conceive the same things, we remember the same words.

But there is no doubt that the bodily conditions that were the first to accompany our thoughts when we came into the world, must have become more closely connected with them than those which accompany them later. This will help to explain the origin of the heat felt around the heart, and the other bodily conditions that accompany love. I observe that it is probable that at the first moment of the soul's union with the body it felt joy, and immediately after love, then perhaps also hatred, and sadness; and that the same bodily conditions which then caused those passions, have ever since naturally accompanied the corresponding thoughts. I think that the soul's first passion was joy, because it is not credible that it was put in the body at a time when the body was not in a good condition; and a good condition of the body naturally gives us joy. I say that love followed because the matter of our body is in a perpetual flux like the water in a stream, and there is always need for new matter to take its place, so that it is scarcely likely that the body would have been in a good condition unless there were nearby some matter suitable for food. The soul, uniting itself in volition to that new matter, felt love for it; and, later, if the food happened to be lacking, it felt sadness. And if its place was taken by some other matter unfit to nourish the body, it felt hatred.

Those four passions, I think, were the first we felt, and the only ones we felt before our birth. I think they were then only sensations or very confused thoughts, because the soul was so attached to matter that it could not do anything except receive impressions from the body. Some years later it began to have other joys and other loves besides those which depend only on the body's being in a good condition and suitably nourished, but none the less, the intellectual element in its joys or loves has always been accompanied by the first sensations which it had of them, and even the motions or natural functions which then took place in the body. Before birth love was caused only by suitable nourishment, which entered in abundance into the liver, heart, and lungs and produced an increase of heat: this is the reason why similar heat still always accompanies love, even though it comes from other very different causes. If I were not afraid of boring you I could show in detail how all the other bodily conditions which at the beginning of our life occurred with these four passions still accompany them. But I will only say that it is because of these confused sensations of our childhood, which continue connected to the rational thoughts by which we love what we judge worthy of love, that the nature of love is difficult for us to understand. And I may add that many other passions, such as joy, sadness, desire, fear, and hope, mingle in various ways with love and thus prevent us from discovering exactly what constitutes it. This is particularly noticeable in the case of desire, which is so commonly taken for love, that people have distinguished two sorts of love: one called *love of benevolence*, in which desire is less apparent, and *love of concupiscence*, which is simply a very strong desire, founded on a love which is often weak.

To treat fully of this passion would take a large volume,

and though its nature is to make one very communicative, so that it incites me to try to tell you more than I know, I must restrain myself for fear this letter may become tediously long. So I pass to your second question, whether the light of nature by itself teaches us to love God, and whether one can love him by the power of that light alone.

I see two strong reasons for doubting that one can. The first is that the attributes of God most commonly considered are so high above us that we do not see at all how they can be fitting for us, and so we do not join ourselves to them in volition. The second is that nothing about God can be visualized by the imagination, which makes it seem that although one might have an intellectual love for Him, one could not have any sensuous love, because it would have to pass through the imagination if it was to reach from the understanding into the senses. Consequently I am not surprised that some philosophers are convinced that the only thing which makes us capable of loving God is the Christian religion, which teaches the mystery of the Incarnation in which God so humbled Himself as to make Himself like us. They say too that those who appear to have had a passion for some divinity without knowing about the Incarnation have not loved the true God, but only some idols to which they gave His name; just as the poets tell us that Ixion embraced a cloud by mistake for the Queen of the gods.

None the less, I have no doubt at all that we can truly love God by the sole power of our nature. I do not assert that this love is meritorious without grace—I leave the theologians to unravel that—but I make bold to say that with regard to the present life it is the most delightful and useful passion possible and can even be the strongest, though not unless we meditate very attentively since we are continually distracted by the presence of other objects.

In my view, the way to reach the love of God is to consider that He is a mind, or thinking substance; and that our soul's nature resembles His sufficiently for us to believe that it is an emanation of His supreme intelligence, *a breath of divine spirit*.[1] Our knowledge seems to be able to grow by

[1] *divinae quasi particula aurae* (Horace, *Satires* II ii. 79).

degrees to infinity, and since God's knowledge is infinite, He is at the point towards which ours strives; and if we considered nothing more than this, we might be so absurd as to wish to be gods, and thus make the disastrous mistake of loving divinity instead of loving God. But we must also take account of the infinity of His power, by which He has created so many things of which we are only a tiny part; and of the extent of His providence, which makes Him see with a single thought all that has been, all that is, all that will be, and all that can be; and of the infallibility of His decrees, which are altogether immutable even though they respect our free will. We must weigh our smallness against the greatness of the created universe. We must reflect how all creatures depend on God, and conceive them in a manner proper to His omnipotence instead of rolling them up in a ball like the people who insist that the world is finite. If a man meditates on these things and understands them properly he is filled with extreme joy. Far from being so injurious and ungrateful to God as to want to take His place, he thinks that the knowledge with which God has favoured him is enough by itself to make his life worthwhile. Uniting himself entirely to God in volition, he loves Him so perfectly that he desires nothing at all except that His will should be done. Henceforth, because he knows that nothing can befall him which God has not decreed he no longer fears death, pain or disgrace. He so loves God's decree, he esteems it so just and so necessary, and is so fully aware of the need to subject himself to it, that even if he expects it to bring death or some other evil, he would not will to change it even if, *per impossibile*, he could do so. He does not refuse evils and afflictions because they come to him from divine providence; still less does he refuse the permissible goods or pleasures he may enjoy in this life since they too come from God. He accepts them with joy, without any fear of evils, and his love makes him perfectly happy.

It is true that the soul must be very detached from the traffic of the senses if it is to represent to itself the truths which arouse such a love. That is why it appears that it cannot communicate this love to the imaginative faculty so as to make it a passion. None the less, I think it can be done.

Although we cannot imagine anything in God, who is the
object of our love, we can imagine our love itself, which
consists in our wanting to unite ourselves to some object.
That is, we can consider ourselves in relation to God as
a minute part of all the immensity of the created universe.
Since objects differ from each other, there are different ways
of uniting oneself to them or uniting them to oneself; and
the idea of such a union by itself is sufficient to produce heat
around the heart and cause a violent passion.

It is true that the custom of our speech and the courtesy of
good manners does not allow us to tell those whose condition
is far above ours that we love them; we may say only that
we respect, honour, esteem them, and that we have zeal and
devotion for their service. I think that the reason for this is
that friendship between human beings makes those in
whom it is reciprocated in some way equal to each other, and
so if, while trying to secure the goodwill of some great
person, one said that one loved him, he might think that one
was treating him as an equal and so doing him wrong. But
philosophers are not accustomed to give different names to
things which share the same definition, and I know no other
definition of love save that it is a passion which makes us
unite in volition to some object no matter whether the
object is equal or greater or less than us. So it seems to me
that if I am to speak philosophically I must say that it is
possible to love God.

And if I asked you frankly whether you love that great
Queen at whose court you now are, it would be useless for
you to say that you had only respect, veneration, and admiration for her; I would judge none the less that you have also
a very ardent affection for her. You write so fluently when
you speak of her that although I believe all you say, because I
know that you are very truthful and I have also heard others
speak of her, still I do not believe that you could describe her
as you do if you did not have a great affection for her, and I
do not think you could be in the presence of so great a light
without being somewhat warmed by it as well.

It is not at all the case that the love which we have for
objects above us is less than that which we have for other
objects. I think that by nature such love is more perfect,

and makes one embrace with greater ardour the interests of the beloved. It is the nature of love to make one consider oneself and the loved one as a single whole of which one is a part; and to transfer the care one previously took of oneself to the preservation of this whole. One keeps for oneself only a part of one's care, a part which is great or little in proportion to whether one thinks oneself a larger or smaller part of the whole to which one has given one's affection. So that if we are joined in volition to an object which we regard as less than ourself—for instance, if we love a flower, a bird, a building or something similar—the highest perfection which this love can properly reach cannot make us put our life at any risk for the preservation of its objects. They are not more noble parts of the whole which we and they constitute than are our nails or our hair; and it would be absurd to risk the whole body for the preservation of the hair. But when two human beings love each other, charity requires that each of the two should value his friend above himself; and so their friendship is not perfect unless each is ready to say in favour of the other *It is I who did the deed, I am here, turn your swords against me.*[1] Similarly, when an individual is joined in volition to his prince, or to his country, if his love is perfect, he should esteem himself as only a tiny part of the whole which he and they constitute. He should be no more afraid to go to certain death for their service than one is afraid to draw a little blood from one's arm to improve the health of the rest of the body. Every day we see examples of this love, even in persons of low condition, who give their lives cheerfully for the good of their country or for the defence of some great person they are fond of. From all this it is obvious that our love for God should be, beyond comparison, the greatest and most perfect of all our loves.

I have no fear that these metaphysical thoughts hold any difficulty for your mind, because I know that nothing is beyond its capacity; but I must confess that my mind is easily tired by them and that the presence of sensible objects does not allow me to dwell on such thoughts for long. So I pass to your third question, whether love or hatred is worse if uncontrolled. I find it more difficult to answer this than

---

[1] *Me me adsum qui feci, in me convertite ferrum* (Virgil, *Aeneid* ix. 427).

the other two, since you have explained less clearly what you mean. The question can be understood in two senses which I think should be examined separately. One passion might be called worse than another because it makes us less virtuous; or because it is more of an obstacle to our happiness; or because it carries us to greater excesses, and disposes us to do more harm to other people.

The first point I find doubtful. If I attend to the definitions of the two passions, I consider that love for an undeserving object can make us worse than hatred for an object we should love; because there is more danger in being united with, and almost transformed into, a thing which is bad than there is in being separated in volition from one which is good. But if I pay attention to the inclinations or habits which arise from these passions, I change my mind. Love, however disordered, has always goodness for its object, and so it seems that it cannot so corrupt our morals as hatred whose only object is evil. We see by experience that the best people, if they are obliged to hate someone, become evil by degrees; because even if their hatred is just, they so often call to mind the evils they receive from their enemy, and the evils they wish him, that they become gradually accustomed to evil. Contrariwise, those who give in to love, even if their love is disordered and frivolous, often become more decent and virtuous than they would if they turned their mind to other thoughts.

I do not find any difficulty in the second point. Hatred is always accompanied with sadness and grief; and if some people take pleasure in doing harm to others, I think their delight is like that of the demons, who, according to our religion, are no less damned even though they continually imagine themselves to be revenged on God by tormenting human beings in Hell. Love, on the contrary, however, disordered it may be, gives pleasure; and though the poets often complain of it in their verses, I think that men would naturally give up loving if they did not find it more sweet than bitter. All the afflictions which are blamed on love come from the other passions which accompany it, from rash desires and ill-founded hopes.

But if I am asked which of the two passions carries us to

greater excesses, and makes us capable of doing more harm
to other men, I think I must say that it is love. It has by
nature much more power and strength than hatred; and
often affection for an unimportant object causes incomparably more evils than the hatred of a more valuable one
could ever do. I can show that hatred has less vigour than
love by a consideration of the origin of each. As I said earlier
our first sensations of love arose because our heart was
receiving suitable food in abundance, and our first sensations
of hatred were caused by a harmful nourishment reaching
the heart, and the same motions still accompany the same
passions. If this is so, it is evident that when we love, all
the purest blood in our veins flows in abundance towards the
heart, which sends many animal spirits to the brain, and so
gives us more power, more strength and more courage; on
the other hand if we feel hatred, the bitterness of gall and the
sourness of the spleen, mixes with our blood and diminishes
and weakens the spirits going to the brain, and so we become
feebler, colder, and more timid. Experience confirms what I
say; because heroes like Hercules and Roland love more
ardently than other men; and contrariwise people who are
weak and cowardly are more inclined to hatred. Anger can
indeed make a man bold, but it borrows its strength from
the love of self, which is always its foundation, and not from
the hatred which is merely an accompaniment. Despair also
calls forth great efforts of courage, and fear can lead to great
cruelties; but there is a difference between these passions
and hatred.

I still have to show that love for an unimportant object, if
disordered, can cause more evil than hatred for another
more valuable. My argument for this is that the evil arising
from hatred extends only to the hated object, whereas
disordered love spares nothing but its object, which
commonly is very small in comparison with all the other
things which it is ready to abandon and destroy to season its
violence. It might perhaps be said that hatred is the proxi-
mate cause of the evils attributed to love because if we love
something we *eo ipso* hate whatever is contrary to it. But
even so love is more to blame than hatred for the evils
which come about in this way, because it is the first cause,

and the love of a single object can give rise in this way to hatred for many. Moreover, the greatest evils of love are not those which are committed through the intermediary of hatred; the chief and most dangerous are those which are done or permitted for the sole pleasure of one's beloved or oneself. I remember an outburst of Theophile, which could be used as an instance: he makes a person mad with love say:

> Dieux, que le beau Paris eut une belle proye
> Que cet Amant fit bien
> Alors qu'il alluma l'embrazement de Troye
> Pour amortir le sien[1]

This shows that even the greatest and most tragic disasters can be, as I have said, seasoning for a disordered love, and make it more delicious the more they raise its price. I do not know if my thoughts on this will accord with yours; but I assure you that they accord in this that as you have promised me great goodwill, so I am with a very ardent passion, etc.

In 1647 the head of the theological college at Leyden caused theses to be defended in a public disputation to the effect that Cartesianism was atheistical. Descartes wrote to protest to the Curators of the university.

## From the letter to the Curators of Leyden University, 4 May 1647[2]

... I have been told that at the disputation, when the opponent[3] asked the respondent and the chairman from what passage in my writings they could prove that I hold God

---

[1] Gods, what a fine victim fine Paris had. How splendidly that lover did, when he lit the fires of Troy to quench his own. *Stances pour Mademoiselle de M. . . .* by Theophile.

[2] AT v. 1; AM vii. 287; in Latin; extract.

[3] The person whose function in the disputation was to attack the theses and defend Descartes.

to be a deceiver, the first passage which they cited and kept on bringing up was the following from p. 13 of my Meditations. 'I will suppose then, not that there is a supremely good God, the source of truth, but that there is an evil spirit, who is supremely powerful and intelligent, and does his utmost to deceive me.' Immediately the opponent showed that in that passage I expressly distinguished between the supremely good God, the source of truth on the one hand, and the evil spirit on the other. He denied that I wanted to hold (there was here no question of that) or even suppose the supremely good God to be a deceiver, and said that I had made this supposition instead about the evil genius. I could not do otherwise, he said, since I had added that God was the source of truth, mentioning an attribute of his that was incompatible with deception. They replied that I had called the deceiver supremely powerful, and that no one was supremely powerful except the true God. At this reply I could exclaim that they must hold all the demons, all the idols, all the gods of the heathen to be the true God or gods, since in the description of any one of them there will be found some attribute which in reality belongs only to God. And I could rightly add that this was a horrible and impious blasphemy, especially as it is no mere supposition but an assertion scandalously taught in a public lecture hall in support of a calumny. But I will merely say that since I knew that good needs a faultless cause while evil follows any defect, and since the context demanded the supposition of an extremely powerful deceiver, I made a distinction between the good God and the evil spirit, and taught that if *per impossibile* there were such an extremely powerful deceiver, he would not be the good God, since he would have the defect entailed by deceitfulness, and could only be regarded as some malign spirit. My use of this supposition cannot be criticized on the grounds that evils are not to be done that good may come; for such a supposition has no moral evil or goodness in it except in virtue of the purpose it serves, because it is an act of the intellect and not of the will, and shows the more that we neither believe it nor want it believed. Now my purpose was excellent, because I was using the supposition only for the better overthrow of scepticism and atheism, and to prove that God is no deceiver, and to establish that as the foundation of all human certitude. Indeed I dare to boast, that there is no single mortal who can less justly and less plausibly be accused of holding God as a deceiver than myself; because nobody before me, whose writings have survived, has so expressly, so earnestly and so carefully proved that the true God is no deceiver. . . .

## Descartes to Chanut, 6 June 1647[1]

Sir,

As I was passing through this place[2] on my way to France I learnt from M. Brasset that he had sent your letters for me to Egmond, and although my journey was urgent, I decided to wait for them; but as they reached my house three hours after I had left they were sent on to me immediately. I read them with avidity, and discovered in them great proofs of your friendship and your tact. I was alarmed when I read in the first pages that M. du Rier had spoken to the Queen of one of my letters and that she had asked to see it. Later, when I reached the place where you say that she heard it with some satisfaction, I was greatly relieved. I do not know whether I was more overcome with admiration at her so easily understanding what learned men find obscure, or with joy that she did not find it displeasing. But my admiration doubled when I saw the force and weight of her objections to the size which I attributed to the Universe. I wish that your letter had found me in my normal abode because the problem is so difficult and so judiciously posed that I would perhaps have unravelled it better in a place where I could collect my thoughts than in the chamber of an inn. But I do not want to use this as an excuse, and I will try to write all I can say on this topic, provided I may be allowed to think that it is to you alone that I am writing, so that my imagination may not be too clouded by veneration and respect.

[1] AT v. 50; AM vii. 435; in French; complete.     [2] The Hague.

In the first place I recollect that the Cardinal of Cusa and many other Doctors have supposed the world to be infinite without ever being censured by the Church; on the contrary, to represent God's works as very great is thought to be a way of doing Him honour. And my opinion is not as difficult to accept as theirs, because I do not say that the world is infinite, but only that it is indefinitely great. There is quite a notable difference between the two: for we cannot say that something is infinite without an argument to prove this such as we can only give in the case of God himself; but we can say that a thing is indefinitely large, provided that we have no argument to prove that it has bounds. Now it seems to me that it is impossible to prove or even to conceive that there are bounds to the matter of which the world is made. For when I examine the nature of this matter I find it to consist merely in its extension in length, breadth and depth, so that whatever has these three dimensions is a part of this matter; and there cannot be any completely empty space, that is, space containing no matter, because we cannot conceive such a space without conceiving in it these three dimensions and consequently matter. Now if we suppose the world to be finite we are imagining that beyond its bounds there are some spaces which are three dimensional and so not altogether imaginary as the philosophers' jargon has it. These spaces must contain matter; and this matter cannot be anywhere but in the world, and this shows that the world extends beyond the bounds we tried to assign to it. Having then no argument to prove, and not even being able to conceive, that the world has bounds, I call it indefinitely large. But I cannot deny that there may be some reasons which are known to God though incomprehensible to me; that is why I do not say outright that it is infinite.

If we consider the extension of the world in this way and then compare it with its duration, I think the only thought it occasions is that there is no imaginable time before the creation of the world in which God could not have created it if He had so willed. I do not think that we have any grounds for concluding that he really did create it an indefinitely long time ago. Because the actual or real existence of the world during these last five or six thousand years is not necessarily connected with the possible or imaginary existence which it might have had before then, in the way that the actual existence of the spaces conceived as surrounding a globe (i.e. surrounding the world as supposed finite) is connected with the actual existence of the same globe. Moreover, if it were possible to infer the eternal past duration of the world from its indefinite extension, it would be even more possible to infer it from its eternal future duration. Faith teaches us that although Heaven and Earth will pass away, that is will change their appearance, none the less the world, that is to say the matter of which they are made, will never pass away. This is clear from the promise of eternal life for our bodies, and consequently for the world in which they will exist, after the Resurrection. But no one infers from the infinite future duration due to the world that it must have been created from all eternity; because every moment of its duration is independent of every other.

The prerogatives which religion attributes to human beings need some explanation, since they seem difficult to believe in, if the extension of the universe is supposed indefinitely great. We may say that all created things were made for us in the sense that we may derive some utility from them; but I do not know that we are obliged to believe that man is the end of Creation. On the contrary, it is said that all things were made for his (God's) sake; God alone is the final as well as the efficient cause of the universe. And since creatures serve each other, any of them might ascribe to itself a privileged position and consider that whatever is useful to it was made for its sake.

The six days of creation are indeed described in Genesis in such a way as to make man appear its principal object; but it could be said that the story in Genesis was written for man and so it is chiefly the things which concern him that the Holy Spirit wished particularly to narrate, and that indeed He did not speak of anything except in its relationship to man. Preachers, striving to incite us to the love of God, often lay before us the various benefits we derive from other creatures and say that God made them for us; they do not consider the other ends for which He might be said to have

made them because this would be irrelevant to their purpose. This makes us very inclined to believe that God made
all these things for us alone. But preachers go even further:
they say that each man in particular owes gratitude to Jesus
Christ for all the blood which He shed on the Cross, just
as if He had died merely for a single man. What they say is
indeed true; but it does not mean that He did not redeem
with the same blood a very large number of other men. In
the same way I do not see that the mystery of the Incarnation,
and all the other favours God has done to men, rule out His
having done an infinity of other great favours to an infinity
of other creatures.

I do not on that account infer that there are intelligent
creatures in the stars or elsewhere, but I do not see either
that there is any argument to prove that there are not. I
always leave questions of this kind undecided, rather than
deny or assert anything about them.

The only difficulty, I think, which remains is that we have
long believed that man has great advantages over other
creatures, and it looks as if we lose them all when we change
our opinion. But we must distinguish between those of our
goods which can be lessened through others possessing the
like, and those which cannot be so lessened. A man who
had a thousand pistoles would be very rich if there was no
one else in the world with so much; and the same man would
be very poor if everyone else had much more. Similarly, all
praiseworthy qualities give more glory to those who have
them, the less people share them; that is why we commonly
envy the glory and riches of others. But virtue, knowledge,
health, and in general all other goods considered in themselves without regard to glory, are no way lessened in us
through being found in many others; and so we have no
grounds for being distressed because they are shared by
others.

Now the goods which could belong to all the intelligent
creatures in an indefinitely large world belong to this class;
they do not diminish those we possess. On the contrary,
when we love God and through Him unite ourselves in
volition to all the things He has created, then the more
great, noble, and perfect we reckon them, the more highly

we esteem ourselves as being parts of a more perfect whole, and the more grounds we have for praising God on account of the immensity of His works. When scripture speaks in many places of the innumerable multitudes of angels it entirely confirms this view; because we regard the least of the angels as incomparably more perfect than men. This is also confirmed by the astronomers when they measure the size of the stars and find them very much bigger than the earth. For if the indefinite extension of the world gives ground for inferring that there must be inhabitants of places other than earth, so does the extension which all the astronomers attribute to it; for every one of them judges that the earth is smaller in comparison with the whole of heaven than a grain of sand in comparison with a mountain.

I now pass to your question about the reasons which often impel us to love one person rather than another before we know their worth. I can discover two, one belonging to the mind and one to the body. The one in the mind pre-supposes too many things concerning the nature of our souls which I would not dare to try to explain in a letter, so I will speak only of the one in the body. It consists in the disposition of the parts of our brain, produced by sense objects or by some other cause. The objects which strike our senses by means of the nerves move certain parts of our brain, and make there certain folds. These folds undo themselves when the object ceases to operate, but the place where they were made afterwards has a tendency to be folded again in the same manner by another object resembling even incompletely the original object. For instance, when I was a child, I loved a little girl of my own age, who had a slight squint. The impression made by sight in my brain when I looked at her cross eyes became so closely connected to the simultaneous impression arousing in me the passion of love, that for a long time afterwards when I saw cross-eyed persons I felt a special inclination to love them simply because they had that defect. At that time I did not know that was the reason for my love; and as soon as I reflected on it and recognized that it was a defect, I was no longer affected by it. So, when we are inclined to love someone without knowing the reason, we may believe that this is because he has some similarity to something in an earlier object of our love, though we may not be able to identify it. Though it is more commonly a perfection than a defect which thus attracts our love, yet, since it can sometimes be a defect as in the example I quoted, a wise man will not altogether yield to such a passion without having considered the worth of the person to whom he thus feels drawn. But because we cannot love equally all those in whom we observe equal worth, I think that our only obligation is to esteem them equally; and since the chief good of life is the possession of friends, we are right to prefer those to whom we are drawn by secret inclinations, provided that we also see worth in them. Moreover, when these secret inclinations are caused by something in the mind and not by something in the body, I think they should always be followed. The principal criterion by which they can be detected is that those which come from the mind are reciprocated, which is not often the case in the others. But the proofs which I have of your affection give me such assurance that my inclination towards you is reciprocated that I would have to be entirely ungrateful, and disobedient to all the rules of friendship, if I were not with much zeal etc.

Descartes spent the summer of 1647 in Paris, where he was awarded a pension by the King of France, which he never drew, and was reconciled with Gassendi.

## Descartes to Christine of Sweden, 20 November 1647[1]

Madame,

I learn from M. Chanut that it pleases your Majesty that I should have the honour to expound to you my view of the

[1] AT v. 81; AM vii. 342; in French; complete.

supreme good understood in the sense of the ancient philosophers. I count this command such a great favour that my desire to obey it turns away all other thoughts; so without making excuses for my insufficiency I will put in a few words all that I have been able to discover on the topic.

The goodness of each thing can be considered in itself without reference to anything else, and in this sense it is evident that God is the supreme good, since He is incomparably more perfect than any creature. But goodness can also be considered in relation to ourselves, and in this sense I do not see anything which we can esteem good unless it somehow belongs to us and makes us more perfect. Thus, the ancient philosophers, unenlightened by the light of faith and knowing nothing about supernatural beatitude, considered only the goods we can possess in this life; and what they were trying to discover was which of these is the supreme, that is, the chief and greatest good.

In trying to decide this, my first observation is that we should not consider as good, in relation to ourselves, anything which we do not possess and is not in our power to acquire. Once this is agreed, it seems to me that the supreme good of all men together is the total or aggregate of all the goods, of soul, of body and of fortune, which can belong to any human being; but that the supreme good of each individual is quite a different thing, and consists only in a firm will to do well and the contentment which this produces. My reason for this is that I can discover no other good which seems so great or so entirely within each man's power. For the goods of the body and of fortune do not depend absolutely upon us; and those of the soul can be all reduced to two heads, the one being to know, and the other to will, what is good. But knowledge is often beyond our powers, and so there remains only our will of which we can dispose outright. I do not see that it is possible to dispose it better than by a regular and constant resolution to carry out to the letter whatever one judges best, and to employ all the powers of one's mind in informing this judgement. This by itself constitutes all the virtues; this alone really deserves praise and glory; this alone, finally, produces the greatest and most solid contentment of life.

So I conclude that it is this which constitutes the supreme good.

In this way I think I can reconcile the most opposed and famous opinions of the ancient philosophers, that of Zeno who thought virtue or honour the supreme good, and that of Epicurus, who thought the supreme good was contentment, to which he gave the name of pleasure. All vices arise only from the uncertainty and weakness consequent on ignorance —and virtue consists only in the resolution and vigour with which a man is inclined to do the things which he thinks good—this vigour, of course, must not stem from stubbornness, but from the consciousness of having examined the matter as well as one morally can. What a man does after such examination may be bad, but none the less he can be sure of having done his duty; whereas, if he does a virtuous action thinking he is doing wrong, or takes no trouble to find out whether he is doing right or wrong, he is not acting like a virtuous man. As for honour and praise, these are often awarded to the other goods of fortune; but because I am sure that your Majesty values virtue more than her crown, I shall not hesitate to express my opinion that nothing except virtue really deserves praise. All other goods deserve only to be esteemed and not to be honoured or praised, except in so far as they are supposed to have been acquired or obtained from God by the good use of free will. For honour and praise is a kind of reward, and only what depends on the will provides grounds for reward or punishment.

I still have to show that the good use of free will is what produces the greatest and most solid happiness in life. This does not seem difficult if we consider carefully what constitutes pleasure, or delight, and in general all the happinesses we can have. I observe first that all of them are entirely within the soul, though many of them depend on the body; just as it is the soul that sees, though through the medium of the eyes. Next I observe that there is nothing that can content the soul except its belief that it possesses some good, and that often this belief is only a very confused representation in the soul. Moreover, the soul's union with the body causes it commonly to represent certain goods to itself as being incomparably greater than they are; but if it knew distinctly their just value, its contentment would always be in proportion to the greatness of the good from which it proceeded. I observe also that the greatness of a good, in relation to us, should not be measured only by the value of the thing which constitutes it but principally also by the manner in which it is related to us. Now freewill is in itself the noblest thing we can have because it makes us in a certain manner equal to God and exempts us from being his subjects; and so its rightful use is the greatest of all the goods we possess, and further there is nothing that is more our own or that matters more to us. From all this it follows that nothing but freewill can produce our greatest contentments. Thus we see that the repose of mind and interior satisfaction felt by those who know they never fail to do their best is a pleasure incomparably sweeter, more lasting and more solid than all those which come from elsewhere.

I omit here many other things, because when I call to mind how much business is involved in ruling a great Kingdom, and how much of it your Majesty attends to in person, I do not dare to ask for longer audience. But I am sending to M. Chanut some papers in which I have expressed my sentiments on the matter at greater length.[1] If it pleases your Majesty to look at them, he will oblige me by presenting them to her, and show that I am etc.

## From the letter to [Silhon], March 1648[2]

. . . First, then, I must tell you that I hold that there is a certain quantity of motion in the whole of created matter, which never increases or diminishes; and thus, when one body moves another, it loses as much of its own motion as it gives to the other. Thus, when a stone falls to earth from above, if it stops and does not rebound, I think that this is because it moves the earth, and thus transfers to it its motion.

---

[1] These were the letters to Elizabeth translated above, pp. 164–181.
[2] AT v. 133; AM viii. 19; in French; complete.

But if the earth it moves contains a thousand times more matter, when it transfers its motion it gives it only a thousandth of its velocity. So if two unequal bodies receive the same amount of motion as each other, this same amount of motion does not confer as much velocity on the greater as it does on the lesser; and so it can be said in this sense that the more matter a body contains the more natural inertia it has. To this one may add that a large body can transfer its motion more easily to other bodies than a small one can, and can less easily be moved by them. So there is one sort of inertia, which depends on the quantity of the matter, and another which depends upon the extension of the surfaces.

You have yourself, it seems to me, given a good answer to your other question about the nature of our knowledge of God in the beatific vision: you distinguish it from our present knowledge in virtue of its being intuitive. If this term does not satisfy you, and if you think that an intuitive knowledge of God will be similar to ours or different only in extent and not in the manner of knowing, that is where, in my opinion, you go wrong. Intuitive knowledge is an illumination of the mind, by which it sees in the light of God whatever it pleases Him to show it by a direct impress of the divine clarity on our understanding, which in this is not considered as an agent but simply as a receiver of the rays of divinity. Whatever we can know of God in this life, short of a miracle, is the result of reasoning and discursive inquiry. It may be deduced from the principles of faith, which is obscure, or it may come from the natural ideas and notions we have, which even at the clearest are only gross and confused on so sublime a topic. Consequently whatever knowledge we have or acquire by way of reason is as dark as the principles from which it is derived and infected with the uncertainty we find in all our reasonings.

Now compare these two kinds of knowledge to see if there is any similarity between such a troubled and doubtful perception, which costs us much labour and which is enjoyed only momentarily once acquired, and a pure, constant, clear, certain, effortless and ever present light.

Can you doubt that our mind, when it is detached from the body, or has a glorified body which will no longer hinder it, can receive such direct illumination and knowledge? Why, even in this body the senses give it such knowledge of corporeal and sensible things, and our soul has already some direct knowledge of the beneficence of our Creator without which it would not be capable of reasoning. I agree that our intuitions are somewhat obscured by the soul's mingling with the body; but still they give us a first, unearned, and certain awareness which we touch with our mind with more confidence than we can give to the sight of our eyes. You will surely admit that you are less certain of the presence of the objects you see than of the truth of the proposition 'I am thinking, therefore I exist'. Now this knowledge is not the work of your reasoning nor information passed on to you by teachers; it is something that your mind sees, feels, and handles; and although your imagination insistently mixes itself up with your thoughts and lessens the clarity of the knowledge, it is nevertheless a proof of the capacity of our soul for receiving intuitive knowledge from God.

I think I can see that what makes you doubtful is your view that an intuitive knowledge of God is one in which God is known by Himself. On this foundation you have built the following argument. 'I know that God is unique, because I know that He is a necessary being; this form of knowledge uses nothing but God Himself; so I know by God Himself that God is unique; and consequently I know intuitively that God is unique.'

I do not think it takes a long examination to show that this argument will not do. You see, to know God by Himself, that is to say by an immediate light cast by the Godhead on our mind, which is what is meant by the expression 'intuitive knowledge', is quite different from using God Himself to make an inference from one attribute to another; or, to speak more accurately, using the natural (and consequently comparatively rather obscure) knowledge of one attribute of God, to construct an argument leading to another attribute of God. So you must admit that in this life you do not see, in God and by His light, that He is unique; but you deduce it from a proposition you have made about Him, and you draw the conclusion by the power of argument, which is a machine which often breaks down. You see what power you have over me, since you make me go beyond the limits I have set for my philosophy, to show you how much I am, etc.

In 1648 Descartes paid another visit to Paris, but found the city in a tumult because of the rising of the Fronde, and soon returned to Holland. While in Paris he received a series of criticisms from an anonymous correspondent, who was in fact Arnauld, following up the themes of the *Fourth Objections*.

## Descartes for [Arnauld], 4 June 1648[1]

The author of the objections which reached me yesterday has chosen to conceal his person and his name: but the better part of him, his mind, cannot remain unknown. This I find to be acute and learned, so that I shall not be ashamed to be worsted in argument or to learn from him. But because he says that he is moved by desire to discover the truth, and not by zeal for argumentation, I shall reply to him here only briefly, and save some things for discussion face to face. I find it safer to treat with argumentative people by letter, but pleasanter to treat with seekers of truth by word of mouth.

I agree with you there are two different powers of memory; but I am convinced that in the mind of an infant there have never been any pure acts of understanding, but only confused sensations. Although these confused sensations leave some traces in the brain, which remain there for life, that does not suffice to enable us to remember them. For that we would have to observe that the sensations which come to us as adults are like those which we had in our mother's womb; and that in turn would require a certain reflexion of the intellect, or intellectual memory, which was not possible in the womb. None the less it seems necessary that the mind should always be actually engaged in thinking; because thought constitutes its essence, just as extension

[1] AT v. 192; AM viii. 45; in Latin; complete.

constitutes the essence of body. Thought must not be conceived as an attribute which can be present or absent like the division of parts, or motion, in a body.

What is said about duration and time rests on the scholastic opinion, with which I strongly disagree, that the duration of motion is of a different kind from that of things which are motionless.[1] I have explained this in article 57 of the first part of the *Principles*.[2] Even if no bodies existed, it could still not be said that the duration of the human mind was entirely simultaneous like the duration of God; because our thoughts display a successiveness which cannot be attributed to the divine thoughts. We can understand clearly that it is possible for me to exist at this moment, while I am thinking of one thing, and yet not to exist at the very next moment, when, if I do exist, I may think of something quite different.

The axiom, *what can do the greater can do the lesser*, seems to be self-evident in the case of first causes that are not otherwise limited; but in the case of a cause determined to a particular effect it is commonly said that it is a greater thing for it to produce some effect other than that to which it is determined and adapted. In that sense it is a greater thing for a man to move the earth from its place than to perform an act of understanding. It is also a greater thing to preserve oneself in existence, than to give oneself some of the perfections one perceives oneself to lack; and this is enough to validate the argument, although it may well be less than to give oneself omnipotence and the other divine perfections all together.

Since the Council of Trent itself was unwilling to explain how the body of Christ is in the Eucharist, and wrote that it was there in a manner of existing which we can scarcely express in words, I should fear the accusation of rashness if I dared to come to any conclusion on the matter; and such conjectures as I make I would prefer to communicate by word of mouth rather than in writing.

---

[1] Arnauld had objected to Descartes' treatment of the duration of the soul in the *Third Meditation* (AT vii. 49; HR i. 168) that the duration of a spiritual being was non-successive.

[2] AT viii. 27; HR i. 242.

Finally, I have hardly anything to say about the void, which is not already to be found somewhere or other in my *Principles of Philosophy*. What you call the hollowness of a barrel seems to me to be a body with three dimensions, not to be identified with the sides of the barrel.[1]

But all these things can be more easily discussed at a meeting, which I would gladly arrange, being the most respectful servant of all men who love honesty and truth.


## Descartes for [Arnauld], 29 July 1648[2]

Recently I was given some objections which appeared to come from an inhabitant of this city. I answered them very briefly, thinking that any omission could easily be remedied in conversation. But now that I realize the writer lives elsewhere,[3] I hasten to reply to his second most courteous letter. Since he conceals his name, I will dispense with any exordium, for fear I commit some solecism in addressing him.

1. It seems to me very true that, as long as the mind is united to the body, it cannot dissociate itself from the senses whenever it is stimulated with greater or less force by external or internal objects. I concede further that it cannot dissociate itself whenever it is attached to a brain which is too soft or damp, as in children, or otherwise ill tempered, as in those who are lethargic, apoplectic, or frenetic, or as in all of us when we are deeply asleep—for whenever we have a dream that we afterwards remember, that means we are sleeping only lightly.

2. If we are to remember something, it is not sufficient that the thing should previously have been before our mind and left some traces in the brain which give occasion for it to come into our thoughts again; it is necessary in addition that we should recognize, when it comes the second time,

[1] Arnauld had suggested that God could destroy the wine in a barrel and leave behind only the hollowness of the barrel without introducing any other substance (AT v. 190).
[2] AT v. 219; AM viii. 71; in Latin; complete.
[3] Arnauld was in banishment at Port-Royal des Champs.

that this is happening because it has already been perceived by us earlier. Thus verses often occur to poets which they do not remember having ever read in other authors, but which would not have occurred to them unless they had read them elsewhere.

From this it is clear that it is not sufficient for memory that there should be traces left in the brain by preceding thoughts. The traces have to be of such a kind that the mind recognizes that they were not always present in us, but were once newly impressed. Now for the mind to recognize this, I think that at their first impression it must have made use of pure intellect to notice that the thing which was then presented to it was new and had not been presented before; because there cannot be any corporeal trace of this novelty. So then, if ever I wrote that the thoughts of children leave no traces in their brain, I meant traces sufficient for memory, that is, traces which at the time of their impression are observed by pure intellection to be new. In a similar way we say that there are no human tracks in the sand if we cannot find any impressions shaped like a human foot, though perhaps there may be many unevennesses made by human feet, which can therefore in another sense be called human tracks. Finally, I make a distinction between direct and reflex thoughts corresponding to the distinction we make between direct and reflex vision, one depending on the first impact of the rays and the other on the second. I call the first and simple thoughts of infants direct and not reflex —for instance, the pain they feel when some wind distends their intestines, or the pleasure they feel when nourished by sweet blood. But when an adult feels something, and simultaneously perceives that he has not felt it before, I call this second perception reflexion, and attribute it to the intellect alone, in spite if its being so linked to sensation that the two occur together and appear to be indistinguishable from each other.

3. I tried to remove the ambiguity of the word 'thought' in articles 63 and 64 of the first part of the *Principles*. Just as extension, which constitutes the nature of body, differs greatly from the various shapes or modes of extension which it may assume; so thought, or a thinking nature,

which I think contributes the essence of the human mind, is far different from any particular act of thinking. It depends on the mind itself whether it produces this or that particular act of thinking, but not that it is a thinking thing; just as it depends on a flame, as an efficient cause, whether it turns to this side or that, but not that it is an extended substance. So by 'thought' I do not mean some universal which includes all modes of thinking, but a particular nature, which takes on those modes, just as extension is a nature which takes on all shapes.

4. Being conscious of our thoughts at the time when we are thinking them is not the same as remembering them afterwards. Thus, we do not have any thoughts in sleep without being conscious of them at the moment they occur; though commonly we forget them immediately. But it is true that we are not conscious of the manner in which our mind sends the animal spirits into particular nerves; because that depends not on the mind alone but on the mind's union with the body. We are however conscious of every action by which the mind moves the nerves in so far as such action is in the mind, where it is simply the inclination of the will towards a particular movement. The inflow of the spirits into the nerves, and everything else necessary for the motion, follows upon this inclination of the will. This happens because of the way the body is constructed, of which the mind may not be aware, and because of the union of the mind with the body, of which it is certainly conscious. Otherwise it would not incline its will to move the limbs.

That the mind, which is incorporeal, can set the body in motion—this is something which is shown to us not by any reasoning or comparison with other matters, but by the surest and plainest everyday experience. It is one of those self evident things which we only make obscure when we try to explain them in terms of others. However, I will use a simile. Most philosophers, who think that the heaviness of a stone is a real quality distinct from the stone, think they understand clearly enough how this quality can impel the stone towards the centre of the earth, because they think that they have a manifest proof from experience of such an occurrence. Now on my view there is no such quality in nature, and consequently there is no real idea of it in the human intellect; and I think that in order to represent this heaviness to themselves they are using the idea they have within them of incorporeal substance. So it is no harder for us to understand how the mind moves the body, than it is for them to understand how such heaviness moves a stone downwards. Of course they deny that heaviness is a substance, but that makes no difference, because they conceive it in fact as a substance since they think that it is real and that it is possible, even if only by Divine power, for it to exist without the stone. Again it makes no difference that they think it is corporeal. For if we count as corporeal whatever belongs to a body, even though not of the same nature as body, then the mind can be called corporeal, since it is made to be united to the body; on the other hand if we regard as corporeal only what has the nature of body, then this heaviness is no more corporeal than the human mind is.

5. I conceive the successive duration of things that move, and of motion itself, no differently from that of things that do not move; for earlier and later in any duration are known to me by the earlier and later of the successive duration I detect in my own thought, with which other things co-exist.

6. The difficulty in recognizing the impossibility of the vacuum seems to arise primarily because we do not sufficiently consider that nothing can have no properties; otherwise, seeing that there is true extension in the space we call void, and consequently all the properties necessary for the nature of body, we would not say that it was wholly void, that is, mere nothingness. Secondly, it arises because we take refuge in the power of God, which we know to be infinite; we attribute to it an effect without noticing that it involves a contradictory concept and is thus inconceivable by us. But I do not think that we should ever say of anything that it cannot be brought about by God. For since everything involved in truth and goodness depends on His omnipotence, I would not dare to say that God cannot make a mountain without a valley, or that one and two should not be three. I merely say that He has given me such a mind that I cannot conceive a mountain without a valley, or an aggregate of one and two which is not three, and that such things involve a

contradiction in my conception. I think the same should be said of a space which is wholly void, or of an extended piece of nothing, or of a limited universe; because no limit to the world can be conceived, without my conceiving extension outside it; and no barrel can be conceived to be so empty as to have inside it no extension, and therefore no body; for wherever extension is, there, of necessity, is body also.

On his return to Holland Descartes received a laudatory letter from the Cambridge Platonist Henry More, who welcomed him as an ally against the materialism of Hobbes, but felt misgivings about the cosmology of the Second Part of the *Principles*.

## Descartes to More, 5 February 1649[1]

Sir,

The praises which you heap on me are proofs rather of your kindness, than of any merit of mine, which could never equal them. Such goodness, however, based on the mere reading of my writings, displays so clearly the candour and nobility of your mind, that though unacquainted with you hitherto I have been completely captivated. So I will answer very willingly the queries which you put to me.

1. The first question was why I defined body as extended substance, rather than perceptible, tangible, or impenetrable substance. It is clear that if body is called perceptible substance, it is defined by its relation to our senses, and thus we explain only a certain property of it, rather than its whole nature. This certainly does not depend upon our senses since it could exist even though there were no men, and so I do not see why you say that it is altogether necessary that all matter should be perceptible by the senses. Just the opposite is the case: all matter is completely imperceptible if it is divided into parts much smaller than the particles of our

[1] AT v. 267; AM viii. 121; in Latin; complete.

nerves and the individual parts are given a sufficiently rapid movement.

The argument of mine which you call cunning and almost sophistical I used only to refute the opinion of those who like you think that every body is perceptible by the senses.[1] I think it does give a clear and definitive refutation of that view. For a body can retain its whole bodily nature without being soft or hard or cold or hot to the feeling, and without having any quality perceptible by the senses. You make a comparison with wax, which although it can be not square and not round cannot be completely without shape. But since according to my principles, all perceptible qualities consist solely in the fact that the particles of a body are in motion or at rest in a certain manner, in order to fall into the error which you seem to attribute to me here, I would have had to say that a body could exist without any of its particles being either at motion or at rest. But this is something which never entered my mind. Body, therefore, is not rightly defined as perceptible substance.

Let us see next whether body if more appropriately called impenetrable, or tangible substance, in the sense which you explained. Tangibility or impenetrability in a body is something like the ability to laugh in man; according to the common rules of logic it is a property of the fourth kind not a true and essential *differentia* such as I claim extension to be.[2] Consequently, just as man is defined not as a risible animal, but as a rational animal, so body should be defined not by impenetrability but by extension. This is confirmed by the fact that tangibility and impenetrability involve a reference to parts and presuppose the concept of division or termination; whereas we can conceive a continuous body of indeterminate or indefinite size, in which there is nothing to consider except extension.

'But,' you say, 'God, or an angel, or any other self-subsistent thing is extended, and so your definition is too broad.' I never argue about words, and so if someone wants to say that God is in a sense extended, since He is everywhere, I have no objection. But I deny that true extension as

[1] The reference is to *Principles* ii. 4 (AT viii. 42; HR i. 255).
[2] On the four kinds of property, see the *Port Royal Logic*, Part i, ch. vii.

commonly conceived is to be found in God or in angels or in
our mind or in any substance which is not a body. Commonly
when people say that something is extended they mean that
it is imaginable—I leave on one side the question whether,
it is a fictional or real entity—and that it has various parts of
definite size and shape, each of which is non-identical with
the others. These parts can be distinguished in the imagination: some can be imagined as transferred to the place of
others, but no two can be imagined simultaneously in one and
the same place. Nothing of this kind can be said about
God or about our mind; they cannot be imagined, but only
grasped by the intellect; neither of them can be distinguished into parts, and certainly not into parts which have
definite sizes and shapes. Again, we easily understand that
the human mind and God, and several angels can all be at
the same time in one and the same place. So we clearly
conclude that no incorporeal substances are in any strict
sense extended. I conceive them as powers or forces, which
although they can act upon extended substances, are not
themselves extended; just as fire is in white hot iron without
itself being iron. Some people indeed do confuse the notion
of substance with that of extended matter. This is because
of the false prejudice which makes them believe that nothing
can exist or be intelligible without being also imaginable,
and because it is indeed true that nothing falls within the
scope of the imagination without being in some way
extended. Now just as we can say that health belongs only
to human beings, though by analogy medicine and a
temperate climate and many other things also are called
healthy; so too I call extended only what is imaginable and
has parts outside other parts of a determinate size and shape,
although other things also may be called extended by
analogy.

   2. I pass to your second difficulty. If we examine what is
this extended being which I described, we will find that it
is no different from the space which is popularly regarded
sometimes as full and sometimes as empty, sometimes as
real and sometimes as imaginary. For everyone imagines in
space—even imaginary and empty space—various parts of
determinate size and shape, some of which can be transferred

in imagination to the place of others, but no two of which can be conceived as compenetrating each other at the same time in one and the same place, since it is contradictory for this to happen without any piece of space being removed. Now since I believe that such real properties can only exist in a real body, I dared to assert that there can be no completely empty space, and that whatever is extended is a genuine body. On this topic I did not hesitate to disagree with great men such as Epicurus, Democritus, and Lucretius, because I saw that they were guided by no solid reason, but only by the false prejudice with which we have all been imbued from our earliest years. As I warned in the third article of the second part,[1] our senses do not always show us external bodies exactly as they are, but only in so far as they are related to us and can benefit or harm us. Despite this, we all decided when we were still children, that there is nothing in the world beside what the senses show us, and so there are no bodies which are imperceptible, and all places in which we perceive nothing are void. Since Epicurus, Democritus, and Lucretius never overcame this prejudice, I have no obligation to following their authority.

I am surprised that a man otherwise so perspicacious, having seen that he cannot deny that there is some substance in every space, since all the properties of extension are found in it, should none the less prefer to say that the divine extension fills up the space in which there are no bodies, rather than to admit that there can be no space without body. For as I said earlier, the alleged extension of God cannot be the subject of the true properties which we perceive very distinctly in all space. For God is not imaginable nor distinguishable into shaped and measurable parts.

But you are quite ready to admit that in the natural course of events there is no vacuum: you are concerned about God's power, which you think can take away the contents of a container while preventing its sides from meeting. For my part, I know that my intellect is finite and God's power is infinite, and so I set no bounds to it; I consider only what I can conceive and what I cannot conceive, and I take great pains that my judgement should accord with my under-

[1] AT viii. 41; HR i. 255.

standing. And so I boldly assert that God can do everything which I conceive to be possible, but I am not so bold as to deny that He can do whatever conflicts with my understanding—I merely say that it involves a contradiction. And so, since I see that it conflicts with my understanding for all the body to be taken out of a container and for there to remain extension, which I conceive in no way differently from the body which was previously contained in it, I say that it involves a contradiction that such extension should remain there after the body has been taken away. I conclude that the sides of the container must come together; and this is altogether in accord with my other opinions. For I say elsewhere that all motion is in a manner circular; from which it follows that it cannot be clearly understood how God could remove a body from a container without another body, or the sides of the container, moving into its place by a circular motion.

3. In the same way I say that it involves a contradiction that there should be any atoms which are conceived as extended and also indivisible. Though God might make them such that they could not be divided by any creature, we certainly cannot conceive Him able to deprive Himself of the power of dividing them. Your comparison with things which have been done and cannot be undone is not to the point. For we do not take it as a mark of impotence when someone cannot do something we do not understand to be possible, but only when he cannot do something which we distinctly perceive to be possible. Now we certainly perceive it to be possible for an atom to be divided, since we suppose it to be extended; and so, if we judge that it cannot be divided by God, we shall judge that God cannot do one of the things which we perceive to be possible. But we do not in the same way perceive it to be possible for what is done to be undone—on the contrary, we perceive it to be altogether impossible, and so it is no defect of power in God not to do it. The case is different with the divisibility of matter; for though I cannot count all the parts into which it is divisible, and therefore say that the number is indefinite, I cannot assert that their division by God could never be completed, because I know that God can do more things

than I can compass within my thought. Indeed I agreed in article 34,[1] that this indefinite division of parts of matter sometimes actually takes place.

4. In my view it is not a matter of affected modesty, but of necessary caution to say that some things are indefinite rather than infinite. God is the only thing I positively conceive as infinite. As to other things like the extension of the world and the number of parts into which matter is divisible, I confess I do not know whether they are absolutely infinite; I merely know that I can see no end to them, and so, looking at them from my own point of view, I call them indefinite. True, our mind is not the measure of reality or of truth; but certainly it should be the measure of what we assert or deny. What is more absurd or more rash than to want to pass judgement on matters which we admit our mind cannot grasp? I am surprised that you seem to wish to do this when you say that if extension is only infinite in relation to us then it will in fact be finite. Not only this, you imagine some divine extension which goes further than the extension of bodies; and thus you suppose that God has parts side by side and is divisible, and attribute to Him all the essence of corporeal substance.

To remove all difficulty, I should explain that I call the extension of matter indefinite in the hope that this will prevent anyone imagining a place outside it into which the particles of my vortices might escape[2]; for on my view wherever such a place may be conceived there is some matter. When I say that matter is indefinitely extended, I am saying that it extends further than anything a human being can conceive. None the less, I think there is a very great difference between the vastness of this bodily extension and the vastness of God's extension, or rather not extension, since strictly He has none, but substance or essence; and so I call the latter simply infinite, and the former indefinite.

Moreover, I do not agree with what you very kindly concede, namely that the rest of my opinions could stand even if what I have written about the extension of matter were refuted. For it is one of the most important, and I

---

[1] AT viii. 59; HR i. 287.
[2] On vortices, see *Principles* iii, lxv, AT viii. 116; HR i. 274.

believe the most certain, foundations of my physics; and I confess that no reasons satisfy me even in physics unless they involve that necessity which you call logical or analytic,[1] provided you except things which can be known by experience alone, such as that there is only one sun and only one moon around the earth and so on. Since in other matters you are well disposed to my views, I hope that you will come to agree with these too, if you reflect that it is a mere prejudice which makes many people think that an extended entity in which there is nothing to affect the senses is not a true bodily substance but merely an empty space, and that there are no bodies which are not perceptible to the senses, and no substance which does not fall within the scope of imagination and is consequently extended.

5. But there is no prejudice to which we are all more accustomed from our earliest years than the belief that dumb animals think. Our only reason for this belief is the fact that we see that many of the organs of animals are not very different from ours in shape and movement. Since we believe that there is a single principle within us which causes these motions—namely the soul, which both moves the body and thinks—we do not doubt that some such soul is to be found in animals also. I came to realize, however, that there are two different principles causing our motions: one is purely mechanical and corporeal and depends solely on the force of the spirits and the construction of our organs, and can be called the corporeal soul; the other is the incorporeal mind, the soul which I have defined as a thinking substance. Thereupon I investigated more carefully whether the motions of animals originated from both these principles or from one only. I soon saw clearly that they could all originate from the corporeal and mechanical principle, and I thenceforward regarded it as certain and established that we cannot at all prove the presence of a thinking soul in animals. I am not disturbed by the astuteness and cunning of dogs and foxes, or all the things which animals do for the sake of food, sex, and fear; I claim that I can easily explain the origin of all of them from the constitution of their organs.

[1] *contradictoria.*

But though I regard it as established that we cannot prove there is any thought in animals, I do not think it is thereby proved that there is not, since the human mind does not reach into their hearts. But when I investigate what is most probable in this matter, I see no argument for animals having thoughts except the fact that since they have eyes, ears, tongues, and other sense-organs like ours, it seems likely that they have sensation like us; and since thought is included in our mode of sensation, similar thought seems to be attributable to them. This argument, which is very obvious, has taken possession of the minds of all men from their earliest age. But there are other arguments, stronger and more numerous, but not so obvious to everyone, which strongly urge the opposite. One is that it is more probable that worms and flies and caterpillars move mechanically than that they all have immortal souls.

It is certain that in the bodies of animals, as in ours, there are bones, nerves, muscles, animal spirits, and other organs so disposed that they can by themselves, without any thought, give rise to all the animal motions we observe. This is very clear in convulsive movements when the machine of the body moves despite the soul, and sometimes more violently and in a more varied manner than when it is moved by the will.

Second, it seems reasonable, since art copies nature, and men can make various automata which move without thought, that nature should produce its own automata, much more splendid than artificial ones. These natural automata are the animals. This is especially likely since we have no reason to believe that thought always accompanies the disposition of organs which we find in animals. It is much more wonderful that a mind should be found in every human body than that one should be lacking in every animal.

But in my opinion the main reason which suggests that the beasts lack thought is the following. Within a single species some of them are more perfect than others, as men are too. This can be seen in horses and dogs, some of whom learn what they are taught much better than others. Yet, although all animals easily communicate to us, by voice or bodily movement, their natural impulses of anger, fear, hunger and so on, it has never yet been observed that any brute animal reached the stage of using real speech, that is to say, of indicating by word or sign something pertaining to pure thought and not to natural impulse. Such speech is the only certain sign of thought hidden in a body. All men use it, however stupid and insane they may be, and though they may lack tongue and organs of voice; but no animals do. Consequently it can be taken as a real specific difference between men and dumb animals.

For brevity's sake I here omit the other reasons for denying thought to animals. Please note that I am speaking of thought, and not of life or sensation. I do not deny life to animals, since I regard it as consisting simply in the heat of the heart; and I do not deny sensation, in so far as it depends on a bodily organ. Thus my opinion is not so much cruel to animals as indulgent to men—at least to those who are not given to the superstitions of Pythagoras—since it absolves them from the suspicion of crime when they eat or kill animals.

Perhaps I have written at too great length for the sharpness of your intelligence; but I wished to show you that very few people have yet sent me objections which were as agreeable as yours. Your kindness and candour has made you a friend of that most respectful admirer of all who seek true wisdom,

Rene Descartes.

The Queen of Sweden wrote to Descartes in December 1648 to thank him for his long letter about the supreme good. The following is Descartes' reply to her letter and to the news that she had been reading the *Principles*.

## From the letter to Chanut, 26 February 1649[1]

... I received as an altogether undeserved favour the letter which that matchless Princess condescended to write

[1] AT v. 289; AM viii. 146; in French; extract.

to me. I am surprised that she should take the trouble to do
so; but I am not so surprised that she read my *Principles*,
because I am convinced that they contain many truths which
are difficult to find elsewhere. It might be said that they are
only unimportant truths about physics which appear to have
nothing in common with the things a Queen ought to
know. But because her mind is universal in its capacity, and
because those truths of physics are part of the foundations
of the highest and most perfect morality, I dare to hope that
she will derive satisfaction from learning them. I would be
glad to learn that she had chosen you in addition to Frein-
sheimius, to lighten the study for her; and I would be most
grateful to you if you would take the trouble to notify me
of the places where I have not explained myself sufficiently.
I would be careful always to reply to you the same day as I
receive your letters. But this would serve only for my own
information, because it is so far from here to Stockholm, and
the letters go through so many hands before arriving there,
that you could have solved the difficulties for yourselves
before you could have had the solution from here.

    I will merely observe at this point two or three things
which experience has taught me about the *Principles*. The
first is that though the first part is only an abridgement of
what I wrote in my *Meditations*, there is no need to take
time off to read my *Meditations* in order to understand them;
many people find the *Meditations* much more difficult and I
would be afraid that her Majesty might become bored.
The second is that there is no reason to spend a lot of time
examining the rules of motion in article 46 and following of
the Second Part[1]; they are not needed in order to understand
the rest. The last is that it must be remembered, while
reading this book, that although I consider nothing in
bodies except their sizes, their shapes, and the movements
of their parts, I claim none the less to explain the nature of
light and heat and all other sensible qualities; because I
presuppose that these qualities are only in our senses, like
pleasure and pain, and not in the objects which we feel, in
which there are only certain shapes and movements which
cause the sensations called light, heat, etc. This I did not

           [1] AT viii. 68–9; HR i. 268.

explain and prove until the end of the fourth part; none the less it is useful to know and observe it from the beginning of the book, so as to understand it better. . . .

In March 1649 Descartes received an invitation to Sweden to teach philosophy to Queen Christine. He replied guardedly and in a covering letter to Chanut explained some of the reasons for his hesitation.

## From the letter to Chanut, 31 March 1649[1]

. . . Experience has taught me that very few people, even if they have an excellent mind and a great desire for knowledge, can take the time to enter into my thoughts; so that I have no grounds for hoping as much of a Queen who has an infinity of other occupations. Experience has also taught me that although my views are found surprising at first, because they are so different from received opinions, once they are understood they appear so simple and so conformable to common sense, that they are no longer admired or regarded as important. For the nature of man is such that men only value things which they admire and which they do not completely possess. Health is the greatest of all the goods which concern our bodies; but it is the one we least reflect upon and savour. The knowledge of truth is the health of the soul; once a man possesses it he thinks no more of it. Although my greatest desire is to communicate openly and freely to everyone all the little I think I know, I meet hardly anyone who will condescend to learn it. But I see that those who boast of possessing secrets, in chemistry or judicial astrology, however ignorant and impudent they may be, never fail to find curious people who buy their impostures very dearly. . . .

[1] AT v. 326; AM viii. 193; in French; extract.

## Descartes to More, 15 April 1649[1]

Sir,

I have received your welcome letter of 5 March at a time when I am distracted by so much other business that I must either write in haste this very moment, or put off replying for many weeks. I have decided on haste: I prefer to seem lacking in skill than in courtesy.

### REPLY TO THE FIRST INSTANCES

*Some properties are prior to others, etc.*[2]

Being perceptible by the senses seems to be merely an external description of sensible substance. Moreover it is not coextensive with such substance; if it concerns our senses, then it does not apply to the smallest particles of matter; if it concerns other senses such as we might imagine God to construct, it might well apply also to angels and souls. I find it no easier to imagine sensory nerves so fine that they could be moved by the smallest parts of matter than to imagine a faculty enabling our mind to sense or perceive other minds directly. Although in extension we easily understand the relation of parts to each other, yet I seem to conceive extension perfectly well without thinking of the relation of these parts to each other. You should admit this even more readily than I, since you conceive in such a way that it applies to God; and yet you deny any parts in Him.

*It has not been shown that tangibility or impenetrability are properties of extended substance*

If you conceive extension by the relationship of the parts to each other, it seems that you cannot deny that each part touches the others adjacent to it. This tangibility is a real

---

[1] AT v. 340; AM viii. 204; in Latin; with omissions.
[2] Here and below the italicized phrases are quotations from More's letter of 5 March (AT v. 298; AM viii. 154). More had argued that body should be defined in terms of perceptibility rather than extension.

property, intrinsic to a substance, unlike the tangibility which is named after the sense of touch. It is impossible to conceive of one part of extended substance penetrating another equal part without *eo ipso* thinking that half the total extension is taken away or annihilated; but what is annihilated does not penetrate anything else; and so, in my opinion, impenetrability can be shown to belong to the essence of extension and not to that of anything else.

*I say that there is another, equally genuine, extension*[1]

At last we agree in substance; there only remains a question of terms, whether this second sort of extension is to be called equally genuine. For my part, in God and angels and in our mind I conceive there to be no extension of substance, but only extension of power. An angel can exercise his power now on a greater and now on a lesser part of corporeal substance; but if there were no bodies, I could not conceive either any space to which an angel or God would be coextensive. To attribute to a substance an extension which is only an extension of power is an effect of the prejudice which regards every substance, including God himself, as imaginable.

### REPLY TO THE SECOND INSTANCES

*Some parts of empty space would absorb others, etc.*[2]

I repeat here that if they are absorbed then half the space is destroyed and ceases to be; but what ceases to be does not penetrate anything else; so impenetrability must be admitted in every space.

*The interval between worlds would have its own duration, etc.*[3]

I think it involves a contradiction to conceive of any duration intervening between the destruction of an earlier

[1] More had admitted that God and angels were not extended in the sense of being tangible and impenetrable, but maintained they were still genuinely extended.

[2] More had said that he could not conceive part of extension changing places unless some parts of empty space absorbed others.

[3] More wrote 'If God destroyed this world and much later created a new one out of nothing, the interval without a world would have its own durations which could be measured in days, years, and centuries.'

world and the creation of a new one. To relate this duration
to a succession of divine thoughts or something similar would
simply be an intellectual error, not a genuine perception of
anything.

I have already replied to what follows when I observed
that the extension which is attributed to incorporeal things is
an extension of power and not of substance. Such a power,
being only a mode in the thing to which it is applied,
could not be conceived as extended once the extended
body corresponding to it is taken away.

## Reply to the Penultimate Instances

*God is positively infinite, that is, exists everywhere*

I do not agree with this 'everywhere'. You seem here to
make God's infinity consist in His being everywhere; which
is an opinion I cannot agree with. I think that God is everywhere in virtue of His power; but in virtue of His essence He
has no relation to place at all. But since in God essence and
power are not distinct, I think it is better to argue in such
cases about our own minds or about angels, which are more
on the scale of our own conception.

The difficulties that follow all seem to me to arise from
the prejudice which makes us too accustomed to imagine as
extended all substances including those that we deny to be
bodies; and which make us philosophize intemperately about
fictional entities, attributing to non-beings the properties of
being or substance. It is important to remember that non-
beings can have no true attributes, nor can they be conceived in terms of part and whole, subject and adjunct etc.
And so you are perfectly right when you conclude that when
the mind considers logical fictions it is playing with its own
shadows.

*A certain and finite number of states would be enough . . .*[1]

It conflicts with my conception to attribute any boundary
to the world; and I have no measure of what I should
affirm or deny except my own conception. The reason I say

[1] More had claimed that a universe of definite dimensions would suffice for
Cartesian physics.

that the world is indeterminately, or indefinitely, great is
that I can discover no bounds in it; but I would not dare to
call it infinite, because I see that God is greater than the
world, not in extension (for I have often said I do not think
He is strictly speaking extended) but in perfection.

## REPLY TO THE LAST INSTANCES

*If you do this*[1]

I am not certain that the continuation of my Philosophy
will ever see the light, because it depends on many experiments which I may never have a chance to perform. But I
hope to publish this summer a small *Treatise on the Passions*,
in which it will be seen how I think that even in us all the
motions of the members which accompany our passions are
caused not by the soul but simply by the machinery of the
body. The wagging of a dog's tail is only a motion accompanying a passion, and so is to be sharply distinguished, in
my view, from speech, which alone shows thought lurking
in a body.

*You could say the like about infants*

Infants are in a different case from animals: I should not
judge that infants had minds unless I saw that they were of
the same nature as adults; but animals never grow up
enough for any certain sign of thought to be detected in them.

## REPLY TO THE QUESTIONS

It conflicts with my conception, or, what is the same, I
think it involves a contradiction, that the world should be
finite or bounded; because I cannot but conceive a space
beyond whatever bounds you assign to the world; and on my
view such a space is a genuine body. I do not care if others
call this space imaginary and thus regard the world as
finite; because I know what are the prejudices that give rise
to this error.

---

[1] An allusion to Descartes' hope of explaining animals' behaviour by the
construction of their organs, which More expected would appear in the Fifth and
Sixth Parts of the *Principles*.

2. When you imagine a sword going through the boundary of the world, you show that you too do not consider the world as finite; because in reality you conceive every place the sword reaches as a part of the world, though you give the name 'vacuum' to what you conceive.

\*     \*     \*

6. I have tried to explain most of what you here ask in my *Treatise on the Passions*. I will only add that I have not yet met anything connected with the nature of material things for which I could not very easily think out a mechanistic explanation. It is no disgrace to a philosopher to believe that God can move a body, without regarding God as corporeal; it is no more of a disgrace to him to think the same of other incorporeal substances. Of course I do not think that any mode of action belongs univocally to both God and creatures, but I must confess that the only idea I can find in my mind to represent the way in which God or an angel can move matter is the one which shows me the way in which I am conscious I can move my own body by my own thought.

Moreover, my mind cannot be more or less extended in place, in virtue of its substance; but only in virtue of its power, which it can apply to larger or smaller bodies.

Father Mersenne had died in September 1648. His place as Descartes' principal correspondent in Paris was taken by Claude Clerselier.

## Descartes to Clerselier, 23 April 1649[1]

Sir,

I will not spend long in thanking you for all the care and precautions you have taken to ensure that the letters which I have been honoured to receive from that Northern country

[1] AT v. 352; AM viii. 222; in French; complete.

should reach me; because I am already so obliged to you, and have so many other proofs of your friendship, that it is nothing new to me. I will only say that none have gone astray, and that I am resolved to make the journey to which the latest letters invite me, though I had at first more repugnance than perhaps you can imagine. My journey to Paris last summer disheartened me; and I can assure you that the extraordinary esteem in which I hold M. Chanut, and the certainty I have of his friendship, are not the least important reasons which have made me decide to go.

I do not expect that the *Treatise on the Passions* will be printed before I arrive in Sweden; for I have been indolent in revising it and adding the things you thought lacking, which will increase its length by a third. It will contain three parts, of which the first will deal with the passions in general, the second with the six primitive passions, and the third with all the others.

As for the difficulties which you kindly put me, I answer the first as follows. My purpose was to base a proof of the existence of God on the idea or thought which we have of him, and so I thought that I was obliged first of all to distinguish all our thoughts into certain classes, so as to observe which are those which can deceive. By showing that not even chimaeras contain falsehood in themselves I hoped to forestall those who might reject my reasoning on the grounds that our idea of God belongs to the class of chimaeras. I was also obliged to distinguish the ideas which are born with us from those which come from elsewhere, or are made by us, to forestall those who might say that the idea of God is made by us or acquired by hearing others speak of Him. Moreover, the reason why I insisted on our lack of certainty of what we are told by all the ideas which we think come from outside, was in order to show that there is no single idea which gives such certain knowledge as the one we have of God. Finally I could not have said 'there occurs a different way'[1] if I had not first rejected all the others and this prepared my readers to understand what I was about to write.

2. To the second I reply that I think I see very clearly

---

[1] In the *Third Meditation*, AT vii. 40; HR i. 161.

that there cannot be an infinite series among the ideas I possess, because I feel myself to be finite, and in the place where I wrote that,[1] I was acknowledging in myself nothing except what I knew to be there. Later, when I do not dare to deny the possibility of an infinite series, it is in the works of God; and I know that God is infinite, and so it is not for me to set any bounds to His works.

3. To the words *substance, duration, number,*[2] etc. I could have added, *truth, perfection, order,* and many others of a class which is not easy to delimit. In each case there might be room for discussion whether or not they should be distinguished from the first which I mentioned; for *truth is not distinct from the thing or substance that is true, nor perfection from the thing that is perfect,* etc. That is why I merely said '*and if there are any other such*'.[3]

4. By '*infinite substance*' *I mean a substance which has actually infinite and immense true and real perfections. This is not an accident added to the notion of substance, but the very essence of substance taken absolutely and bounded by no defects; these defects, in respect of substance, are accidents; but infinity or infinitude is not.* It should be observed that I never use the word 'infinite' to signify the mere lack of limits (which is something negative for which I used the term 'indefinite') but to signify a real thing, which is incomparably greater than all those which are in some way limited.

5. I say that the notion[4] I have of the infinite is in me before that of the finite because, by the mere fact that I conceive being or that which is, without thinking whether it is finite or infinite, what I conceive is infinite being; but in order to conceive a finite being, I have to take away something from this general notion of being, which must accordingly be there first.

6. *This idea, I say, is supremely true.*[5] Truth consists in being, and falsehood only in non-being, so that the idea of the infinite, which includes all being, includes all that there is of truth in things, and cannot contain anything false; and

---

[1] Ibid., AT vii. 42; HR i. 163.
[2] Here and below, italics denote Latin words in a French context.
[3] AT vii. 44; HR i. 165.    [4] AT vii. 45; HR i. 166.
[5] AT vii. 46; HR i. 166.

this is so even if you want to suppose it untrue that that
infinite being exists.

7. *It is sufficient for me to understand this.*[1] I mean, that it is
sufficient for me to understand *the fact that God is not
comprehended by me* in order to conceive God in very truth
and as He is, provided that I judge also that there are in
Him all perfections which I clearly conceive, and also many
more which I cannot comprehend.

8. *As for my parents, even though.*[2] That is, even though
everything we were accustomed to believe of them is perhaps
true, i.e. that they begat our bodies, still I cannot imagine
that they made me, so long as I consider myself only as a
thinking thing, because I see no relation between the corporeal action by which I am accustomed to believe they begat
me, and the production of a thinking substance.

*That every deception depends on some defect is manifest to me
by the light of nature; because a being in which there is no
imperfection cannot tend to non-being, that is, cannot have non-
being, or non-good, or non-true as its end or purpose; for these
three things are the same. It is manifest that in every deception
there is falsehood, and that falsehood is something non-true and
therefore non-being and non-good.* Forgive me for having
interlarded this letter with Latin; the brief time I have had
to write it has not allowed me to think of words, and I only
want to assure you that I am, etc.

In April 1649 a Swedish admiral was sent to Descartes, and in June Chanut
visited him and persuaded him to accept the invitation to Stockholm. In the
same month he wrote to Queen Christine's librarian.

## From the letter to Freinsheimius, June 1649[3]

... I have one more favour to ask you. I am being urged
by a friend[4] to give him the little *Treatise on the Passions*,
which I had the honour of offering to her Majesty some time

[1] AT vii. 47; HR i. 167.    [2] AT vii. 50; HR i. 170.
[3] AT v. 361; AM viii. 228; in French; extract.    [4] Clerselier.

ago. I know that he plans to have it printed with a preface
of his own, but I have not yet dared to send it to him,
because I do not know whether her Majesty will approve of
something which was presented to her in private, being
published without a dedication to her. But because this treatise is too small to deserve to bear the name of so great a
Princess, to whom, if this sort of homage is not unpleasing to
her, I might some day be able to offer a more important
work, I thought that perhaps she would not object to my
granting this friend's request. That is what I ask you most
humbly to tell me, because the first of my cares is to try to
obey and please her. . . .

Descartes put the final touches to the *Treatise on the Passions* in Augus t
and it appeared in November with a dedication to Queen Christine.

## Descartes to More, August 1649[1]

When I received your letter of 23 July I was just on the
point of sailing to Sweden,[2] etc.

1. *Do angels have sensation, properly so called, and are they
corporeal or not?*[3]
I reply that the human mind separated from the body
does not have sensation strictly so called; but it is not clear
by natural reason whether Angels are created like minds
distinct from bodies, or like minds united to bodies. I never
decide about questions on which I have no certain reasons
and I never allow conjectures into my system. I agree that
we should not think of God except as being what all good
men would wish there to be if He did not exist.
    Your illustration of the acceleration of motion, to show
that the same substance can occupy different amounts of

---

[1] AT v. 401; AM viii. 261; in Latin; with omissions.
[2] Descartes left on 31 August.
[3] Italics denote quotations from More's letter (AT v. 376; AM viii. 241).

space at different times, is ingenious[1]; but there is a great disparity, because motion is not a substance but a mode, and a mode of such a kind that we can inwardly conceive how it can diminish or increase in the same place. Now there are notions appropriate to each type of being, which in judging about it must be used instead of comparisons with other beings; thus what is appropriate to shape is not the same as what is appropriate to motion; and neither of these is the same as what is appropriate to extended substance. Remember nothing has no properties, and that what is commonly called empty space is not nothing, but real body deprived of all its accidents (i.e. all the things which can be present or absent without their possessor ceasing to be). Anyone who has fully realised this, and who has observed how each part of this space or body differs from all others and is impenetrable, will easily see that no other thing can have the same divisibility, tangibility, and impenetrability.

I said that God was extended in virtue of His power, because that power manifests itself, or can manifest itself, by acting on extended substance. It is certain that God's essence must be present everywhere for His power to be able to manifest itself everywhere; but I deny it is there in the manner of an extended thing, that is in the way in which I just described extended substance.

\*       \*       \*

The translation which I call motion, is a thing of no less entity than shape: it is a mode in a body. The power causing motion may be the power of God Himself conserving the same amount of translation in matter as He put in it in the first moment of creation; or it may be the power of a created substance, like our soul, or of any other thing to which He gave the power to move a body. This power is a mode in a creature, but not in God; but because this is not easy for everyone to understand, I did not want to discuss it in my writings. I was afraid of seeming inclined to favour the view of those who consider God as a world-soul united to matter.

---

[1] More had argued, 'numerically the same motion can occupy now a larger body, now a smaller one, on your own principles'.

I agree that *if matter is left to itself and receives no impulse from anywhere it will remain entirely still*. But it receives an impulse from God who preserves the same amount of motion or translation in it as He placed in it at the beginning. This translation is no more violent to matter than rest is: the term 'violent' refers only to our will, which is said to suffer violence when something happens which goes against it. But in nature nothing is violent: it is equally natural for bodies to collide with each other, and perhaps to disintegrate, as it is for them to be still. I think that what causes you difficulty in this matter is that you conceive a force in a quiescent body by which it resists motion, as being something positive, namely, an action distinct from the body's being at rest; whereas in fact the force is nothing but a modal entity.

You observe correctly that a *motion, being a mode of a body, cannot pass from one body to another*. But that is not what I wrote; indeed I think that motion, considered as such a mode, continually changes. For there is one mode in the first point of a body A in that it is separated from the first point of a body B; and another mode in that it is separated from the second point; and another mode in that it is separated from the third point; and so on. But when I said that the same amount of motion always remained in matter, I meant this about the force which impels its parts, which is applied at different times to different parts of matter in accordance with the laws set out in article 45 and following of the Second Part.[1] So there is no need for you to worry about the transmigration of rest from one possessor to another, since not even motion, considered as a mode which is the contrary of rest, transmigrates in that fashion.

You add that body *seems to you to be alive with a stupid and drunken life*. This, I take it, is just a fine phrase; but I must tell you once for all, with the candour which you permit me, that nothing withdraws us from the discovery of truth so much as setting up as true something of which we are convinced by no positive reason, but only our own will. That is what happens when we have invented or imagined something and afterwards take pleasure in our fictions, as you do

[1] AT viii. 67; HR i. 268.

in your corporeal angels, your shadow of the divine essence, and the rest. No one should entertain any such thoughts, because to do so is to close the road to truth against oneself.

Descartes reached Stockholm at the beginning of October 1649 and wrote the last of his letters to Princess Elizabeth to assure her of his safe arrival. He had only four months to live; during this period he wrote a ballet for Queen Christine's birthday but no letters of philosophical interest. He suffered greatly from the Swedish winter, especially as he was obliged to rise at five to teach the Queen philosophy. He contracted pneumonia while nursing a friend and died on 11 February 1650.

# INDEX OF PERSONS

# SUBJECT INDEX

# Subject Index

water 39
wax 66, 148, 155
will 32, 84, 160, 209
— and ideas 93
— and understanding 102, 144, 209

will, weakness of 32
word of God 14
words 206
world, *see* universe
world-soul 114, 257

# INDEX OF CITATIONS OF DESCARTES' WORKS

Anthony Kenny, Master of Balliol College, Oxford,
is the author of *Action, Emotion, and Will*;
*Descartes: A Study of His Philosophy*;
*Aristotle's Theory of the Will*;
and other books and articles.